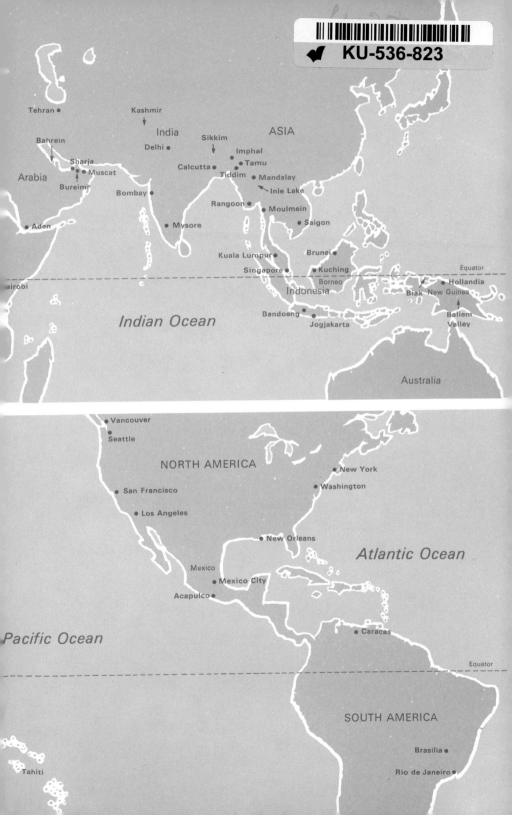

A.W. Rose.

Dunwood
Luncarty
Perth.

Travel Warrant

Bernard Fergusson

TRAVEL WARRANT

COLLINS · St James's Place, London, 1979

William Collins Sons & Co Ltd
London · Glasgow · Sydney · Auckland
Toronto · Johannesburg

First published 1979
© Bernard Fergusson 1979
ISBN 0 00 216792 1
Set in 11 pt Monotype Baskerville
Made and Printed in Great Britain by
William Collins Sons & Co Ltd Glasgow

For Geordie Fergusson

Contents

Illustrations

Chapter One

'AS IT WAS IN THE BEGINNING'

My old home of Kilkerran lies in the Girvan Valley, in that southernmost district of Ayrshire which has rejoiced in the name of Carrick since long before the word Ayrshire was coined. It is a large, imposing but benevolent house, of four storeys and a basement, built of a local stone which has the magic property of sometimes looking grey, and of sometimes glowing with the vague pinkness of a trout. Sometimes in the setting sun it takes on the colour of a rose.

It stands on the slope of a hill, looking south-westwards down the valley across open fields dotted with the occasional elm, oak and beech. Behind it the hill at once rises more steeply, planted with hardwoods dating from the early eighteenth century. The present house dates primarily from the 1680s, when it was enlarged to embody an old tower which is known to have been standing in 1517. Later, the middle of the house was gutted to afford space for a graceful staircase; Regency wings of great elegance were added in 1815; and my grandfather made further additions in the 1850s and 1870s.

But this beloved house is not the original Kilkerran. What is left of 'Old Kilkerran' – three storeys of one wall, and the rest tumbled rubble, with a fallen turret lying on its side – still stands two miles further up the next hill to the south, on a promontory jutting out eighty feet above the deep Dobbing-stone Burn. Half a mile away is the farm of Knockcrochar, a euphonious name which to those ignorant of Gaelic (as I am) will mean nothing sinister; but its significance was explained to me fifty years ago by that greatest of authorities, Sir Herbert Maxwell of Monreith. It means 'Hangman's Hill', and supports the probability that the Fergussons of Kilkerran in those days exercised their baronial rights of 'pit and gallows'.

How long we have actually lived on Kilkerran we don't know, nor is it of much interest to anybody but ourselves. The continuous documentation goes back to John Fergusson in 1434; but his father and grandfather, Duncan and Colin, were there before him, and a Fergus, son of Fergus, on record in the 1320s, was presumably of the same stock. The point is that it has furnished us with an abode in which we are fortunate enough to have enjoyed some permanence over the years, and with a base from which to make sorties. The earliest of such sorties were mostly local; but gradually they spread more widely, whether in the service of the Crown, or in efforts, mostly unsuccessful, to feather individual nests. We never managed to produce a real Nabob, such as feature in the novels of John Galt.

The first to venture far afield, and disastrously, was William, an eldest son who was killed in his father's life-time at the Battle of Pinkie in 1647, one of over forty landed gentry from Ayrshire to fall on that dismal day. His son, my belligerent namesake Bernard, who eventually succeeded his grandfather, was a bonnie fighter in his own right, and largely in his own interests, although he was also a vigorous supporter of Lord Cassillis in the Kennedy feud, which split that powerful family and the whole of Carrick into two camps for close on half a century. He attempted to oust some neighbours, the Craufurds of Camlarg, from a mill of which both he and they claimed the ownership. Summoned for this misdemeanour to the Sheriff Court in Ayr, he duly attended, but accompanied by fifty-five armed supporters, including two of his five brothers. The Sheriff appears to have been reasonably impressed by this show of force, since he acquitted him; and Bernard's future sorties were limited to Edinburgh, where he pursued his case more conventionally, but without success, in the High Court over several years.

The first of the family to go overseas was Bernard's eldest grandson John, and that was not of his own volition, so much as from having backed the wrong political horse in the Civil War. Having been knighted by the King in 1641, he deemed it his duty to join Montrose, with two of his younger sons; and I remember as a boy my mother pointing out to me the little paddock of Gettybeg, beside the Dobbingstone Burn a few hundred yards downstream from Old Kilkerran, where they are reputed to have tethered the horses of the troop they had raised for the expedition the night before they set off for Selkirk. Montrose was defeated at Philiphaugh before they reached him; but their absence was noted, the family heavily fined for this lapse, and Sir John obliged to flee abroad, where he died in 1647.

Apart from the fines, Sir John had run up heavy debts, saddling his son and grandson, both called Alexander, with a burden they never succeeded in paying off. In 1700 the second Alexander and his son sold out to a cousin, another Sir John and a grandson of the old Royalist, who had made a fortune as an advocate in Edinburgh. The writ still survives by which father and son 'cheerfully renounce all interest and title they in any manner of way pretend to the above lands, and wish a happy enjoyment thereof to the said Sir John and his'. Their line survived for three or more generations before apparently flickering out, though it possibly survived a little longer in Ireland. Each traceable generation included an Alexander, one of whom died in 1698 in the ill-fated expedition to Darien, that graveyard of many young Scottish hopefuls; his brother John died in Jamaica thirty years later.

'The said Sir John' must have been a pretty fly performer in his chosen profession of advocate: not for him the discomforts and dangers of Darien or the West Indies. He had been at the Bar for less than ten years when he had amassed enough money to buy the present Kilkerran (then a Kennedy place called Barclanachan) and to convert it from a tower into a peaceful dwelling-house; and for less than twenty before paying off the Kilkerran debt to their neighbours at Bargany, and taking over both the place and the headship of the family. Three years later, he became a Baronet of Nova Scotia, an honour which had to be paid for in hard cash as surely as any of those retailed by Lloyd George two centuries later. Finally, in 1719, ten years before he died, he was recognized by the Lord Lyon as Chief of the Name of Fergusson: despite the fact that his cousins were senior to him in line, and that the Fergussons of Craigdarroch in Dumfriesshire could trace their descent further back than the 1430s, the earliest date that the Kilkerran stock could prove, whatever they might claim.

As soon as he had acquired the house and lands of Old Kilkerran, Sir John transferred the name to Barclanachan, and allowed the old tower to tumble down. His eldest son James followed him to the Bar, did well, married an heiress, became a judge with the title of Lord Kilkerran; and was allowed by his father, for at least twenty years before he succeeded, to indulge his fancy for silviculture and agriculture on a generous scale, and to acquire ever yet more land. It was he who commemorated the Act of Union in 1707 by planting six silver firs in the Lady Glen at Kilkerran, of which three, 140 feet in height, still survive.*

The years passed, and the estate prospered: it also grew. Successive heads of the family continued to follow the law in Edinburgh, to their great profit, taking two days to ride there on horseback by way of Hyndford Bridge, and inhabiting a series of town houses, several of which still survive. One is 'the old house with the peartree', at the corner of West Nicolson Street, vacant at this moment of writing, but until lately in use as a whisky-store: Lord Kilkerran died in it one afternoon in January 1759, having apparently had a stroke after sitting on the bench that morning. Another, No. 5 Charlotte Square, is now the headquarters of the National Trust for Scotland. They chose their wives with circumspection, selecting heiresses without fail: a knack which recent generations seem lamentably to have lost. Various younger brothers and cousins sought their fortunes furth of Scotland, in London, India or elsewhere, with varying degrees of success; several loyal ones, who either failed to marry or whose unions were not blest with progeny, bequeathed modest fortunes back to the trunk of the family tree.

The regency enlargements to the house, the canalization of

---

* Alas! Since these words were written, early in 1978, these three survivors have had to be felled, at the very moment when the Scottish Devolution Bill was being debated in the House of Lords.

14

three miles of the river, the establishment of a six-acre walled garden a mile away, the construction of a dozen miles of amenity paths through the woodlands complete with stone or wooden bridges over the burns, the re-routing of the public highway from Girvan to Ayr on the far side of the river to keep the *hoi polloi* away from the policies and ensure greater privacy for the house, the building of model cottages designed by fashionable architects: all this had cost £70,000, but was paid off easily in a few blithe years. Everything looked rosy: too rosy, perhaps, for my grandfather Sir James, who succeeded his father Sir Charles in 1849 at the tender age of seventeen, without undue encumbrance of trustees. He died four years before I was born, but the evidence makes it clear that he was an eager, energetic youth of high spirits and extravagant tastes: in contrast to his rather staid father, whose obelisk monument on Kildoon Hill, 'erected by public subscription', can still be seen for many miles around.

'Staid' he may have been; but he bequeathed also one splendid row, in full swing, to his son, my grandfather. It turned on whether or not the incipient Glasgow & South-Western Railway might run its new line down the far side of the valley, on Kilkerran land. Sir Charles had dug his toes in: had not *his* father shifted the high road, with none daring to say him 'Nay'? Nobody was going to run noisy railway trains, belching filthy smoke, down his valley. The railway company promoted a bill in Parliament, which was passed, granting them rights of compulsory purchase; and their surveyors began working out their trace along a line which ran below Kildoon Hill, past Kilhenzie and Craigfin, along the brae-face of the Burning Hill, above Carsloe, below Dalzellowlie, above Drumburle, and so on to the neighbouring lands of the Kennedies of Dalquharran and the Dalrymple-Hamiltons of Bargany. Each working day they stuck in their pegs. Each evening Sir Charles's men howked up the pegs as though they were tatties, and chucked them into the river.

The *impasse* was coming to a head when it was resolved by Sir Charles's death. The young Sir James, displaying a tactical eye for the main chance and realizing that he was bound to lose in the end, drove an excellent bargain, which the Company, on the principle of 'anything for a quiet life', gratefully accepted. It included the right to stop express trains at Kilkerran Station, a right from which I occasionally benefited as a schoolboy; alas, it has not only been eroded long since, but could not now be exercised, since Kilkerran Station was an early casualty in the Battle of Beeching. The first train ever to stop there was the one which brought Sir James and his bride to Kilkerran on their return from their honeymoon in 1859; the last, sadly, was in 1965. But there still remain trophies from that tussle of long ago: the station buildings, the booking-office, the waiting-room, the lamp-room, the stationmaster's house, now constitute the estate office from which my nephew the current Sir Charles directs the manifold activities of present-day Kilkerran. The diesel-driven trains thunder disdainfully past without stopping. They seem to me to stink much more than their predecessors the steam trains, whose smoke used to rise so gracefully above the trees.

The Sir James who was my grandfather was the first head of the family to break the tradition of five generations of practising at the Scots Bar. Like my father after him, he joined the Grenadiers, and went out to the Crimean War as Assistant Adjutant to their 3rd Battalion. The Adjutant was George Higginson, who became a full general: he celebrated his hundredth birthday, which was also the eightieth anniversary of his joining it, by addressing that same Battalion on the same barrack square at Victoria Barracks, Windsor: this was in 1926. A few weeks later, at the Henley Regatta, my Eton tutor Henry Marten introduced me to him; and he said: 'You must be young Jim Fergusson's son.' I had to confess that I was his grandson; and that 'young Jim' had been killed in an earthquake before I was born.

My grandfather, born in 1832 and killed in the Jamaica earthquake of 1907, had a distinguished career in his own right; but he ruined the fortunes of Kilkerran. His friend and neighbour, Hunter Blair of Blairquhan, which marches with Kilkerran, died in his arms from a mortal wound at the battle of Inkerman; and Sir James, without even returning home, was elected to Parliament in his stead. As soon as the campaign was over, he left the Army for politics: a career to which he was not consistently faithful, but to which he was later to return.

The bride whom he brought to Kilkerran in that inaugural train was Lady Edith Ramsay, younger daughter of the first and last Marquess of Dalhousie. Tragically widowed and broken in health, Dalhousie was to die a few months later. His own father had been Governor-General of Canada; his father-in-law Lord Tweeddale Governor of Madras; and Lord Tweeddale's father-in-law, the fifth Duke of Manchester, Governor of Jamaica for nineteen years. Dalhousie himself had been appointed Governor-General of India at the youthful age of thirty-five, when he had what must have been the rather embarrassing satisfaction of being greeted by his subordinate father-in-law on his first arrival in that country.

One would have thought that with such a family tradition behind her, with her father, grandfather and great-grandfather having all held vice-regal appointments, my grandmother would have been reconciled to life in a Colonial Government House; but when Sir James, after a spell as Under-Secretary for India, accepted in 1868 the Governorship of South Australia, she was thoroughly miserable, as her letters reveal, and desperately homesick for the company of her beloved elder sister Susan. Susan herself was to have an even more miserable time when her husband was created Lord Connemara and appointed Governor of Madras, his elder brother Lord Mayo having become Viceroy* in the same year as the Fergussons went to Adelaide. Neither brother's tenure can be said to have ended happily: Connemara was divorced by Susan for adultery while in office, and Mayo was fatally stabbed by a convict whose jail in the Andaman Islands he was visiting. These are therefore not to be reckoned among the more successful proconsular appointments held by the family, and those other families with whom it was linked by marriage.

By contrast, Dalhousie's nine years in India, although he remains a controversial figure, were reckoned to be successful. He built 2000 miles of roads and 4000 miles of telegraph; he constructed railways, finished the Ganges Canal, embarked on

---

* The title 'Viceroy' was substituted for that of 'Governor-General' after the Mutiny of 1857.

vast schemes of irrigation; waged war on thuggery, suttee and the slave-trade; set up the Legislative Council; and did much for education. He was ruthless in annexing huge territories whenever an excuse offered: during his time, the Punjab, Nagpur, Oudh, Jhansi, Berar and Lower Burma passed under British rule; and yet he is still regarded in India (though not in Burma) as an enlightened liberator rather than as an oppressive imperialist. It was he who exacted the Koh-i-noor diamond from the Punjab as part of the spoils of war, and, after sitting on it for a year, sent it to Queen Victoria, to the fury of the Directors of the East India Company, who considered that it should have reached her through them. On 16 May 1850, he wrote to his friend Sir George Couper:

> The Koh-i-noor sailed from Bombay in HMS *Medea* on 6 April. I could not tell you at the time, for strict secrecy was observed, but I brought it from Lahore myself. I undertook the charge of it in a funk, and never was so happy in all my life as when I got it into the Treasury at Bombay. It was sewn and double-sewn into a belt secured round my waist, one end through the belt fastened to a chain round my neck. It never left me day or night . . . My stars! What a relief it was to get rid of it.

Some good authorities blame him and his policies for contributing to the frustrations and resentments which led to the outbreak of the Mutiny. On this I am not qualified to pronounce. But however tough he was as an administrator, his letters and diaries reveal him as a soft-hearted man of high liberal principle and devoted to his family, from whom the exigencies of his office separated him for so many years.

How much the Dalhousies missed their home and children during that long separation – and Lady Dalhousie was never to see either again – is evident from the following letter from Dalhousie to Susan, who had written to report how she and her sister had celebrated his birthday in a pious pilgrimage to Dalhousie Castle from their lodgings in Edinburgh in honour of the day:

> I am doubly pleased when I see that you thought no way so pleasant of spending that day as in going to the old Castle, and

enjoying yourselves on the banks of your own home. It is a foolish vanity in some people to be always talking of their own house as superior to anything in the world, to be always praising everything of their own, and thinking all their geese swans. But it is pleasant and right to be attached, as you are, to your own home, and to prefer it for your enjoyment to any other spot in the world . . . But I want you to know the names of the woods and places about Dalhousie which you don't seem to know and to which you give new names. There is not a glen or a burn or a field or a wood about the place which has not its own name. Get Main [the factor] to tell them to you. Tell him to take you to the Annah Park and to shew you the Edgewell Tree and to tell you its story, and to carry you over the Bridge at Prestonholm and round to the Kirk Bank and so among the flowers on the island, and then in return you may pull his old bones up Blawloun, and help him to the old Manse thro' the Sclaters' Croft.

The death of his wife on her way home for reasons of health, while he remained at his post in India, broke Dalhousie's heart. For three days he shut himself up in his office in the height of the hot weather in Calcutta, refusing to see anybody, before resuming his work, writing: 'Surely, surely God will pardon me if for a time I feel it almost too hard to bear . . . I have gone on as usual, but oh! it is hard, heartless and objectless toil now.' He stuck it out with failing health for another three years before coming home to die, aged only forty-eight.

When Sir James and Lady Edith went out to Adelaide, they took with them two daughters and a son: my father Charles, aged three. Another son was born there: my uncle, the future Admiral Sir James. From his birth, she never recovered, dying six months later; and my father, now six, was taken riding pommel in front of a groom on horseback to see her on her death-bed. Two years later, my grandfather went on to be Governor of New Zealand, accompanied by a newly-acquired Australian wife, who also predeceased him; and, as Nanny to the children, a girl who had come out with them from Scotland as nursery-maid. Ninety-four years later, my wife and I went to call on an old lady in the Bay of Islands in New Zealand: a widow with a Maori name, totally blind, and living in a spotlessly clean house all by herself. We were electrified to find photographs of Kilkerran, and of my father, his brother and sisters as children. We had no idea of her identity when we went to see her, but she turned out to be the daughter of that family Nanny of long ago.

After only two years in New Zealand, my grandfather returned to Britain. He made two unsuccessful efforts to re-enter Parliament, but was rejected by the electors of both Frome and Greenock. In 1880 he accepted an offer from his old chief, Disraeli, of the Governorship of Bombay, where he spent the next six years, consciously pursuing the policies of his father-in-law thirty years earlier, especially in matters of education. His physical energy was proverbial, and he is reputed to have ridden thousands of miles on horseback throughout the Presidency, probing into every corner of the administration. Among other things, he founded Fergusson College, Poona, which still retains his name; and which, paradoxically, has been the Alma Mater of some of the most prominent Indian nationalists during turbulent times, including such men as Tilak. Several proposals since Independence to divorce his name from the College's have been defeated, owing to the recognition of his own and his father-in-law's devotion to the cause of Indian education. It brought them both some obloquy among the British in their own day, but widespread gratitude among Indians ever since. Fergusson College, which I have visited twice in the last forty years, has produced several statesmen, Ambassadors, High Commissioners and at least one general; and at the moment of writing the Indian High Commissioner in London is an Old Fergussonian.

Sir James may have been a good and successful public servant; he seems to have done well in his colonial appointments, and as Under-Secretary of State for India and for Foreign Affairs, and as Postmaster-General; but as Laird of Kilkerran he was a disaster. He grew little less spendthrift as he grew older, although his physical energy never diminished. When the safety bicycle became the current craze, he adopted it with the same enthusiasm as that with which later generations were to adopt the pogo-stick, or judo, or jogging. Instead of travelling home from Westminster by way of St Pancras and Kilkerran Station, he used to bicycle all the thirty-five miles from Kilmarnock; and not merely to Kilkerran, which was usually let to English tenants in the vain effort to recoup his finances, but to his more favoured little shooting-box of Balbeg, high up in the hills near the head of the Girvan Valley. That old bicycle of his, a real iron-clad and sheer murder to pedal, still leaned up against the wall in the little room off the front hall of Kilkerran (known as 'The Hall's Own Child', and the repository of all sorts of junk) throughout my youth.

After his second wife died, he married a third, a widow, of whom no kindly word has ever been said. Once again in Parliament, as Postmaster-General, he lived with her in London; but the day came when his two sons, my father Charles and my uncle James, decided that she was too much of a termagant. They met him at Victoria Station on his return from some official visit to the Continent; told him that they had found him some more congenial, and independent, quarters; and led him submissively off to them. He and his third wife never met again.

In the great political landslide of 1906, he lost his seat, North-East Manchester, to a young and unknown Labour candidate, the future Cabinet Minister J. R. Clynes, who came from a very different background: his father was an illiterate Irish grave-digger in Oldham. Sir James went off to Jamaica, partly on business, partly to relax after his political defeat: he was now seventy-five. He was buying cigars when there was an earthquake: the shop collapsed, and he was killed outright.

This happened in January 1907. My mother was at Kilkerran; my father was travelling south on the night train, back to Windsor, where he was commanding his battalion of Grenadiers. He woke up suddenly in his sleeper from a vivid dream, in which his father had apologized for the financial mess in which he had left Kilkerran, and discussed in detail such things as the rent arrears of one particular tenant-farmer (whose grandson is still the tenant today). Next morning at St Pancras Station, my father met his cousin Lord Balfour of Burleigh; and while they shared a taxi to their mutual club for bath and breakfast, my father told him of this especially sharp impression of Sir James. After breakfast, my father sat down and wrote a full account of it to my mother, posting the letter before catching the train to

Windsor. There in his little house at Datchet the telephone rang. It was old Thom, Sir James's butler in London, reading out a cable from Jamaica announcing his death.

I believe that I have had two telepathic experiences in my life, but cannot be completely sure of either. The fact that my father told Lord Balfour, and wrote to my mother, of his dream before the news came through seems to make this case more authentic than most.

Sir James's death called forth many tributes, some graceful, some frivolous. 'Sir James's idea of Paradise will be reading Family Prayers with his arm round a pretty girl.' When the flag fluttered down from the statue in Ayr which was being unveiled in his honour (from the nose of which to this day hang dewdrops or icicles in wet or snowy weather), revealing the potted summary of his career inscribed on the plinth, his old friend and neighbour Sir Hugh Shaw Stewart of Ardgowan said to those around him: 'There was no need to put all that: all they needed to say was that it took an earthquake to kill him.'

No bad epitaph; but he left Kilkerran grievously burdened. At some time in the nineties, he was compelled to call what was almost a Council of War to decide what was to be done: at which my father, my uncle the future Admiral and the family lawyers were present. Even the ultimate horror was discussed: the disposing of Kilkerran altogether, if need be, to satisfy the creditors. He had been slow indeed to learn: while in Australia he had built a sumptuous yacht; while in New Zealand he had bought 8000 unprofitable acres, which for all the efforts of his cousin Robert Fergusson whom he had installed as manager were a running financial sore; and while in Bombay he had directed that an elaborate rose-garden be laid out on the slope south of the house against his return: this alone had cost £5000, a large sum in those days. In the event, Kilkerran was salvaged; but my father succeeded to only half of the acres which had been my grandfather's inheritance, and during his lifetime had to part with another 12,000, including Balbeg and six good hill farms surrounding it. My brother James during his tenure was obliged to sell still more, including two farms tenanted by families whose names appear in a 1727 rent-book: they were as loath to buy as he to sell. The New Zealand property was disposed of at a poor price as part of the salvage operation; and the irony is that these particular acres near Cambridge are now, with the development of modern methods of fertilizing, some of the most valuable in the whole of the rich Waikato country.

It is now time for my father, of whom we have already had a glimpse, to step formally on to the stage. The physical resemblance between him and my grandfather, by all accounts and as seen in their portraits, was startling, but in character they were very different. My father was a martinet, and reputed to be the fiercest Adjutant and Commanding Officer that even the Grenadiers had ever known. He could be stern, and he never compromised; but he was a father to revel in, to be proud of, and to love. He was tall, handsome, and always well-groomed; he had a magnificent military bearing, even when he became a little bowed towards the end of his life: he died in 1951, soon after his eighty-sixth birthday, when we buried him, like Joshua, 'in a corner of his inheritance'. We certainly held him in awe; and as for his standards perhaps I can best illustrate them by recalling that when in 1931 I passed out of Sandhurst third out of 150, having originally passed in second, and thought I had done pretty well, he asked me quite seriously why I had dropped a place.

He was born in Edinburgh in 1865, and spent some of his boyhood, as I have described, in South Australia and New Zealand, returning home, with clear memories of both, with his father and stepmother at the age of nine. His childhood was not happy, since his father was little at home, and the schoolroom was presided over by a real sadist of a governess. Her rule came to an end when Sir James 'discovered that she had condemned my father to writing out the word 'BEAST' 10,000 times for calling her that when she repeatedly hit his sister on the knuckles with a ruler for playing her scales badly on the piano. He was then sent to school at Wixenford, where the local Rector and school chaplain was Charles Kingsley, the novelist, who befriended him. I cannot discover where he spent his holidays during his last two years in the famous Miss Evans's house at Eton, when his father was in Bombay; but he paid a brief visit to Bombay between Eton and Sandhurst, whence he was gazetted to the Grenadiers in 1883.

In 1896, after his stint as Adjutant, he was seconded to the Egyptian Army, with which he remained for the next seven years. He commanded a Sudanese battalion at Omdurman, and was so severely wounded in the chest at the skirmish at Roseires on the Blue Nile on Boxing Day of 1898 that he was actually being buried. A well-timed, unconscious grunt revealed to those concerned the fact that they were being premature, thus enabling him to survive for another fifty-two years, and to breed a family.

In 1901 in the Guards' Chapel he married my mother, Alice Boyle, daughter of Lord Glasgow, and his own second cousin: Sir James's mother had been a Boyle, and he and Lord Glasgow were first cousins: Lady Glasgow was a Hunter Blair of Blairquhan. To this in-breeding, no doubt, may be traced many of my own eccentricities. The Glasgows lived, as their grandson the present Admiral Lord Glasgow still lives, in the lovely old house of Kelburn – part sixteenth, part eighteenth century – in the far north of Ayrshire, looking out across the upper Firth of Clyde at the delectable islands of Arran, Bute and the two Cumbraes. Lord Glasgow was a retired naval officer who had himself been Governor of New Zealand from 1892 to 1897, so that my parents shared, among many other things, memories of their respective New Zealand childhoods. The Boyles had the same tradition of brothers and cousins serving overseas: my great-uncle Berto had soldiered for twenty-eight years in the Indian Army before his first leave Home, and some Boyle cousins were settled in New Zealand.

My father was still serving with the Egyptian Army, so that my parents' first married home was in Cairo, where my sister was born. They came back to Britain in 1902, with my father, although a brevet full colonel, commanding a company of Grenadiers before assuming command of the 3rd Battalion, in which both he and his father had spent all their Grenadier service. He rose rapidly thereafter, becoming a major-general in 1910, the youngest in the Army by several years; and in 1912 went to Command the 5th Division at The Curragh in Ireland. Here, in March of 1914, he became involved in the unhappy business of 'The Curragh Incident', when General Gough and almost all the officers in his Cavalry Brigade, which came under my father for administration, opted to send in their papers rather than march to impose Home Rule on Ulster. The whole business was a muddle and a misunderstanding, and it proved possible to cancel all the hasty decisions that had been taken, though not entirely to heal the wounds. The verdict of history, or rather of such historians as are still interested, is that my father came out of it well: he took the line that it was the duty of officers to obey orders, and not to allow personal political views to affect that basic concept; and he persuaded his infantry officers to follow his lead. But by and large, the cavalry officers of the Army never forgave him; and when later on, in the war, Gough succeeded to the Army in which my father was commanding the IInd Corps, Haig transferred him to command the XVIIth in the Army under Plumer, the only Infantry Army Commander in the field. In the First War, all the senior commanders except Plumer and Horne (a Gunner) were cavalrymen: French, Haig, Byng, Rawlinson, Allenby and Gough; whereas in the Second no cavalryman reached the summit, although a handful came near it.

When war broke out in August 1914, and my father went off with his division to take part in the Mons Retreat and the Battle of Le Cateau, in which it had heavy losses, we remained for two or three months at The Curragh. My mother and the two elder children must have crossed to England ahead of us, for I recall clearly my own voyage across the Irish Sea, in company with Nanny Dunning (who wasn't much taller than I was), my brother Simon (four years my senior) and a Scots nursery-maid called Chrissie, from Kingstown to Holyhead, in a blacked-out ship and a gale of wind, and with Nanny and Chrissie both out for the count.

We wintered in London, and went north to Kilkerran 'for the duration' in April 1915. We must have travelled by a day train, for I well remember my first impressions of that happy house, a month short of my fourth birthday. We arrived at Kilkerran Station after dark, and I was wrapped up in rugs for the two-and-a-half-mile journey in a horse-drawn wagonette. I looked up at what seemed to me an enormous building, black against the starlight; I was led up two flights of wide stairs, and appraised the long passages which I hoped – in vain – that I might be allowed to use for my new scooter; Simon and I were fed on bread-and-brown-sugar in the big, square day nursery with its huge leaping fire, before being put to bed side by side in the night nursery next door, and listening half-asleep to Nanny and Chrissie still chatting. I remember also, when daylight came, being lifted up to the bathroom window to see Simon (whom I still suspect of having skipped his ablutions) picking daffodils on the lawn below; and beholding for the first time in my life, on the far side of the valley, the wooded shoulder of the northern end of the Burning Hill.

That view has been on the retina of my mind's eye all my life all over the world. Often when homesick, or between war-time periods of fear, I have switched it on as one might switch on one of those transparencies in a projector, the exhibition of which puts such a strain on happy friendships. And to my mind's ear I have called the roll of the hills and the houses, from Craigfin to the Mulloch, from Heckleburnie to Drummochreen: just as, when a homesick schoolboy, I used to call the majestic roll of the high hills to the eastward of us: Lamachan, Benyellary, The Merrick, Kirriereoch, Tarfessock and Shalloch-on-Minnoch. Some of the smaller and older houses no longer exist. My father prided himself on the quality of his housing; and although he could not bring himself to pull down the older ones while their inhabitants still dwelt in them contentedly, he could equally not contemplate putting new tenants into them, and razed those which could not be improved. In those days, such decisions still rested with the laird rather than with any local authority; but at least no Kilkerran pensioner ever wanted for a roof over him or his widow so long as they lived. And for as long as they could wield a hoe or a billhook, they could earn a few extra shillings keeping the amenity paths in order. One of the joys of my childhood was in joining them at this task with my tiny spade, confident that I was being of real help, and listening to their tales and talk in an antique tongue which is now long silent.

Our greatest hero was Mungo McInnes, an elderly forester who preferred to work on his own. We were spell-bound by his mostly apocryphal tales. There were on Kilkerran Meg's Hill and Meg's Cave, the latter a modest cavern a few hundred yards up the Toddy Burn above the house. No record of Meg, whoever she was, existed; but Mungo inevitably claimed to remember her, as 'an auld wifie, wi' *fangs*'. We were not alone among the children on the place in accepting as Gospel everything that Mungo told us. Once my mother, launching a new intake of Sunday-school children on their religious education, opened the bowling by asking a small boy: 'Who made the world?' With the triumphant air of one who knows the right answer, he replied: 'Mungo McInnes!' When my mother retailed this to Mungo the next time she saw him, he looked thoughtful; and leaning on his axe he said: 'Weel, I wadnae say but whit I had a hand in it!' Many is the time that I have taken that as my text in what was intended to be an uplifting speech for youth.

The war years at Kilkerran seem very long in retrospect. The house quickly filled up with 'convalescent officers', as the phrase was – only I pronounced it 'Conva Lesson Tofficers' – dismissed from hospital, and building up their strength before returning to the trenches, all too often to be killed. Some were Scots, some Australian, but the great majority were for obvious reasons New Zealanders. My father's younger brother James, whose wife was a New Zealander, was at sea, commanding the battleship *Thunderer* at Jutland and elsewhere; but his elder daughters were at Kilkerran with us, doing lessons with my sister under a charming old Alsatian governess who looked like a duchess, and whose aged mother, from whom she received occasional messages through the Red Cross, was in German-occupied territory. They were red-letter days for us all when those rare communications came through.

Twice a year, my father came home for a week's leave. When he was expected, Simon and I (James being away at school) used to crouch on the gravel sweep in front of the house, each with an ear to the ground, hoping that like Red Indians we might hear the wagonette's wheels bringing him from the station long before it came into sight. Since the drive emerged from the woods a good half-mile short of the house, our filial optimism was never rewarded. He would arrive in uniform – red cap, red tabs, three rows of medal ribbons, white hair – in time for a late breakfast; but this was always preceded by a formal ceremony, mock to him but deadly serious to us, called 'Greeting the Ancestors'. He would enter the dining-room, and bow solemnly, in turn and in strict seniority, to each head of the family whose portrait hung there, while we trotted at his heels and did likewise.

For the rest of his leave, most of which he spent calling on his tenants and the families of men away at the war, there followed the normal family routine. After sixty years I still shudder with shame at one episode. One morning when he was reading prayers I behaved so badly that he rose from his chair at the breakfast-table, where the big Bible lay before him; strode across to where I was sitting; picked me up; carried me from the dining-room; deposited me on the bottom step of the stairs just outside; and returned to his place to resume the family devotions. But before he could shut the door, my voice was heard, wailing: 'Well, all I can say is, I shall be jolly glad when you go back to France!'

That must have been the only time in my life when I dared to be cheeky to my father. Even the greatest wilted at his potential wrath. Lord Chandos in his memoirs described an occasion in 1915 when, as Oliver Lyttelton, he was ADC to Lord Cavan, a former Grenadier commanding a division in my father's Corps. He wrote of my father:

> . . . the very image of a Guardsman, tall, good-looking, beautifully turned out, white moustache and a quilt of medals. One day, Sir Charles came into our HQ, and I saw him take the major-general on one side. I could not help hearing that he was taking the general's name for wearing the gold spurs of a Guardsman. 'You are no longer a regimental officer, please remember that, Fatty.'

Twelve years later, when my father was Governor-General of New Zealand, the Duke and Duchess of York paid a royal visit to that country. Lord Cavan was head of their suite, and among the junior equerries was Tim Nugent of the Irish Guards: one of the best-loved men who ever lived. The day before the party, travelling in HMS *Renown*, was due in that country, Tim had occasion to put his head into Lord Cavan's cabin, and was horrified to find him polishing his boots.

'Good heavens, sir!' he said: 'you shouldn't be doing that. Can't I get hold of your servant?'

'Now don't laugh, Tim,' said Cavan. 'I know it's absurd. I know I'm a Field-Marshal, and that I've been CIGS; but the fact is, I'm still terrified of Sir Charles Fergusson, and I'm not going to entrust my boots to anybody else!'

My father was well into his eighties, and rather deaf, when Tim Nugent told me this story, and I retailed it when I was next on leave. By then he had much mellowed. He listened, with his hand cupped to his ear, and was obviously delighted. The few times that I saw him again between then and his death, he used to ask me, rather shyly: 'What was that silly story that your friend Nugent told you about me?'

When I was an instructor at Sandhurst in 1938, one of my brother officers told me that a man called Kew, the Foreman of Indoor Servants, had a tale which would interest me. I got him to come and see me in my quarters, and found him a pleasant, shy, modest man: it was not until afterwards that I discovered that he held the MC, the DCM and the MM. His story was that in 1916, during the war, a man had been left out wounded in no-man's-land during a night patrol; that next morning he had seen the man's arm sticking up, and had crawled out over the parapet, to find him in a shell crater actually within the German wire, suffering from multiple wounds.

It was a difficult job to get him out of the wire, but eventually I got him on my back and started back. On my way I heard somebody calling. I looked up and saw someone coming over our parapet with a stretcher. I could see it was not our stretcher-bearer. I waited until the man with the stretcher got nearer and I got the shock of my life when I saw it was General Fergusson. When he reached me, he opened the stretcher and I placed the wounded man on it. I remember telling the General we had better get a move on, because the enemy were sniping us and I was afraid the General would get hit. Anyhow we reached the trench safely. Our doctor was there to attend the man, but unfortunately he died soon after.

I discovered afterwards how General Fergusson came to be in the adventure. It appears that he was paying a visit to the front line trenches and arrived at the same time as the stretcher-bearers. General Fergusson enquired their business and was told what was happening. He immediately threw off his steel helmet and started over the parapet, telling the stretcher-bearers to wait in the trench. I should like to say that General Fergusson's action was the topic of the day in the Regiment. It proved to everyone that a General was prepared to risk his life to help a comrade.

The foregoing is taken from the account which Kew wrote out at my request, but he omitted one detail. He told me that when he first saw my father he mistook his grey hairs for a white bandage, and was bowled over when he realized who it was.

This story, too, I retailed to my father, half expecting him to deny it. He was then only seventy-three, and still very much on the ball. He said at once: 'I remember it well. I remember arriving at a point in that trench, and seeing a lot of people looking through periscopes. They told me that there was a man out there trying to bring in a wounded man, and not a soul was trying to give a hand. It was a disgraceful performance.'

It was for my brother James's carefully compiled archives that I got Kew to put his story on paper. So much for the tales one often hears: that Generals in the First War never went round their trenches. It is significant that Kew recognized my father, and did not have to be told his identity. My father never missed a day except for occasions when he had 'flu, and once when he had had a whiff of gas.

Chandos has another tale about my father when he arrived in Cologne in December 1918, to take over as Military Governor. The Oberburgermeister was none other than Dr Adenauer, who treated my father to a long speech, tracing the history of Cologne from Charlemagne onwards, and expressing his apprehensions for the immediate future. To quote Chandos again:

The Military Governor stood up, the very personification of a senior general. With the ghost of a smile he said: 'I am a soldier, and therefore the political history of Cologne does not concern me. As for the rest, my troops will keep your city in order. You may go now.' The Oberburgermeister and the Town Council filed out in some dejection and seemed aware that they had taken no tricks.

Still, when my father left a year later Adenauer, in bidding farewell, told him that, though strict, he had been fair and courteous; and he sent me a message of sympathy on his death.

In 1919 my father returned from Germany on half-pay, and although promoted to full General was never again employed by the Army. In his later years, when he grew more communicative, he ascribed this partly to the shadow of the Curragh Incident, and partly to the hostility of Winston Churchill, who was Secretary of State for War at the material time. They had first crossed swords over some incident at Omdurman; more remotely at the time of the Curragh Incident when Churchill was involved as a member of the Government; and more directly when Churchill was in temporary command of a battalion of Royal Scots Fusiliers in my father's Corps during the First War. It could well be that he had in fact reached his ceiling, and he certainly never grumbled about it; but it must have been galling for one who, when first promoted Major-General, had been the youngest in that rank by three years, and of whom Byng had written in a Confidential Report at the end of the war that 'his name will ring for ever in history as one of the most successful of our Corps Commanders'. Inactivity must have irked him, for he was still only fifty-six; but he had a measure of compensation when in 1934, eleven years after leaving the Army, he was created GCB, an unusual distinction after being so long in retirement. It filtered through to us long after that this was due to the King himself, who had had great sympathy for him over that wretched Curragh business, and the clove hitch in which he had found himself.

Naturally I was unaware at the time of all these ins and outs.

31

I only remember those immediately post-war years as halcyon, although from early 1921 I was spending two-thirds of each miserably at a prep school in Middlesex, long since disappeared and built over. Some summers my father let Kilkerran and the grouse-shooting for August and September to prosperous Americans such as Otto Kahn, while we moved down to Ladyburn, the dower-house two miles away; sometimes he shot it himself, entertaining old Grenadier friends like Sir Harold Ruggles-Brise and Lord Edward Gleichen, who had been one of his brigade commanders in the 5th Division in 1914. And in the evenings we used to play single-wicket cricket on the lawn.

Some features of that period, close on sixty years ago, seem remote today. To begin with, we had nine indoor servants: 'I can't think how your mother does it,' I remember my father saying; 'we used to have thirty.' We had no car until 1921, although we had briefly had one at The Curragh before the war; no telephone until 1930; electric light was not installed until 1955, up till when the house was lit by acetylene gas, regarded originally as one of my grandfather's more outrageous extravagances. Telegrams, costing sixpence, came to Kilkerran Station, whence they were brought by a boy on a bicycle. The post also came by bicycle, all the five miles from Maybole, brought by Mr Rogers, who was also a watchmaker: once a week he stayed on after delivering the letters, to wind all the clocks in the house. There was a memorable Sunday afternoon when on a family walk we spotted him poaching the river on the Barcully side, just downstream from Hamilton Bridge: he was so startled when my father tapped him on the shoulder that he nearly fell in. I am not sure which was the greater offence: the poaching or the Sabbath-breaking.

The lawns were mown with a mower drawn by a horse wearing leather boots; and the hay on either side of the drive with a scythe wielded by the shepherd who looked after the Home Parks: originally Wright, and then Tom MacTaggart, who lived to be ninety, and who had been born and laid in a manger, in accordance with the best of precedents, in the shepherd's house of Doughty (pronounced 'Dochty'), far back in the hills. There were family prayers every morning at

8.50 a.m., with the servants ranged on one side of the room, and the family and guests on the other. Every Sunday, wet or fine, the family walked to church and back, two-and-a-half miles each way, in bowler hats and stiff collars. Every Sunday evening between tea and dinner we would sing hymns and metrical psalms around the harmonium in the 'vestibule', as the hall was called where the staircase reached the first floor. (As in all Scots houses of that date, all the 'public rooms' were one stair up). The harmonium was played by my father, peering through the old-fashioned *pince-nez* that he wore only for reading. We were forbidden to read secular books or to hum secular tunes, yet we never found Sundays dreary.

It was an ordered and happy life. We children paid frequent calls on the nearer farms, where we ate vast teas, and on the many old widows who seemed to abound in various cottages, some of them thatched: Mrs Barton, a carter's widow, who was always good for a biscuit or two out of the old tea-caddy in which she kept them on her chimney-piece; 'old Mrs Jones', who lived to be a hundred, with a tremendous celebration which included a telegram from the King; and, above all, 'Nanny' Happle at the Poundland. Years later, when my parents were abroad and I was staying with the English tenants of Kilkerran during my holidays from school, I went to call on her; and she said: 'Hoo are ye?' Puzzled at not being recognized, I said: 'I'm Bernard.' Her voice rose in wrath: 'I didnae speir "*Wha*" were ye?" I speired "*Hoo*" were ye?" ' I felt black ashamed at having become so anglicized as not to recognize what should have been my own tongue.

One morning in August 1924, we were at breakfast at Ladyburn, Kilkerran being let for the shooting. Mr Rogers arrived with the post and the newspapers; and I was about to open the latter, when my father announced, quite casually, that in them we would see the announcement that he was to be Governor-General of New Zealand. It dawned on us why, some days before, he and my mother had paid a mysterious visit to her sister, Lady Augusta Inskip, who lived fifty miles down the coast at Dunskey, near Portpatrick. It now came to light that the purpose of that visit had been to ask whether she and her husband would be prepared to act as guardians to us boys if my parents were to accept this appointment. They had agreed, and consequently my parents had taken it on.

So it came about that they were faced with the same problem as had confronted their families in earlier generations. Dalhousie and his elder brother (who died young) had been left behind when their father went off to be Governor-General of Canada in 1819; he himself had had to leave his daughters in Scotland when he went to India in 1847, and did not see the younger one for nine years (the elder joined him in India after his wife's death); when Sir James Fergusson went to Bombay in 1880 he had had to leave his sons behind; and finally when Lord Glasgow went to New Zealand in 1892 he was able to take his six younger children with him, but had to abandon his two elder sons, who were already respectively in the Navy and Army.

It was decided that my sister Helen, aged twenty-two, would accompany my parents; and from this much happiness came to her, since she married their Military Secretary in New Zealand a year later. My brother James at Balliol, my brother Simon at Sandhurst, and I, nearing the end of my first year at Eton, were all the wrong ages, and it was ruled that we should remain in Britain. Each of us was able to have a short spell in New Zealand, mine of six months being the most generous; but this was the end of our family life together. By the time my parents returned, six years later, all of us were embarked on our various careers; and life at Kilkerran was never to be quite the same again.

Chapter Two

LANDFALLS OF THE PAST

The first foreign soil that ever my eye beheld was, improbably, the islet of Sombrero, in the Leeward Islands. I say 'soil', but it looked more like solid and arid rock; and I say 'foreign', but it is in fact a British possession. With its lighthouse, flashing dutifully throughout the hours of darkness, it marks the northern entrance to the Anegada Passage, pointing the way to Curaçao, 450 miles to the south-westward; but when I saw it that August morning in 1925, the light was extinguished, and the sun, already high in the heavens, was rendering the light-house and its attendant buildings a dazzling white. It was obvious to my eager boyish eye why the place was called Sombrero, for it was the shape of just such a hat: with a symmetrical lump in the middle, and an equally symmetrical broad brim around it, a little above sea-level. It is, in fact, a mile long and two cables wide, and the light is manned by four keepers from Anguilla, twenty miles to the south-eastward.

The next time I saw Sombrero was thirty-seven years later, in October 1962, when I was once again on my way to New Zealand, in a ship of the same line, the New Zealand Shipping Company (now no more), the *Rangitane*. It was in a previous *Rangitane*, sunk by enemy action in November 1940, that my parents returned from New Zealand in 1930. This time I was following in the footsteps of my father and both my grand-fathers, on my way to take up office in my turn as Governor-General of New Zealand; but there was a shadow of doubt as to whether the voyage might not be interrupted. There was crisis in the air, and we were listening eagerly to every news bulletin: which were a great deal more frequent, more urgent

35

and more pregnant than the flimsy sheets of useless news that had been their scanty equivalent in 1925. President Kennedy and Mr Khrushchev were having their show-down over Cuba; and there was a distinct possibility that our progress through the Caribbean and the Panama Canal might be interrupted by events outside our control. At Curaçao we were entertained by the Dutch (in fact, a half-caste) Governor, and also by a British frigate, which happened to be paying a courtesy visit, but which was at three hours' emergency notice for sea. At Panama, a few days later, the American Governor, though discreet, was also *distrait* while he entertained us; and he confessed to me, in a corner of his Residence, that, as soon as I took my leave, he was to fly to the Pentagon for urgent consultations. I took the hint at once, and my leave three minutes later.

No such cloud hung over the voyage of 1925. The day after the *Ruahine* passed Sombrero, there came in sight the beautiful Dutch island of Bonaire, with a jagged mountainous silhouette reminiscent of Arran on my native Clyde. Scudding along close under our lee, heeling well over in a fresh breeze on the same course as ourselves, was a beautiful half-decked cutter: her hold full of great hooped barrels containing I don't know what, and her crew a dozen Negroes, clad in enormous straw hats and little else. A few hours later, I was ashore on Curaçao: 'abroad' for the first time in my life.

It was appropriate that my first overseas landfall should have been in the West Indies, for (apart from the poor Royalist exile Sir John) the first of the family to develop itchy feet and venture abroad was, like myself, the youngest son of three: the Alexander who joined, and died in, the disastrous Scottish expedition to Darien. The little more that we know about him was that he was once a Captain in the Army, and that he never married.

But the Caribbean bug was not thereby eradicated from our bloodstream. I have already told how my grandfather Sir James was killed in an earthquake in Jamaica; and my father, in 1932 and 1933, was Chairman of a Royal Commission, the 'West Indies Closer Union Commission', which advocated, ahead of its time, the Federation which was eventually set up in 1958, but which lasted only a few years. Late in the eighteenth century, Sir Adam, the 3rd Baronet of Kilkerran, inherited to his embarrassment an estate in Jamaica, which he never visited, and of which he rid himself as soon as he reasonably could. There is still at Kilkerran a list of his slaves, all of whom bore Roman names such as Pompey, Cato, Catullus and so on. Sir Adam had succeeded his father, Lord Kilkerran the judge, because of the early death at the age of twenty-three of his elder brother John. John had run away from the school which he was attending at Northampton in England, run by Dr Philip Doddridge (author of 'O God of Bethel', and other hymns) in 1745, in order to join the Army to fight against the rebels; and there remain at Kilkerran copies of the acrimonious correspondence between his father and his headmaster concerning the incident. Sir Adam never married; and my brothers and I are descended from Sir James the 4th Baronet, whose father was the third brother Charles, wine merchant in London, whose second son, also Charles, a bachelor Nabob in a small way in India, bequeathed £30,000 to support Kilkerran.

Sir Adam was only twenty-six when he succeeded his father, and it fell to him to look after his seven surviving brothers and five sisters. These included the eccentric George, who became immortalized in contemporary memoirs as Lord Hermand the judge: he once interrupted the proceedings of the court by reading a whole chapter of *Guy Mannering* from the Bench, Walter Scott the still anonymous author being present. The youngest brother James was a bit of a rolling stone. Born in 1746, the year of Culloden, he eventually stopped rolling when he settled in Tobago in 1774, having already reconnoitred eight other West Indian islands, including Carriacou, just north of Grenada in the Windward Islands. On 7 February of that year, he wrote to Sir Adam from Tobago: 'I can not possibly at present explain the nature of the bargain I have made with Mr Wilson for want of time. I have bought his lot on Bloody Bay which I formerly mentioned to you; it consists of 300 acres of as good land as any in the West Indies, for which I am to pay two thousand pounds sterling in bills at 3, 6, 9 and 12 months, and 2000£ to lay at four years' interest at

5 per cent interest for which I have likewise granted him bills to draw upon you.' Poor Sir Adam!

Ten days later, he wrote to his brother Charles, inviting him to take a share; saying that he only intended to put on ten Negroes at first, and asking Charles to send him '2 dozn. Kilmarnock caps, 2 dozn. cutlasses, 2 dozn. coarse earthenware bowls', plus tools, bedding, medicines, and wine. 'Please to direct the goods to be landed at Bloody Bay.' It was perhaps little wonder that Charles forwarded this letter direct to Sir Adam.

These were only the first of a torrent of letters, pouring forth optimism, plans, apologies for being precipitate, and requests for more financial help, in almost equal proportions, along with protestations that his next-door neighbour George Ferguson (of the Aberdeenshire family of Pitsligo) approves of his purchase, his investments, his plans for planting cotton, indigo and other crops, and his selection of slaves. 'I have purchased ten new Eboe Negroes for which I have drawn on you . . . I have built a house for myself and two Negroe houses capable of containing 40 Negroes . . . I have purchased ten prime Mandingo* slaves for £430 for which I have given bills on you . . . I am this moment returned from performing one of the dirtiest offices of a surgeon on one of them, for I dress them all male and female with my own hands, as the doctor whom I employ lives at a distance, and only visits us once a week, for which I allow him £15 per year . . . I have actually since I sat down to write given two injections and one emetic, and dressed about twenty sores, but I assure you that I wash my hands with warm water and soap directly after these operations, so that you need not fear the paper being polluted.

'My house is situated on a very centrical situation on a fine flat topped hill which extends itself to the river and intersects the bottom. From this situation I not only command the bay but also the whole estate which I assure you contributes not a little to the dispatch of work, as I took some pains with the

---

* 'Eboes' are, of course, Ibos, from the Eastern Region of Nigeria, not far from the Niger delta; Mandingos came from 1500 miles up that river, in what is now Mali.

most knowing of my Negroes to show them that with my glass I could at any time tell who was idle altho' I was not with them . . . I could write on this subject with pleasure for a month were not my spirits damped at the reflection that I am obliged to pester you with money matters. For tho' I make no doubt of this estate soon refunding all that is layed out on it yet the subject is the most disagreeable I could possibly write about – and I dare say not very agreeable for you to read. Was I subject to the vapours I should certainly begin to fancy myself a cart horse. I am sometimes a month without seeing a soul but my own people.'

'I have taken the liberty of drawing on you for £114 for provision and lumber.' 'I have struck a bargain with Mr Fullerton for his seasoned gang, consisting of 28 slaves, very fine young people, healthy and thoroughly seasoned.' 'I think the gang now remaining work admirably, more than their original cost. The difference between a thoroughly seasoned Negroe and a raw one is in general estimated much too low. But besides all our Negroes being now seasoned, consequently less subject to sickness, they are vastly improved in every respect.' The price in 1777 for a 'Seasoned Negroe' was £50, and for a 'new' one £38.

The last, sad letter in the bundle is from one William Bruce, writing from Shirvan, Tobago, and dated 8 October 1777, to whom James refers in several letters. (All the neighbours to whom he refers bear Scots names: Bruce, the George Ferguson already mentioned, Fullerton, Gilbert Petrie of Englishman's Bay.) Bruce's letter to Sir Adam begins: 'Sir, it is with the deepest concern, I acquaint you of the death of my worthy and invaluable friend, your brother James Fergusson . . . He expired upon Saturday the 27th Septr. last, about four o'clock in the morning, after a long and painful illness, which he bore with the same good temper and spirits, which was usual to him in good health . . . About sixteen hours before his death, at his own desire, I wrote to his brother Charles . . .' Bruce goes on to say that thrice in the last twelvemonth James had come to Shirvan for reasons of health, it being drier than his own estate, and that at the moment of his death he was planning to go to Bermuda for a temporary change of climate. He writes of James in terms more affectionate than would seem to be called for in a merely conventional letter of condolence. He adds that he and Petrie had sought in vain for a will among James's effects, and offers the services of them both in winding up the estate, and in marketing and shipping the imminent crop. He sounds like a very good chap and faithful friend, signing himself 'Your most afflicted and most obedient servant'.

Bound up in the bundle is Sir Adam's endorsement of the whole correspondence, which reads pathetically across the span of two centuries, and seems to hint at some of the cares of a tender but troubled eldest brother. He wrote:

> The within letters are my only apology for engaging in that unfortunate business of Tobago. Those who do not know what it is to be anxious to procure an establishment for a beloved brother will think them none. Those who do, though they may not think them a sufficient excuse for the folly, will perhaps allow that they extenuate it.
>
> Janry 19th, 1781.

In 1964, there came as our guests to New Zealand for a few days Sir Solomon and Lady Hochoy, who were enjoying a sabbatical from Sir Solomon's twelve-year stint, first as Governor and then as Governor-General of Trinidad and Tobago. Sir Solomon is a Chinese – the tallest I have ever met – who was born in Jamaica, but taken by his parents to Trinidad in his infancy. There he had an illustrious career in the Civil Service, ending up with four years as Chief Secretary, before becoming his country's first Governor. They were the most congenial of guests. When Peter Gibaut, my naval ADC, offered Sir Solomon a pink gin, he replied: 'Pink's no good to me: I'm colour-blind. Could I have a whisky-and-soda?' And when he asked a footman: 'What's that fruit? It's a new one to me'; and the footman said: 'Those are Chinese gooseberries, Your Excellency'; Sir Solomon fixed him with a mock glare, and said: 'Are you making fun of me, young man?'

I told Sir Solomon of my remote Tobago connection, and as a result we found ourselves spending three days with him in Trinidad the following year, on our way back to New Zealand from our mid-term leave in Britain. He and his wife flew over to Tobago with us, and they despatched us up the coast to Bloody Bay, which proved to be about thirty miles up the northern coast of the island, in a swift, impeccably smart Coastguard vessel. I had with me typescripts of James's letters, furnished by my eldest brother; a photostat of James's sketch-map of the property; and a map of the island, dated 1799. My wife and son, then aged ten, were with me. All went well until we reached Bloody Bay, when the heavens opened, and the rain poured down on us solidly.

We were put ashore, in defiance of the weather, in a small boat with an outboard motor, and found six or eight black fishermen hauling a net on the beach. I explained who I was, and why I was there; and they gave me a hearty welcome, with the warm rain splashing off their bare shoulders, and told me that the families living just round the point, 'coloured people, you know', were also called Fergusson. They pointed out the path at the head of the beach, which they said led up to the ruins of the old 'barracks': this was the word they used; and so we set off, up the hill.

The site of the 'barracks' was exactly on the spot which my sketch-map indicated; but we were defeated by the elements. The rain intensified; the track, which was steeply uphill and overgrown anyhow, became more and more of a butter-slide; and after fifteen minutes, aware of the pressure of time, of the Coastguard vessel awaiting, and the aircraft also, we simply and sadly gave up, slid down the hill (taking seconds where we had taken minutes), and re-embarked, wet to the skin. That is the nearest that any member of the family is ever likely to get to where poor James struggled so hard, so far from Kilkerran, two hundred years ago, to make a living, to justify himself, and to pay back his brothers for their evidently minimal confidence in him, aged only thirty-one when he died.

I stumbled on two other things before we left Tobago. The first was the painful fact that the Bloody Bay property had just been bought by a prosperous Chinese for exactly the same sum in pounds sterling as that to which James had committed Sir Adam all these many years ago, and not a penny more. The second was a baptismal record dated 29 August 1796 of

one Mattie, daughter of James Fergusson, deceased, by a
black woman also called Mattie. I found four other Ferguson
or Fergusson entries in the same record, referring to three
girls and one boy, all specified as 'black', and all between
1792 and 1800: records before 1782 having been destroyed
during a brief French occupation. There is nothing to indicate
whether these were of Pitfour, or Kilkerran, or of some other
origin; but presumably they account for the families living
'just around the point', whom I would dearly have loved to
have met, had time and weather permitted. 'Mattie' is recorded as having been born in January 1786, ten years before
her baptism, which would rule out 'our' James as being her
father, since this was nine years after his death; and the fact is
well established that slaves often adopted the names of their
owners, all considerations of paternity apart.

I am not ashamed of being the collateral descendant of
slave-owners. Why should I be? It was normal in their time. I
like to believe that James was a kindly master, despite his use
of his spy-glass to make sure that his men were not idling, and
that his medical attentions upon them, as described in his
letter, were inspired by something more than a mere veterinarian
instinct. There was still some time to pass before slave-owning
became a matter for shame. James Newton the hymn-writer,
and the author of 'How Sweet the Name of Jesus Sounds', was
still engaged in the slave trade a mere twenty years before
James Fergusson bought his first team of 'Negroes', and
continued to command slave ships for several years after his
conversion to Evangelical Christianity. It was the British who
first awoke to its iniquities, and strove, with eventual success,
to abolish it, in the teeth of the opposition of many entrenched
vested interests: not least the vested interest of black Africans.

Slavery is still more rife than many people realize. I have
myself been waited on by slaves in at least four countries, all
of them Arab, during the last twenty years, and have met
several former slaves who have been 'manumitted'. Indeed, I
have met one man who has been manumitted twice. 'Manumitted' literally means 'to set forth from one's hand'; legally, it
means 'to set free from slavery'; and it can be accomplished by,
say, a British Resident with certain quasi-consular powers in

certain States giving the equivalent of a passport to a slave who has managed to slip away from his master. My acquaintance who was manumitted twice had the misfortune to be snapped up again by his former owner, and the good fortune to succeed in slipping away again, and back into the British Resident's office. This time he had the good sense to move further along the Persian Gulf, to a new abode and a new life.

Twenty years ago I visited two small Arab countries in succession, in both of which there were slaves. In the one, the slaves seemed to be for ever cowering for fear of a blow, or of a cuff on the side of the head. In the next, not fifty miles away, the slaves, both male and female, seemed to have the same relationship towards their masters as that of a treasured family retainer, privileged to scold or to be teased in the same fashion as a beloved Nanny; and from the enquiries that I made of the British Resident, I found that my assessment was not far adrift. In more recent years, I have spent several days in an Arab country where some of the slaves owned and drove Cadillacs, and had slaves of their own. They were not their own masters: far from it; and if they were to put a foot wrong, they would be seriously at risk. But they knew on which side their bread was buttered, and took good care not to drop it wrong side up.

I seem to have got well off course since calling at Curaçao. The Panama Canal was as hot and steamy in 1962 as in 1925: in our cabin, even steamier, since a stewardess inadvertently allowed our bath to overflow, and it took three days to get the temperature back to normal. Fortunately, soon after entering the Pacific you encounter for several days the surprisingly cool Humboldt Current. In 1925, ten days out from Panama, and still twenty short of Wellington, we hove to for an hour and a half off Pitcairn, while the Islanders came off to pick up mail and to sell us fruit. I was eager-eyed to meet all these Christians and Adamses and other bearers of *Bounty* names. Years later, it fell to me as Governor-General to invest with the MBE John Christian, sixth generation in descent from Fletcher who led the mutiny; very civilly, he invested me in return with two small wooden turtles, of his own carving. I was proud of this link; but my eye was well and truly wiped a little later by my successor Sir Arthur Porritt, the distinguished New Zealand-born surgeon and former Rhodes Scholar. On his way to take up the appointment, his ship diverted to Pitcairn in response to an SOS, and the Governor-General-designate whipped out an Islander's appendix as easy as wink. I accused him at the time, and have never withdrawn the charge, of having staged the whole thing as a public relations gimmick.

The man I remember most clearly in the old *Ruahine* was the dark, saturnine, Scots Chief Officer, Jock Laird. He rarely smiled, and some thought him dour; but I found him kind and patient, and he often allowed me to accompany him on his rounds of the ship. In a certain seaport in New Zealand, there is a memorial to him, and the two reasons why do credit both to him, and to those who erected it. The first was this. Apparently he was a guest at some local function, at which the speaker, with the approval of those present, was inveighing against Britain for not buying more New Zealand goods. Jock rose from his chair, lumbered over to the window, looked out of it, grunted, and returned to his place. Pressed to say what was on his mind, he made a speech of one sentence: 'I've just looked at all the cars parked down there in the street, and every one is American.'

The second was rather different. On 20 August 1940, the *Turakina* (8700 tons gross, Master, Captain J. B. Laird), in the Tasman Sea 250 miles off Cape Egmont, bound from Sydney to Wellington, encountered the German commerce raider *Orion*, which ordered her to stop and not to use her wireless. Jock promptly began reporting his position and the fact that he was being shelled; he turned stern on, and opened fire on *Orion* with his single little pop-gun of a 4·7 mounted on the poop. *Orion*'s armament consisted of six 5·9-inch guns, one 3-inch, six AA guns and six torpedo tubes. *Turakina* is thought to have scored one hit; but within twenty minutes she herself had been hit repeatedly, including by two torpedoes; she sank two minutes after the second torpedo, and Jock Laird and thirty-three of his men went down with her. Twenty-one were rescued, of whom one, badly wounded, died.

The other memorable person aboard *Ruahine* was a passenger,

Edgar Stead, a noted New Zealand naturalist from Canterbury, who had been asked, with his wife, to keep an eye on me during the voyage. His interests ranged widely; but on this particular trip he was bringing out rhododendrons and azaleas to plant in New Zealand, from those three notable gardens, all within fifty miles of Kilkerran: Bargany, Lochinch and Logan. Thrice daily he had made it my duty to help him water these damn things, half-way across the world; but I had my reward in the 1960s, when his by now legendary garden of Ilam, bequeathed to Canterbury University, blazed in glory each November. I am not sure that anybody believed me when I said that the ancestors of these superb shrubs came from my corner of Scotland, and that I had watered them three times a day all the way out to New Zealand; but the happy convention that nobody contradicts a Governor-General sustained me.

It was Edgar Stead, wearing his familiar Sherlock Holmes fore-and-after hat, who awoke me early in the morning of Sunday 6 September 1925, and chased me on deck for my first look at New Zealand. We were approaching Cape Palliser, and I noted in my diary, the only one I have ever kept: 'Country seems very desolate.' I hung over the rails all morning, even while the coast receded, but became wildly excited as we approached Orongorongo and Pencarrow Head. Pencarrow, I knew, was where the barque *Halcione*, 878 tons, had piled up in January 1896, and become a total loss. It was in *Halcione* in 1875 that my father and his brother and sisters had sailed home from New Zealand as children round the Horn, thus enabling them to boast for the rest of their lives that they had been round 'both Capes' under sail: for they had made the outward voyage round Good Hope. In those days, to have done this endowed you with the privilege of putting both feet on to the table after dinner. My father's eldest sister, my Aunt Susan Georgina (known less reverently to us her nephews as 'Aunt Caledonia', because she was stern and wild) was an extremely dignified, indeed forbidding, old lady, who was a friend of Queen Mary, whom she resembled, and on whom my generation thought she modelled herself. Once, at a smart dinner in London at which several Admirals were present, she electrified the company by saying: 'How many of you are entitled to do this?' and swung her satin shoes up on to the festive board. Those who knew her only as a public figure were shocked and horrified; those who knew her well loved her and were proud of her all the more. As for the Admirals present, they were tickled to death: the more so because not one of them could rival her claim.

My mother came off to greet me in the harbour tug, the *Janie Seddon*, before *Ruahine* berthed. I must have been a horrid shock to her, since during the year since we had said goodbye to each other I had grown three inches, and my voice had broken. There was a shock for me, too, at Government House two hours later, when I learned that my sister Helen had become engaged to the Military Secretary, Major Leonard Haviland of the Bengal Lancers, whom I had scarcely heard of, let alone met; but that was the beginning of a long and happy story, which was to last close on fifty years.

Even after more than half a century, I remember clearly those blissful six months of boyhood in New Zealand: the more clearly, perhaps, because after my reluctant return to Eton I was so homesick for that paradisal country. I was constantly drawing nostalgic maps of it from memory in the end pages of my schoolbooks, when I should have been better employed: sketchmaps of sheep stations on which I had spent a few days, and charts of waters on which I had sailed.

I had had trouble at school with my eyes, as a result of which my hours of reading were strictly rationed, and I was excused all lessons while in New Zealand. The only lessons I had were for a period of four weeks, when a rather pathetic, down-at-heel, elderly Old Etonian exile was engaged, while we were spending a month in Dunedin, to give me some oral lessons in Latin for a couple of hours a day (and I suspect that this was an act of charity towards him by my parents rather than for my direct benefit); and when an elderly Maori, at my own suggestion, came up to Government House in Wellington to teach me something of his language. (My mother spoke it a bit, with more enthusiasm than accuracy; she had learned some as a girl.) The experiment was not successful, since he

46

used to get carried away into telling long legendary tales in either Maori or English, or reciting endless *whakapapa* or genealogies. To these I listened, as bewildered as I was fascinated, but learned little more than an approximate pronunciation. However, I did carry back with me to Eton a Maori Bible, which I still possess, and which I put to good use by irritating my neighbours in College Chapel, following the Lessons in it while they were dutifully doing the same in their Greek Testaments.

I pleaded with my parents to let me stay on in New Zealand rather than go back to Eton: to allow me instead to attend Wanganui, where two of my mother's brothers had been educated when their father was Governor in the nineties; or Christ's College, where many of my New Zealand cousins had been; or Timaru Boys High School, which had deeply impressed me when I went there with my father. But my father was adamant, taking the line that, since my life would be based on Britain rather than on New Zealand, I should complete my schooling at Eton. Not until after he died, when I had access to his diaries, did I realize that he had given serious consideration to my plea, and had only decided against it after much thought. In retrospect, I am sure that he was right, but at the time I was deeply disappointed.

Although I missed two halves at Eton, that New Zealand episode was unquestionably more than a mere substitute for them: it was a far richer contribution to my education. In 1925, it was a mere eighty-five years since New Zealand had first come under the British flag at the Treaty of Waitangi, on 6 February 1840. Pioneers of the first generation were still in evidence; and there was an abundance of people who had been children when their parents had landed, to use one of my father's favourite phrases, 'with little more than a hammer and a bag of nails'. With my father, I attended gatherings of veterans of the Maori Wars: veterans of both sides, who chuckled amicably over this victory or that defeat, as though they were memories of this or that Rugby match for the Ranfurly Shield. At such reunions there was still to be seen the odd wearer of the New Zealand Cross, the decoration for gallantry illicitly instituted by the Governor, Sir George

Bowen, in 1869 by an Order in Council, and reluctantly legitimized by Queen Victoria a year or two later. Only twenty-three were awarded, about a quarter of them to Maori, and the last surviving holder died at Whakatane in 1933, aged eighty-five.

I had the good fortune to meet, under my father's aegis, most of the leading Maori figures of the day. Three of them had in common a high proportion of Irish blood. These were Sir James Carroll (Timi Kara), who was rather older than the others, having been born in 1853, and who had at one time been Acting Prime Minister; Sir Peter Buck (Te Rangi Hiroa), doctor, DSO, anthropologist, former Member of Parliament, and the author of several learned, witty and readable books about his people; and the Rev. F. A. Bennett, who subsequently became the first Maori Bishop, and with whom I continued to exchange Christmas cards until he died many years later. My mother and I attended more than once his beautiful church at Ohinemutu, near Rotorua, and several of his sons became friends of mine in after years. Then there was Sir Apirana Ngata of the Ngatiporou on the East Coast, who did so much for the renaissance of Maori culture, and Sir Maui Pomare of the Ngatiawa, the doctor, who did more for Maori health than any other individual. All except Bennett were at one time Members of Parliament, and I came in due course to know the children and grandchildren of all except Buck, who was, sadly, childless. There were also the other Maori MPs, the huge H. W. Uru and Tau Henare. The latter was the grandson of Robert Wynyard, who succeeded Sir George Grey as Governor in 1864; Tau's son James, who won the DSO commanding the Maori Battalion in the Second War, a magnificent figure of commanding influence among both Europeans and Maori in the far north of New Zealand, was knighted in 1978. I met others as well, such as Mita Taupopoki, the eccentric old Arawa chief, and his kinsman Kepa Ehau, who used to interpret for my father when in Arawa country, and several of the chiefs in Poverty Bay and the Bay of Plenty.

Long after I was back at Eton, I used to recall the day when my father unveiled the War Memorial at Tikitiki in the Ngatiporou country on the East Coast. Our party was staying

Old Kilkerran

Kilkerran today

Captain John Bollons

at Matahiia with Ken Williams, a scion of the great Williams
family who are part of the tapestry of New Zealand history.
The original Henry Williams was a naval officer who had
taken Holy Orders, and settled as a missionary in the Bay of
Islands in 1823, being joined soon after by his younger brother
William. Between them they had bred twenty children, and
the two of them had been instrumental in the negotiation of
the Treaty of Waitangi, which had bound the two races
together into a single nation. My father's younger brother,
Admiral Sir James Fergusson, had married one of Henry's
granddaughters, which conferred on us a sort of collateral link
with that illustrious clan. Ken and his cousin Arnold between
them had done much to open up the East Coast; but far from
alienating the Maori inhabitants had helped and inspired
them in the arts of agriculture and husbandry: so much so that
when the Williams family came under political attack in
1916 for having allegedly exploited their peculiar advantages
in the matter of acquiring Maori lands, Sir Api Ngata sprang
passionately to their defence in Parliament, declaring that no
family anywhere had ever done more for anybody than the
Williamses for the Maori of the East Coast.

That hot February morning, our party drove in a convoy of
old-fashioned open 'tourer' cars, as they were then called, to
the great *hui*, or gathering, at Tikitiki. Long before we arrived,
we could hear the glorious, open-throated singing of the several
thousand Maori gathered there: it still remains one of the
corners of New Zealand where Europeans are in the minority.

It was a moving and memorable occasion. Three hundred
and fifty of the Ngatiporou and kindred East Coast tribes had
gone to the war. Of these eighty-seven, almost a quarter, had
been killed, and every one was a volunteer. This tradition
carried on into the Second War, and Ngarimu the posthumous
Maori VC was also a Ngatiporou.

But the day was not without its lighter moments. We, by
which I mean the Vice-Regal party, were met by the traditional challenge, led by a belligerent group ('their tongues
hanging out a fathom', as Captain Bollons, of whom more
later, used to say). They were led by a half-naked savage,
brandishing a *taiaha* and yelling the odds within a yard of my

father: who, knowing the form, stood his ground with good-humoured dignity. This seemingly barbaric greeting over, the leader suddenly relaxed, saying: 'I'll be back in a moment, Your Excellencies'; and disappeared round the corner, to return within three minutes, impeccably dressed in a bowler hat and all that goes with it, as Sir Apirana Ngata, MP.

Meanwhile, the Vice-Regal party had been led towards the covered stand erected for it: a temporary building which in India would have been called a *chamiana*, but which was known in New Zealand as a *raupo* hut: poles, a grass roof and no walls. The rising sun had melted the varnish on the newly varnished chairs. As everybody got up to greet us, a very old Maori lady of ancient lineage and with a tattooed chin found that her chair had stuck to her. Her children and grand-children tried to separate her from it by pulling her like a cracker, with devastating results; she was hustled away round the corner, and brought back later in a different dress. A long day ended with the sounds of hymn-singing as the Maori wended their various homeward ways on foot or horseback, while the sun went down behind the high, venerated hill of Hikurangi.

That was part of a tour lasting three and a half weeks; but the day after Tikitiki my parents took me aside, and explained to me with delicacy one tiny fraction of the facts of life. They told me that my sister, who was of the party, was pregnant, and that the trip was proving too strenuous for her; the roads at that time in that district were too rough for anybody in her condition; her husband being on duty must carry on with the tour, but I was to escort her back to Auckland by sea, in the little coastal vessel *Wainui*, that called once a week at near-by Tokumaru Bay. I must treat her with tender care; she must not lift a suitcase, or risk any bump. I received my instructions with a solemn sense of importance, and felt highly responsible as the diminished party set off on their onward journey to Gisborne and beyond.

It was a shock at Tokumaru Bay two days later to find that there was no jetty, and that we would have to be slung on board *Wainui* in a net, of all things, out of a small surf-boat. There was a heavy sea running, and after all these parental warnings it was with horror that I watched my beloved sister thus soaring aloft. We had the dickens of a rough voyage round East Cape and across to Cape Colville. That evening on the bridge, long after dark, while my sister lay miserably below being sick, Captain Grey regaled me with a grisly story of the days when he was apprentice in a windjammer. One of the men had died, and his body was consigned to the deep; his effects, including a knife to which he was known to be particularly attached, had been auctioned among the ship's company. That evening at dusk he was observed to be clambering back over the taffrail at the starboard bow, obviously in search of his precious knife; its purchaser flung it over the side in terror, whereupon the ghost followed it, and never troubled them again. I postponed for as long as possible leaving the well-lit bridge, and the company of the captain and the man at the wheel, for the dark of the deck and the ten yards or so to the companion that led below. When at last I ventured, and just as I set foot on the deck, the ship pitched yet again, and a little lick of white spray came over the taffrail at the starboard bow, for all the world like the long-dead mariner come back in search of his knife. I plunged down the companion and along to my cabin as fast as I could lick, slammed the door, and kept the light on all night.

That trip to the East Coast, which had also included Rotorua and the Bay of Plenty, was my last in New Zealand. I had already accompanied my parents on tours to Taranaki and New Plymouth, to Hawke's Bay and Canterbury and Westland; I had spent a fortnight each on stations in Hawke's Bay (Horonui) and the Wairarapa (Te Parae). Te Parae was the home of Guy Williams, one of Henry's many grandsons, and Guy's son Alister had become a close friend; he had been one of our party when we camped for five days on Little Barrier Island, a jealously guarded bird sanctuary in the Hauraki Gulf, north of Auckland. There had also been the month in Dunedin, where among other things my father had opened the South Seas Exhibition, which included many of the exhibits from Wembley the previous year.

The Dunedin Exhibition had been both ambitious and successful, though its opening was not without incident. An arm of the harbour, now known as Logan Park, had been reclaimed to form a perfect showground. The opening ceremony was marked by the singing of a large choir, recruited for the occasion, and by the playing of the Band and the Pipes and Drums of The Argyll and Sutherland Highlanders, specially imported from Scotland. Their joint activities had unfortunately not been fully co-ordinated. When choir and band combined in the rendering of the *Old Hundredth*, from opposite sides of the ground, the former used the old-fashioned 'gathering notes' at the beginning and end of each line, whereas the band did not. As neither could hear the other, each carried on regardless, so that the band reached the end a clear verse ahead of the choir. Worse was to follow when, through a second misunderstanding, the choir sang *God Defend New Zealand* as soulfully as they knew how, what time the band cheerfully marched up and down to the strains of *Colonel Bogey* (of which, incidentally, the Bandmaster, Ritchie, *alias* Ken J. Alford, was the composer). And on visiting the exhibition a day or two later my father, invited to sample one of the New Zealand wines on show, found himself sipping a glass of coloured water, to the lasting embarrassment of the exhibitor.

From Dunedin we sailed, at the end of November, for a voyage of more than three weeks in the Government steamer *Tutanekai*. She was a vessel of about eight hundred tons: no beauty, to be frank, but I loved her dearly. She had the dual role of servicing lighthouses, inspecting buoys and beacons, searching for castaways on remote islands and renewing the caches of food maintained for them, on the one hand; and serving as the Governor-General's official yacht on the other. In her, for instance, shortly after I left for home, my parents did a cruise of more than six weeks to the Cook Islands, to western Samoa (which had been taken over from Germany in 1914, and was to remain under New Zealand administration until 1962), to Pago-Pago and to Tonga; and, later on, to the Chatham Islands.

Tutanekai's Master was Captain John Bollons, who has remained one of my greatest heroes all my life. Many years later I wrote a novel around him (*Captain John Niven*), embodying all I knew of him and a good deal else besides. As an orphan English boy of sixteen, he was wrecked in the barque *England's Glory* when, in 1881, she missed stays trying to enter Bluff Harbour, always a tricky entrance, and piled up about a mile to the westward. The crew were succoured by the local Maori, with whom they lived for a few days; and young Bollons so liked the life with them that when a rescue party arrived, he hid and never rejoined his shipmates. He continued to live for several years with his adopted tribe, but eventually took service in the Government steamer *Stella*, *Tutanekai*'s predecessor at two removes. When my mother's father Lord Glasgow became Governor in 1892, Bollons was Second Mate in *Hinemoa*, *Stella*'s successor; and my mother and her sisters were captivated by this shy young man, in many ways more Maori than European. She was naturally overjoyed to find him now the captain; and he became almost my father's closest friend in all New Zealand.

To me, he was romance personified. Like his crew, I was a little frightened of him: he once sent me away from the table (my parents being ashore somewhere) for having dirty fingernails; but I adored him without reservation. His language was a mixture of English, of Maori, and of sea-faring terms. Once, when he came to tea at Government House, my mother expressed the hope that he hadn't got wet in the rain-squall that had just passed over. 'Oh no, Your Excellency,' he said, 'I hove to under the lee of the Post Office.' And once, when he had told his steward to bring him some fresh tea, because what he had just brought was 'five-fathom tea', I asked him what this mysterious phrase meant. 'Tea that's too weak,' he replied: 'you can see the bottom at five fathom.' He knew the invisible floor of the sea around New Zealand as well as a taxi-driver knows the streets of London. He was known and loved by all the lighthouse-keepers and their children; by everybody who dwelt on islands, or at the head of remote bays to which no road reached; by innumerable coastal Maori, who would swarm on board, whether to laugh at his sallies in their own tongue, or to ask him to arbitrate in some local dispute. I can see him now, with his neat grey beard, clipped in the same shape as that of King George the Fifth; with his hands in his jacket pockets, and his feet set well apart, whether ashore or afloat, in case some sudden movement of the ship might upset his balance. He was pure Conrad.

We cruised, that time, to Bluff and to Stewart Island, and in leisurely fashion all the way up the South Island Sounds, in the wake of the great Captain Cook. We had intended to go down to the Snares, a group of uninhabited islands, and lying sixty miles south of Stewart Island, discovered by Vancouver in 1791, to collect some sea lions for the Wellington Zoo; but the weather was against us, and after two false starts from Stewart Island we cut our losses, and shortly after midnight on 10 December made for Preservation Sound and Chalky Inlet, finishing up for the night in Cook's old anchorage in Dusky Sound. During the two or three days that we dodged between various harbours on the northern and eastern coasts of Stewart Island, we learned much from Captain Bollons's lips, apart from visiting a group of Norwegian whalers in Port Pegasus. We spent a morning on the site of the long-abandoned Maori village on The Neck, 'fossicking' among its remains, with old Bollons mumbling away *sotto voce* in Maori. I imagine that he was intoning, Maori-fashion and in Maori tradition, greetings to his long-dead friends from that settlement, 'in the long village from which there is no return'.

In Dusky Sound he showed us the tree-stumps cut by Cook's men to afford platforms on which to mount his instruments, and pointed out the remains, in Facile Harbour, of the *Endeavour* (not Cook's): the first recorded shipwreck, in 1795, in New Zealand waters. (I sought it again in vain in the 1960s: I had the place clearly in my mind's eye, and I am sure I was within a couple of cables of it, but I failed dismally to find it.) Sound by Sound, he told us of Cook's association with each place, and the adventures of those who came after him. At the head of Breaksea Sound, for instance, two arms go off into the high interior as though to form the letter Y. In his voyage of 1773, Cook had no time to investigate either, faced as he was with the prospect of a dead beat out of the Sound to regain open water; so he wrote on his draft chart the words 'Nobody Knows What.' On board as a midshipman was George Vancouver, who had already done one voyage with Cook before

54

the mast. Eighteen years later, in 1791, Vancouver, now himself in command of two exploring ships, *Discovery* and *Chatham*, had the satisfaction of resuming where Cook had left off, 'as it was moderate and pleasant weather'. The job was done in ships' boats. Vancouver himself explored the northern arm, which now bears his name, and the Chatham pinnace the southern, now called Broughton Arm after *Chatham*'s youthful captain. Vancouver, returning triumphantly to his ship, had the delight of writing against the original annotation of his famous captain: 'Somebody Knows What.' And when the two boat parties joined up with each other again, 'we drank a cheerful glass to the memory of Captain Cook, whose steps we were now pursuing'. This entry in the log demonstrates what glorious and generous men these venturous sailormen were, and what good pickers such people as Admiral Palliser were who chose them. Who but Cook would have immortalized his first landfall of New Zealand by calling it after the humble ship's boy who first spotted it from aloft, 'Young Nick's Head'?

All this and much more was told to us by Captain Bollons during those seemingly timeless days of cruising in the Sounds; and our cruise added further to the local nomenclature. One day of dripping rain, when we were steaming slowly up Doubtful Sound, he asked me whether I would like an island to be called after me. Naturally I said that I'd love it; and he pointed at a little round rock, covered with bush, shaped like a plum pudding and perhaps seventy feet high, and said: 'Would that one do?' Ecstatic, I accepted; and for a few years at school I kidded myself that, back in New Zealand, there was an island, however small and remote, called after me. As I grew older, I dismissed this miasmic thought from my mind; but when I returned to New Zealand in 1962 I found that he had been as good as his word, as I should have guessed that he would be. Fergusson Islet in Doubtful Sound now has a light on it, to lead vessels up to the elaborate hydro-electric works on Deep Cove, at the Sound's head: I regard that light as the equivalent of the Red Hackle, which I wore on my bonnet for nearly thirty years in The Black Watch.

Those 'seemingly timeless days of cruising' were limited only by the fact that my father had to be in Greymouth, some two hundred and fifty miles north of the northernmost Sound, Milford, by a certain date: a date which was duly met, although it involved lying off, rolling in a heavy Tasman swell, for a couple of hours before there was enough water to allow *Tutanekai* over the Grey River bar. But the 'timeless days' in the Sounds were wonderfully happy, and enabled my parents – although the phrase had not then been coined – to 're-charge their batteries'. The Sounds were then, as they almost remain today, totally uninhabited: the only exceptions now being the hydro-electric activity at the head of Deep Cove in Doubtful Sound, and the tourist development at the head of Milford Sound. Otherwise they remain largely as in my day – or as in Cook's.

There are these deep fjords: fjords so deep that, in one place that I know of, a substantial waterfall plunges over a cliff more than two thousand feet above sea level, and is blown away by the time it should have reached one's up-turned face. There is one sheer cliff of the same height, below which a depth of 212 fathom is registered 30 yards off-shore. It was about another, but more feathery, waterfall, in one of the other Sounds, that my mother so appropriately quoted the Tennysonian lines of her youth:

A land of streams: some, like a downward smoke,
Slow-dropping veils of thinnest lawn did go . . .

It was country unchanged since the dawn of time. Even the Maori had scarcely penetrated it, apart from the occasional coastwise search for greenstone on its beaches. The half-dozen frightened folk whom Captain Cook encountered in Dusky Sound in 1773 will have been one of the last tattered remnants of Ngati-Mamoe, a humble, peaceable and unbelligerent little clan, chased from pillar to post by tougher people from the north. Some trickle of their blood may still survive today, but little more than that.

A curious tale circulated at the time of Bollons's death in 1929. He had remained ashore for a minor operation, and *Tutanekai* had sailed without him, for a routine inspection of buoys and beacons, under his mate, Barney Buller, his lifelong Maori friend from his own tribe in the far south. That night, as she lay at anchor in complete calm, she began to pitch for no reason. A large moth flew on board, visiting the saloon, his cabin, the bridge; and the Maori members of the crew, shattered, at once exclaimed that the Captain must be dead. According to Maori legend, this particular moth would appear if anybody died away from home; it represented the spirit of the dead man taking leave of his familiar haunts, before setting out on the traditional journey of a departing soul by way of Spirits' Bay in the far north of the North Island. Bollons had indeed died that evening, a few hours after my father had visited him in hospital. I retold this story in my novel, and received three letters from old friends of Bollons who had heard it at the time.

In March 1926 I sailed for home and Eton with a heavy heart, from Auckland in the old *Niagara*, by way of Suva, Honolulu and Vancouver. The last I saw of New Zealand was the Hen and Chicken Islands, so named by Captain Cook: one of the latter was later christened 'Lady Alice Island' after my mother, who had camped on it for a week. It was in this very stretch of water, just off the Chickens, that *Niagara* was to strike a mine and to sink, fortunately without loss of life, fourteen years later. Once again she was bound for Vancouver; and she was carrying 295 boxes, each holding two gold ingots to the total value of £2½ m, which were being transferred to the United States. The wreck was located seven months later in over seventy fathom of water; and 94% of the bullion was recovered in a ten-month operation by a team of divers headed by two Australian brothers called Johnstone. At the time, this was the deepest successful salvage operation ever undertaken, and for all I know the record still stands.

Chapter Three

HOME AND FRANCE

I travelled home under the benevolent wing of Sir Francis Bell, the Grand Old Man of New Zealand politics. He was then aged seventy-five, but, like Moses, 'his eye was not dim, nor his natural strength abated'. When Massey the great war-time Prime Minister of New Zealand died in May 1925, my father tried hard to induce Bell to take over; he had been *de facto* Prime Minister during the many months of Massey's terminal illness, and was something of a world figure. But Bell was adamant. He had ceased to be an MP as far back as 1896, professing himself disgusted with political intrigue, and had only consented to come back to lead the Upper House (abolished in 1950) at Massey's earnest request when the latter came to power in 1912. In 1925 he was unwilling to return to the Lower House, and refused to contemplate the idea of a Prime Minister in the Upper. He agreed only to act for a couple of weeks (thus becoming the first New Zealand-born Prime Minister) until a new Leader had been chosen; and the choice fell upon Gordon Coates, a cattle-farmer from the Kaipara Harbour, north-west of Auckland, with an outstanding war record, aged a mere forty-seven. But Coates knew little of Britain, whereas Bell knew it well, having been up at Cambridge and a member of the English Bar, with a wide British acquaintance. The Imperial Conference of 1926 was about to take place, and Bell agreed to support the new Prime Minister at its deliberations. Hence his journey.

Lady Bell had died many years before, and he was reluctant to travel to Britain with only his Private Secretary, Stanley Hunter, for company. When he heard that, for reasons of economy, I was to return to Britain by the same rather dull route *via* Panama, he at once asked my parents to let me accompany him, insisting on paying the difference. I am a little surprised, in retrospect, at my father agreeing, for he hated being under an obligation to anybody; but agree he did, and in consequence I had a memorable journey. I found my cabin full of books provided for the voyage by Dame Clara Butt, who had lunched at Government House a few days before and heard of my impending journey; but I was much nettled by her assessment of my mental age, since she had sent a selection of G. A. Henty and R. M. Ballantyne, whom I had long outgrown.

Suva was sultry, Honolulu was heaven; and I had a happy hour on a surfboard with a professional. Victoria and Vancouver were blotted out by rain, but we saw a remarkable run of salmon in the Fraser River, jostling each other like whitebait. From Vancouver to Seattle we travelled by overnight steamer, with the high snow-covered mountains to the eastward dazzling in the moonlight. Union and Washington, the two fresh-water lakes at Seattle, were crammed with sailing-vessels, the like of which I have never seen, built during the war and laid up ever since: some rigged as barques and others as ships: five-masters, six-masters and one astonishing seven-master, all fitted with labour-saving electric winches. I remember nothing of Portland, Oregon, and little of San Francisco, except for a vast number of seals lying on a rock near the Golden Gate, and the yarns spun by Stevenson Smith, the New Zealand Government Agent, who had fought against the Maori warrior Te Kooti, and had lived for some years in the Chathams. In the train between San Francisco and Los Angeles, we ran through a vast cloud of black smoke at least fifteen miles across, rising from the oil-wells of San Luis Obispo, which had been on fire for several days. The line ran within half a mile of them, and at the heart of the smoke we could see the flames leaping and swirling a hundred feet high, and hear their roar. At Hollywood we had luncheon with Tom Mix the cowboy film star (I have a photograph of him, with Sir Francis, Stan Hunter and me, to witness that I do not lie), and tea with Dolores Del Rio. Ten minutes out of Los Angeles in the New Orleans train, on a level crossing, we ran over an old jalopy crammed with a large Mexican family, killing two of them, and hurling a small boy some thirty yards. It was the first time I had encountered sudden death, and it shook me quite a bit.

Three sweltering days and two nights across Arizona, New Mexico and Texas brought us to New Orleans. There was of course no air-conditioning, and the sand penetrated everywhere; I found it even among my clothes in my heavy luggage when unpacking at Eton weeks later. I nearly got left behind at El Paso. Noticing that the train was scheduled to stop for an hour and ten minutes, I thought it would be fun to put a foot across the frontier, to enable me to boast that I had set one in Mexico. What I hadn't realized was that the clock was put forward an hour at El Paso, and that the train's stop was for a mere ten minutes. I was rescued in the nick of time by the Negro car conductor, and rushed back breathless to the train. Crossing the Mississippi – it was a mile wide – on the train ferry, I was thrilled to see alligators again, eight months after my first sight of them in the Gatun Lake of the Panama Canal. Of New Orleans, I remember only that it had open sewers and stank to high heaven.

Returning to Eton after all this was the anti-climax of a lifetime. It was made clear to me early on that nobody was in the least interested in my stirring adventures of the past nine months. I went to report myself to my tutor, the notoriously absent-minded Henry Marten ('C.H.K.M.'), and it was evident that he had never noticed that I had been away. His greeting when I knocked on his door was: 'Come in! Go 'way! Very glad to see you, though.' My arrival back at my Aunt Augusta's house in Eaton Square, exactly 272 days after I had left it to sail for New Zealand, happened just on the eve of the General Strike, which at least a third of the boys at Eton made their excuse for not coming back to school: whereas my Uncle Tom and my Aunt Augusta made very sure that I was one of the two-thirds who did. Their motive in so doing may not have been entirely disinterested. They could scarcely have wanted me hanging around No. 10 Eaton Square, quite apart from the fact that at the time Uncle Tom was Solicitor-General, and must have had quite a lot on his plate.

So back to Eton I went, and there I remained for the next

three and a half years; blissfully happy on the whole, but woefully missing my parents and New Zealand. The best thing about Eton in those days, and I hope today, was the degree to which it was actually run by the boys. Pop and the Library, the equivalent in other schools of School and House Prefects, were self-elected, and the detectable hand of authority sat light on the place. When war broke out in 1939, boys tended to leave younger than before: so that possibly the boys at the top of the school were marginally less mature than in my time; and the tendency to leave younger has continued. But when I was an instructor at Sandhurst in 1938 and 1939, the Etonians arriving there were infinitely more mature than their contemporaries from other schools. I don't say that they were necessarily nicer.

Provost James wrote, in his *Eton and King's*: 'Though no boy is going to pass through Eton without woes – very often of his own making – he is not going to find any other five or six years in his life which will pile up more memories that he is glad to keep.' I had my woes; and among them was the fact that, having gone to Eton very young, I out-stayed my contemporaries, and was therefore rather lonely, within my own house, during my last year, my sixth. But the woes are long forgotten, the joys still fresh in mind; the friends have to some extent been superseded, but the acquaintance remains wide.

My tutor, Henry Marten, was a true English eccentric and a glorious character: a bachelor, for whom his sister Isobel (who bore a strong resemblance to a woodcock) kept house. He had substantial private means; and having gone up from Eton to Balliol to read history, he wrote to the then Head Master, the formidable Dr Warre, to offer his services as a whole-time teacher of history. The story goes that Warre, a traditional classicist, replied that to have a master on the strength teaching nothing but history was unthinkable, whereupon Marten offered to come and teach history for no salary at all. Not for ten years was history recognized as a subject for full-time specialist study, with Marten as its presiding genius: a concept which soon spread to other schools. Marten built up a corps of really inspired history masters, which included in my day such men as Robert Birley (a close friend of my eldest brother

James at Balliol, and subsequently Head Master both of Charterhouse and of Eton itself), J. D. Hills (later Head Master of Bradfield: whose affectionate soubriquet at Eton, where he commanded the OTC, was 'The Man Who Won The War'), and Dick Routh, my Modern Tutor during my last two years, when I was myself a history specialist. Besides being a passionate historian, Routh had a genius for indoctrinating the young with a taste for literature, for pictures, and for some sort of style in the writing of English. I had already had an introduction to such tastes at the hands of George Lyttelton, my original Classical Tutor, who had divested himself of me and many others during my absence in New Zealand, when he succeeded 'Jelly' Churchill as a housemaster. Lyttelton was the last housemaster who had to buy his house off his predecessor: thereafter such buildings were the property of the school. Lyttelton, Marten and my father had one inheritance in common: they had all 'boarded' in their day with Miss Evans, the last in the long line of Eton Dames; and Lyttelton resurrected the House Colours which Evans's had rendered illustrious: a red cap, with a black skull-and-crossbones above its peak. There were some who thought such exhumation blasphemy; but George Lyttelton trod down this opposition with his booming voice and his considerable physical weight.

Henry Marten boomed too, in a voice which we all rejoiced in imitating. He was clean-shaven, with a boyish complexion; he had a bald and shining pate, ringed with a halo of white hair. He became Lower Master in succession to A. B. Ramsay, who went off to be Master of Magdalene, and to write and publish exquisite verses in Latin, Greek and English: I cannot judge the former, but I have always been sad that Ramsay's English verses never won wider acclaim. Witness these scathing lines on Pétain in 1940:

> 'They shall not pass! They shall not pass!' he cried,
> And answering legions faced the fire, and died.
> He lived; and, later, crawling from the grave,
> Surrendered what his soldiers died to save.

When eventually Marten came on to the pay-roll, he diverted his salary to the purchase of books on an enormous scale. He bequeathed them to the school, where they now occupy two rooms of the Provost's Lodge (diminished in size these days) as the Marten Library. For his History Specialists, one school-time a week was devoted entirely to reading, and to encouraging us to borrow books to read in our own time. 'Why not tackle something big, now?' he used to cry; 'Why not tackle Lecky?' Guy Burgess the eventual traitor, an ebullient bore, wanted to read Philip Guedalla: Marten sought to dissuade him with the words: 'Fireworky stuff, y'know, fireworky stuff!'

He always addressed his pupils as: 'Gentlemen!' The rumour was that when King George the Sixth engaged him to go to Windsor Castle twice a week to teach constitutional history to the two Princesses, as they then were, Marten addressed them in the same manner; and I have been able to confirm, from the most authoritative of sources, that this is true. I also learned from the same impeccable authority that the Princesses' nickname for him was 'The White Rabbit', which describes him to a T. When Lord Hugh Cecil, later Lord Quickswood, was appointed to succeed James as Provost, I ventured to deplore this to Marten. He looked embarrassed, and replied in his explosive voice: 'Purely a temporary measure! Purely a temporary measure!' Whether or not he knew that he was himself destined to succeed 'Linky' Cecil, I have no idea; but he did, in 1945; and a few weeks later was dubbed KCVO by the King in the presence of the whole school, on the steps of College Chapel.

The Head Master throughout my time was Cyril Alington, a figure of whom we were all proud. He was the first Head Master for centuries who was not himself an Etonian, though he had been a notable Master in College years earlier, before going as Head Master to Shrewsbury. It would not be true to say that he was widely loved, since to those who did not know him he was remote, and there was a barb in his tongue which some feared. But as one rose to the top of the school and came closer under his influence, one came to appreciate him more and more. He consciously rejoiced in being a link between Eton and the wider world outside, and in bringing together public figures and boys with whom they might find a mutual interest. He knew that I was Scotch, the son of a soldier and a Governor-General, and interested in writing: consequently I was invited to his table to meet such people as Lord Plumer, Lord Lloyd and John Buchan. There were sequels to the first and last of these meetings. Years later, John Buchan offered me an appointment – which for various reasons I refused – as one of his ADCs in Canada; and Lord Plumer, partly because of his friendship with my father, invited himself to tea in my room, sending a postal order for ten bob to cover the financial outlay. With this subsidy, I went down town to buy the sort of things that I thought suitable for a Field-Marshal's tea; but when he arrived he exclaimed: 'What? No eggs, no sausages? This isn't the sort of tea we used to have when *I* was at Eton!' We went down town again together, and bought the items which he specified; and while I was cooking them, he jostled with me among the tea-fags who were ministering to their masters' needs, giving them culinary advice. 'Scrambled eggs? Cover the bottom of the saucepan with just a film of milk, and beat up the eggs well before you spill them in!' He was a dear little man, portly and ugly, with a white moustache like a waterfall. It was not until years later that I realized what a staunch friend in trying times he had been to my father, who was eight years younger than he. He died two years after I left Eton, and I never met him again.

My generation remembers Alington best for his 'Bed-time Stories', as we dubbed his Sunday evening sermons in chapel. We never quite knew what was coming. It might be a potted biography about somebody, Etonian or not, the anniversary of whose birth or death fell in that week. It might be a straight homily on a subject either topical or ageless. It might be one of the 'Fables', for which he was famous. It might even be partly in verse. Certainly we were never disappointed, and every man-jack of us listened rapt. The light from the candles on either side of the pulpit shone on his dramatically handsome face and silvered hair; and the deliberation with which he blew out each candle as he finished, before he proceeded back to his place in chapel in the wake of the 'Holy Poker', as the saintly-looking verger was known, was a masterpiece of

NZGS Tutanekai

NZGS Hinemoa

HMNZS Lachlan in Captain Cook's old anchorage in Dusky Sound

With the Kachins from Saga, who guided us during the war. Taken in 1960

At a feast with Queen Salote of Tonga

presentation. He was a showman, certainly; but indubitably a great man, and a lasting influence on us all. And his wife, born Hester Lyttelton, who looked like a cross between the Ugly Duchess and the Red Queen, was a darling, and the perfect foil to her husband. Having begun life as a loyal Lyttelton Liberal, she voted steadily Labour for the last thirty years of it. Like Henry Marten, she was something of an eccentric; and her son-in-law, Lord Home, has told some endearing stories of her in his autobiography.

Even more remote, until one came to know him, was the Provost, Dr Montague Rhodes James. I came within his orbit purely by chance. I happened to know the preacher in College Chapel one Sunday morning, and went to greet him in the Ante-Chapel after the service. He was bidden to coffee with the Provost, and the Provost told me to come along with him. So began a friendship which lasted until his death ten years later. It may sound like a curious bracket, but I couple the Provost with Captain Bollons as the two men whose memories I cherish most from before my twentieth year. Soon he was inviting me to Sunday breakfast; later I graduated to dinner; and for the rest of his life, until he died in 1936, I was often invited, and as often as possible accepted, to spend a week-end at the Provost's Lodge.

I find it difficult to convey how much he meant to me. He, like Henry Marten, was a bachelor, with a sister – in his case, a childless widow – keeping house for him. He was the son of a country parson, brought up initially in a Rectory near Canterbury, and subsequently in East Anglia, where I think he really felt his roots to be: he used to rejoice in assuming a rich Suffolk accent. He was born in 1862, and won scholarships first to Eton, and then to King's, of which he became first a Fellow and then Provost; but it is on record that once, outside King's one evening at dusk, he looked towards Eton, and confessed that his heart lay there. To Eton he returned as Provost in 1918, and was still in office when he died. I went to say good-bye to him three days before the end, and got special leave from Wavell to attend his funeral. In popular memory he is renowned chiefly for his eerie *Ghost Stories of an Antiquary*, and their sequels; but his real claim to fame rests on his distinction as a palaeographer, an authority on old stained glass, and a cataloguer of ancient manuscripts, in which – although many of his findings have been overturned by those who followed in his footsteps, but who still pay grateful tribute to his pioneering – he led the way along uncharted paths. 'A Continental Reputation, Gentlemen!' Henry Marten used to say.

Both came to stay at Kilkerran. Marten used to include it in his annual grouse-shooting circuit: first to the Craig-Sellars at Ardtornish, at the head of Lochaline in Morven, opposite Mull; then to the Drummond-Morays at Abercairney in Perthshire, where the sons, Jamie and Andy (both, alas, now dead), had been in his house; and finally to Kilkerran. He shot with more enthusiasm than skill ('Phut-phut-phut!' said the head keeper at Abercairney, 'and he's up tae's knees in cairtridges, and no' a bird tae pick!'); but he loved it, and we all, including my father, loved having him.

Provost James was a different matter. He had never fired a gun, or fished, or taken any exercise in his life: apart from bicycling long miles in France with boon companions like F. Anstey, the author of *Vice Versa*, Gurney Lubbock and others, to visit cathedrals. I invited him to stay at Kilkerran, without first asking my parents' permission, shortly after their return from New Zealand. My father was furious, and my mother had difficulty in dissuading him from cancelling the invitation. The Provost made a sedate northward progress by rail, breaking his journey twice *en route*. My brother Simon and I met him with the car off the train at Ayr; and as we drove the sixteen miles to Kilkerran, I felt more and more as James Boswell must have felt as he conveyed Dr Johnson to stay with his formidable old father Lord Auchinleck: the more so because the Boswells and we have been neighbours and allies for centuries past.

Dinner on the first evening went only moderately well. My mother did her best, chattering away as was her wont; my father was polite but reserved. We forgot to warn the Provost that breakfast at nine was preceded by family prayers ten minutes earlier; and the atmosphere was not improved when the door opened, and the Provost came in when we were all on our knees, our hands on our chins, our elbows on our chairs, and our rumps facing the door. The dining-room at Kilkerran was, and still is, hung with the portraits of those same ancestors as my father used to greet on his periodical returns on leave from the First War, but interspersed with Italian scenes brought back by Sir Adam from his Grand Tour in mid-eighteenth century. As my father, still in rather grim mood, was doling out the porridge, the Provost was standing in front of one of these pictures, which portrayed a number of men and women with no clothes on eating grapes in a woodland grove, mumbling to himself.

'I didn't quite catch what you said, Mr Provost?' said my father, his porridge ladle in mid-air.

'I was saying,' said the Provost, 'that I like the picture, but I wouldn't have liked the party.'

There was a pause; then my father guffawed; and from then on my father took him to his heart. I heard him say to my mother after breakfast: 'I don't mind how long that man stays.' In fact, having come for a long week-end, he stayed for three weeks; and came back again at my father's insistence the following year. Thereafter, we were badly hit financially by the economic crisis of 1931. Most of the house was put under dust-sheets, and we lodged in odd corners of it; and entertained only humbler guests, such as brother-officers of Simon and myself, whom my father was prepared to allow to come knowing that they wouldn't mind roughing it. There were no more house-parties; the shooting was let, apart from some rough walking on the Burning Hill, and little scraps of woodland on the marches, where one could walk up the odd wild pheasant or woodcock; the grouse in any case were diminishing in numbers, and blackgame had become so rare that there was an embargo on shooting them. My father, who had been a first-class shot in his day, was determined not to deteriorate: so he gave up shooting himself on his seventieth birthday in 1935, and contented himself thereafter with criticizing in blistering terms the performance of his sons.

Yet Kilkerran continued to be a happy home, and its family as united as it was happy. There were few changes among the employees, and even fewer among the tenant-farmers and smallholders: some of whom, like the Andrews of

Rowanstone, of Barcully and Moorston, the Hazels of Craigfin, the Breckenridges of Ballochbroe, the Irvines of Lochspouts, the Kennedies of Carsloe, and mad old Rewcassel of Billybeg, the last of his line (who, when one of his two horses died, harnessed his equally mad housekeeper to the shaft of his cart opposite the survivor), had been on the place for two or three centuries, since before the records began. Among the employees there were dynasties like the Hopsons (two of whose daughters went out to New Zealand to help my parents in Government House as housemaids), the Morrisons (some of whom also faithfully served the Glasgow & South-Western Railway for three generations), the Thomsons, the McVeys, and another family of Andrew, kin to Rowanstone, who were the hereditary estate joiners. Kenneth Andrew, the present incumbent, should have a few years still to run. His grandfather, old John, who died soon after the First War, and who wore white mutton-chop whiskers, lived entirely off oatmeal; and David his son and Kenneth both inherited his intimate knowledge of every house on Kilkerran, including the Big House itself: where every beam lay, where every lum ran, and every drain.

Then there were the shepherds: the Galloway family, for three generations in the remote Garleffan but-and-ben – sold, alas, during these last few years, and Sandy Galloway has come down out of the snows and out of the hills into the valley proper; and old Tom MacTaggart, already mentioned, born in the hills at Doughty, three miles from Garleffan with no other house between them. Tom spent all his life herding on Kilkerran, except for a few years with my cousins at Dunskey in Wigtownshire; and my brother Simon (who became the Church of Scotland Minister in Barr, the next-door parish to Kilkerran, after retiring as a lieutenant-colonel from The Argyll and Sutherland Highlanders) buried him from his house, which you can see from the windows of Kilkerran, when Tom died aged ninety. Tom's daughter still helps to keep the Big House running, and her husband is one of my nephew's right-hand men.

By now, Kilkerran was no longer our perpetual base so much as a parental doo'cote to which we flew back whenever we could. My sister's husband had retired from the Indian Cavalry, and was working for the Lord Chancellor in London; my eldest brother James, who had married in 1931, was working first as a bookseller in London and then in a publisher's in Edinburgh, living in Haddington; my brother Simon was stationed sometimes in Edinburgh and sometimes at the Argylls' depot in Stirling Castle; and I was variously at Colchester, at Maryhill Barracks in Glasgow, and as ADC to General Wavell in Aldershot: a wonderful experience about which I have written elsewhere. We all winged homeward whenever possible. But we also enjoyed, gregariously, the fleshpots of country-house parties in Scotland: attending Highland Games and Highland Balls: the Argyllshire Gathering at Oban, the Northern Meeting at Inverness, Portree, and all the others. House-parties on the grand scale were still possible for people of modest means, although my budget, carefully assessed (for I was very broke), had to take into account whether or not I would have enough left over, after paying for my cartridges, to tip the head keeper and the butler on the scale to which I feared they were accustomed. I once had to refuse an invitation to Goodwood Races because I calculated that I wouldn't be able to cope with the butler. On the subject of butlers, I recall that in three consecutive houses where I stayed and shot – Monreith, Murdostoun and Carberry – the butlers were called respectively Shepherd, Lamb and Fox; but I could hardly ask for a rebate because of that. Poor Fox eventually dropped down dead in the act of handing round the coffee.

Since coming back from New Zealand, my only ventures abroad had been modest incursions into France. The first had been when my parents were still absent. I spent two full summer holidays from Eton 'learning French in a family', as the phrase ran; but in fact 'the family' was a childless couple – delightful, middle-aged, and bourgeois – plus six to eight young British or American schoolboys or undergraduates who were also supposed to be learning French, presumably from each other. The establishment consisted of three houses in a single garden, of diminishing size like Chinese boxes, known as *Les Trois Pavillons*, in the suburb of Saint-Symphorien on the opposite side of the Loire above Tours. The sanitary needs of the whole household had to be met by a single earth privy in the garden, one's progress to and from which could be witnessed by the rest of the community, so that there was rarely any rattling on the door: a hiss of '*Occupé!*' – and *Occupé* is a word that *can* be hissed, despite its lack of sibilants – forestalled any such waste of time. Monsieur Giraud was sardonic and cadaverous, with a Charlie Chaplin moustache: he had been too badly gassed in the war to do anything much beyond repairing and oiling his inverted bicycle, which seemed to occupy him, in his black beret, all and every day. Madame was roundabout and jolly, dressed always in black, liable to gales of laughter, and to become stern only if she caught us speaking English (or American), when she fined the offender a franc, to be inserted in a money-box in the form of a porcelain pig. '*Le Cochon!*' she would shout, and there was no argument about paying up.

Their hatred for the Germans was almost pathological. Monsieur had been a prisoner, and Madame a nurse, during the First War. They would point out the hole in the roof of the Musée des Beaux Arts near the Pont de Pierre over the Loire (the hole carefully conserved by the City Fathers as a memorial of German 'frightfulness') caused by a single minatory German shell in 1870. My heart bled for them both in 1940, when France was overrun, and throughout the war I constantly wondered how they were faring. In 1945 I had a chance to go and investigate. The house had changed hands, but I sought out an elderly maiden lady whom I remembered as a close associate of Madame in all her Catholic good works. From her I learned that Madame had died during the war, as much from a shamed and broken heart as from any other cause; Monsieur had entered a religious order, stipulating that no effort should be made to trace him, or to forward any correspondence.

But those shadowed years lay far ahead: I was still only fifteen years old. I hired a bicycle; and, sometimes in company with two French brothers of roughly my age from just over the road, I set out to discover and explore the many Châteaux of the Loire. I must have covered hundreds of hot and dusty kilometres during those two summers. I recall how shocked the brothers were when, on one really broiling day between Tours and Langeais, I suggested a swim in the Loire. '*Mais sans maillot?*' they said, appalled – so disapprovingly that I didn't dare bathe naked even by myself. I hadn't expected such an entrenched degree of modesty.

The formal Châteaux with their sedate gardens were certainly lovely: Amboise, Azay-le-Rideau, Chenonceaux with its graceful arches over the Cher, Villandry, Chaumont. Chenonceaux belonged to 'Meester Menier, Chocolate-Man', as the woman guide said in bad English with a sneer; Villandry to M. Carvalho, whose grandson I was to meet more than forty years later as a reporter during the civil war in Nigeria; Chaumont to its original owners, one of the few Loire Châteaux of which that could still be said. I had met a younger brother of its owner, and to this I owed an invitation to luncheon. I had failed to make it clear to my prospective host and hostess that I was aged only fifteen, and proposed to arrive, hot and sweaty, by bicycle after a forty mile ride up-Loire and mostly uphill; but they welcomed me as civilly as though I had arrived in formal clothes and a coach-and-six.

Beautiful as these Châteaux were, I greatly preferred, at my romantic age, the more warlike ones: those with battlements, dungeons and portcullises, such as Luynes, Langeais and Loches. Luynes, like Chaumont, was still lived in by its original owners. Langeais, on the right bank of the Loire downstream from Tours, had a curious resemblance, although it was much larger, to Lord Ailsa's Castle in the High Street of Maybole, now occupied by his factor. Loches was, and is, the most impressive of the three. I had been briefed by my mother's family to look out for the mysterious inscription carved deep in the wall of one of its dungeons, reading simply: EBENEZER KELBURN. The guess was that he might have been a cadet of their family belonging to the *Garde Ecossaise* who had got himself into trouble, although they had no record of anybody of his name. I duly found it, and saw it again twice more before the war, enjoying the sensation that it might constitute some sort of link between me and Quentin Durward. But when I sought it again when the war was over, it was no longer traceable. After the passage of centuries, prisoners had once again been lodged in the dungeons of Loches, this time Frenchmen incarcerated by Germans. In the age-long tradition of prisoners, they too had resorted to carving their names and other *graffiti* on the walls; and the endeavour of Ebenezer Kelburn, whoever he was, to ensure that posterity should know of his imprisonment, had been obliterated for ever.

In 1932 I returned to Tours, lodging in the bosom of the same family; but this time I was attired in the uniform of a 2/Lieutenant in the Black Watch, on a three months' attachment to the 32nd Regiment of Infantry. Their barracks were on the far side of the town, necessitating two changes of tram. My initial appearance in the kilt at the first tram-stop took away the collective breath of all Tourangeaux within hundreds of metres. I had thought my appearance unmistakably Scotch; but one man at the tram-stop, raising his hat with all politeness, asked me whether I was Greek or Yugoslav. By the time my attachment ended, I had become a familiar figure on the tram-routes of Tours: regarded with an affectionate tolerance not unlike that accorded to 'Prince Monolulu', the Abyssinian tipster on pre-war English racecourses.

There was nothing glamorous about soldiering in metropolitan France, unlike service with the Colonial Infantry or the Foreign Legion. Apart from a small regular cadre, the men were all conscripts, serving for precisely one year, on a programme laid down centrally. If for any reason, such as adverse weather, a day or two had to be skipped, that part of the programme was simply omitted. There was no mess life. Married officers came to their work in the morning and went home at night, carrying brief-cases, just as though they were attending an office. Unmarried officers lived in lodgings in the town, though they dined occasionally in the *popotte*, which was no more than a private room in a second-rate restaurant. There was little light-heartedness about the life, and even the young officers were desperately solemn. I found things very different when later on I did an attachment to a Moroccan regiment, and for a short time to a battalion of the Legion, in Damascus in 1937–8, or even when I took twenty Gentlemen Cadets from Sandhurst for a fortnight's skiing to the 6th Chasseurs Alpins in Savoy in January 1939. These last were admittedly a metropolitan, conscript unit, but with a cheerful *panache* about them which was sadly lacking in the 32nd Infantry.

Nevertheless, I enjoyed my attachment at Tours, and the hospitality of several people in the neighbourhood. There were the de la Panouse family, who had lived long in London, where the father had been Military Attaché: a son-in-law who was staying with them was a captain in the Irish Guards, for all his French name; and the de Brantes, who lived in a large house called Les Fresnes, set in policies of broad fields studded with occasional hardwood trees, reminiscent of the view from the windows of Kilkerran. It turned out that old General de Brantes, a man of exquisite manners, had commanded a cavalry brigade on the flank of my father's division during the Mons retreat; and I struck up a friendship with his eldest son François, a serving cavalry officer, whom I was to meet again in London in 1939–40, when he was Assistant Military Attaché. He was destined to be taken prisoner, to escape, to join the Resistance, to be captured, and to die bravely in a concentration camp. His daughter became Madame Giscard d'Estaing, and three of his grandchildren have stayed with us at Ballantrae.

I did at least learn French, which has been a joy to me ever since. To my grief, I have no aptitude for languages. At different times in my life, I have tried to learn Arabic, Turkish, Urdu, Burmese and Maori. I can make some sort of shift in Maori, and I wouldn't starve for lack of Arabic or Urdu; but rational conversation in any of these tongues is far beyond me. Only in French am I at home. Once, when a new French Ambassador came to present his credentials to me in New Zealand, he sent a message to ask whether he might do so in French. I agreed. After the ceremony, breaking into rather bad English, he thanked me, adding: 'I had heard that Your Excellency's French was quite notorious!'

In March of 1937, I returned from Wavell's Staff at Aldershot to the bosom of the Regiment in Glasgow, so as to proceed to Palestine with them that autumn. I travelled to Southampton twenty-four hours ahead of the Battalion, in charge of the baggage and the eighty men who were to handle it, and proceeded to load it on board the troopship *Nevasa*. To the horror of the Staff Captain Embarkation, a very tall Cameron Highlander called Barber, who subsequently became a General, I promised the men a run ashore if they finished the job in time. 'You idiot!' said Tiny Barber, 'you'll never get 'em back!'

I bet him a fiver that I would, and duly paraded the men; I told them about the bet, and begged them not to let me down: they were to be back on board by 11 p.m. without fail. At 10.55, they were all back bar six, and I very nearly handed over my fiver, while Tiny Barber gloated. At 10.57 we heard the sound of raucous singing; and round the corner of a dockside shed came four of the Jocks, carrying the other two. It was Tiny's fiver that changed hands, not mine.

And so we sailed for Port Said, the first of many times that I was to see it. The last was in very different circumstances, in 1956.

Chapter Four

FOOTLOOSE

I had been barely three months in Palestine when I had cause to regret my vaunted proficiency in French. Soon after our arrival, I had been appointed to the congenial job of Brigade Intelligence Officer, South Palestine. I was roaming the country, pretty well my own master, and seeing myself as an embryo T. E. Lawrence. The 'Arab Troubles' were below the level they had reached in 1936, and were to reach again in 1938 and 1939, but there was still plenty of excitement. In December, out of the blue, came a signal ordering me to report to Sandhurst in February to teach French; and even an intervention by Wavell, now GOC Palestine and Trans-Jordan, failed to win me a reprieve. After a fortnight brushing up my knowledge of the language with the French Army in Beirut and Damascus, and discovering something of both Lebanon and Syria, I sailed ignominiously for home in the luxurious new troopship *Dilwara*, returning from her outward maiden voyage with a battalion of the Royal West Kents from India. They celebrated their arrival in Southampton Water in the traditional manner, by casting their sola topis overboard.

I did not sail again for overseas until December 1940, a tour which was to last for four years. I have already written about those years at inordinate length, and will not repeat myself. There were the good moments and the bad, but they certainly, in Provost James's phrase, 'piled up many memories that I am glad to keep'. Like everybody else, I found myself in all sorts of places of which I had never heard, but which became familiar names in the course of the war: Tobruk, Mersa Matruh, Ranchi, Imphal, Kohima; and in countries which I had always thought so remote and exotic that I never expected to see them: Kenya, Turkey, Iraq, the Persian Gulf, Baluchistan, Burma. Nowadays, Turkey has well-trodden tourist tracks; the Gulf is crammed with British business men, air-conditioning and high-rise buildings; and Burma is closed to foreigners except for a single tourist route, Rangoon-Pagan-Mandalay-Rangoon, designed for package tours and strictly limited to seven days.

In January 1941, I flew down to Kenya with Wavell. On the way south, we stopped for a day in Khartoum to see General Platt, the Sirdar, who was commanding in the Sudan, and successfully campaigning, though with slender resources, against the Italians, under the chivalrous Duke of Aosta, later to die as a prisoner of war in British hands. His forces had erupted from Ethiopia the previous year, over-running British Somaliland and some of the Sudan itself. We stayed in the picturesque Palace, the scene of Gordon's death in 1885, with the Governor-General, Sir Hubert Huddleston, who had just been brought out of retirement as Lieutenant-Governor of the Royal Hospital at Chelsea to return to the Sudan, in which he had spent most of his career. 'No better appointment could have been made,' says his notice by Sir Harold Mac-Michael in the Dictionary of National Biography, 'for his name was honoured and respected throughout the whole vast country.' Wavell and he were old friends, for Huddleston had commanded a brigade under Allenby in Palestine when Wavell was Allenby's Brigadier, General Staff, and there were only three years between them in age. For all the pressing matters that now concerned them, they found time to reminisce about the past, while I sat fascinated to hear them.

I was fascinated also by the mere fact of being in Khartoum, having heard so much about it from my father. That morning, for the first time in my life, I had seen the city of Omdurman from the air, as we lost height descending towards Khartoum, and marvelled at its expanse: it sprawled over the desert like a vast ant-heap, flattened but not destroyed by a steam-roller, and a myriad white-clad figures scuttled about in its crevices. My brother Simon was now serving with the Sudan Defence Force, to which he had got himself seconded in 1937. Unfortunately he was far away in the south with the Equatorial Corps, and I did not get a chance to see him until a year later.

I had not been in Nairobi for more than an hour before dropping one of the bricks for which I have a well-earned reputation. We had been met at the airport by and carried off to luncheon with Lord and Lady Delamere, the acknowledged leaders of Kenya society. At my humble place at the foot of the table, during the first course, I was asked by my neighbours whether I knew anybody in Nairobi, to which I replied that I had some acquaintance with Lord Erroll and Sir Delves Broughton. There was a slight *frisson*, and it was broken to me that, on that very morning, the latter had been arrested and charged with the murder of the former. He stood his trial, was acquitted, and subsequently died by his own hand.

A mishap to the aircraft on take-off – in fact, it caught fire, but we all scrambled out, and the flames were extinguished before much damage was done – meant that Wavell had to fly back north in a smaller one, leaving me behind. I spent one happy day looking at beasts in a game reserve with Ritchie, the *doyen* of white hunters, before flying in a small civilian aircraft to Kisumu on Lake Victoria to await a flying-boat. There I was made an honorary member of the pilots' mess, and had a happy time listening to their tales and gossip. The world of civilian pilots was small in those days, and everybody knew everybody. One story concerned 'Tich' Atchison, a minute flying-boat pilot, whose navigator had sent a spoof panic message over the air: 'Can you tell me my position? Am blind-flying at six thousand feet.' 'Why are you blind-flying? Visibility should be perfect.' 'I know, but the pilot's air-cushion is busted!'

The old Imperial Airways flying-boats were the most civilized method of travel conceivable. They were slow, and not too silent; but you could smoke, and you could walk about, luxuries unknown in other aircraft in those days. You flew low, and you could savour the country over which you were passing: unlike modern flying, when you are so high that you can see little, and when islands such as Cyprus look no bigger than a postage-stamp. During 1941 and 1942, I travelled at one time or another every stage of the flying-boat route that was still operational, all the way from Kisumu to Calcutta. Unlike modern airports, which might all have come from the same mould, every stopping place was different from the next; starting at first light, you arrived at your halt for the night a reasonable time before sundown, so that you could go for a walk, a swim, or even a sail. Thus on the Nile you alighted at such contrasting places as Rejaf, with jungle down to the water's edge; at Bor in the great marsh of the Sudd, or at Malakal; at Khartoum itself, where the White Nile and the Blue mingle their contrasting waters, or at Luxor, with the tombs and temples all around; at Cairo, where we used to pause in our tennis at the Gezira Club to watch the huge aircraft, as it was by the standards of those days, putting down gently behind the houses. (My parents' first married home had been on Gezira Island, in days when there were only three houses on it.) There was the halt at the Dead Sea where you emerged gasping in the heat 1300 feet below sea-level, later switched to the lovely Tiberias on the Sea of Galilee; the lake at Habbaniya, whose waters lapped the desert; the Tigris at Basra, Dubai on the Gulf, Karachi; Udaipur, where each island boasted its own white palace; the Ganges at Allahabad, the Hooghli at Calcutta. It was always a thrill to sink down towards the water, and to await the *swoosh* of foam washing past the portholes, and the nodding motion when you finally rode to your moorings. I was delighted to find, when I reached New Zealand in 1962, that she still had two squadrons of Sunderlands in commission. I made use of them quite a lot, and we managed to keep them going until 1967, when we had sadly to relinquish them, partly because of the increasing difficulty of obtaining spare parts. They were in much demand, among other things, for 'mercy flights' to the islands of the South Pacific.

I had some other fairly 'hairy' flights in the Middle East, as well as elsewhere. There was a particularly light-hearted and casual Egyptian pilot who became a close friend, with whom I used to fly via Lydda and Nicosia to Turkey, when I was doing frequent liaison trips between Cairo and Ankara in the first half of 1941. (He wrote himself off in the end in a spectacular crash, and I was more sad than surprised.) Once in 1943, when I was visiting the Middle East from India lecturing about the First Wingate Expedition, from which I had just returned, he ran out of petrol half-way across the Sinai Desert, on our way to Lydda. We were in a De Havilland Rapide, and I had vaguely noticed that there were two other passengers. He put down safely on a smooth bit of sand not far from the main road, and radioed back to base asking for another aircraft to fly up with some spare cans, but was told that it couldn't reach us for three or four hours. It was July, and the day was getting abominably hot; so we got out and settled down to wait in the shadow afforded us by one of the wings.

I took stock of my fellow-passengers. One was a stout, jovial Irish priest; the other a plump, well-dressed woman whom I guessed to be in her late fifties. She was considerably shaken by our forced landing, so I sought to comfort her; she replied in a strong French accent, and I suddenly realized that she was Alice Delysia, the distinguished actress who was entertaining Free French troops in the Middle East. The more frivolous the priest got, the more distressed she became; and when he said: 'Sure, time's hanging very heavy on our hands: would ye like me to marry you to this lady?' she looked like having hysterics. She swore that nothing would ever induce her to fly again, so I walked the half-mile to the road, and flagged down an Army truck which was heading towards Palestine. I saw that the driver was wearing the Red Hackle of my Regiment, and recognized Private Abercromby, who had been wounded in Tobruk, and had not recovered in time to travel to India with the rest of our Battalion when we were transferred there eighteen months before. Mlle Delysia viewed him with some suspicion when I introduced them, but decided that he was the lesser of two evils, and clambered with her abundant luggage into the truck. 'A *French actress*?' Abercromby remarked incredulously when he saw her; but he drove off in the direction of Beersheba with a great grin, all the same, and I saw her later in Jerusalem.

It had been just after the relief of Tobruk, where I had been a company commander with my Regiment for the last month of the siege, that I managed to get down to the southern Sudan to see my brother Simon. We were all given two weeks' leave, and General Theron, the South African liaison officer at GHQ in Cairo, arranged for me to fly down on his plane that ran every week to Pretoria, for the plane to make a special stop for me at Juba, the capital of the Equatorial Province, and to pick me up on its way back a week later. The grass airstrip at Juba was only rarely used; and when we got over it I was dismayed to see it occupied by a herd of grazing elephants. 'Don't worry!' said the pilot, 'we'll soon shift them!' and he buzzed them, within a few feet of their huge, hanging ears. They lumbered away into the jungle, we went round once more, and touched down. There was Simon, whom I had last seen at Kilkerran in August 1939, when telegrams had arrived simultaneously ordering us back to our respective stations: mine at Sandhurst, his in the Sudan. He didn't look as welcoming as I had expected. 'Get your kit into the car quick,' he snapped; 'we can talk later.'

Three miles down the red laterite track, he pulled up his station-wagon, and explained why we were in such a hurry. The Governor of Equatoria had only one hobby, his garden, and we had just stampeded forty elephants into it. I saw the point.

Simon's boss at Torit, Headquarters of the Equatorial Corps, 80 miles east of Juba and 4500 feet up, was Colonel 'Katie' Cave of the Rifle Brigade, who had stayed at Kilkerran: a splendid man, who had been in the Royal Flying Corps in the First War, and who had flown his own aircraft all over Equatoria until war-time difficulties made it impossible. He had then handed it over to the Royal Air Force as a gift. Three years later, to my embarrassment – he was fourteen years older than I – he was posted to me as Second in Command to my Brigade, to run my Rear Headquarters when I was in Burma. At first, because of our difference in age, I refused to accept him, but yielded to his pleading. Not only did I never regret it: I never ceased to rejoice. After the war, he went to Bede College in Rome to study for the Catholic priesthood as a 'late vocation', coming back to Britain every summer break, buying a Jaguar and taking a gun in a grouse-shoot. He returned to Equatoria as a missionary, only to be expelled with all the others when the newly independent Sudan decided that they must go, and spent his last few years in a religious house at Sunningdale, a much honoured Monsignor. When he stayed with us in New Zealand in 1964 or thereby, I asked some of the Catholic hierarchy to meet him; and the late Bishop Foley of Suva asked him, with a twinkle, how he had become a Monsignor so soon after his ordination so late in life. 'Well,' said Katie modestly – he always had trouble with his Rs – 'I can only suppose that it's because I happen to know the wight people.' I have known many saints in my life, but Katie was at the top of the league. He died after a series of heart attacks in 1974.

Those six days at Torit were great fun, but they gave me one major fright. On the Sunday, Simon and I were having luncheon in his *tukhl* – the round thatched house which is the standard residence in those parts – when I heard a remote roaring noise, and brought it to his attention. Years of quinine had made him deaf, and he shrugged it off with: 'As I was saying . . .' Within another minute, even he could hear it; and when we went outside we could see a wall of smoke a hundred feet high approaching us from the eastward. Simon rushed off to his car, in the smaller garage *tukhl* thirty yards away, and drove like Jehu the half-mile to the barracks to turn out his troops for fire-fighting, while I scrambled on to the roof and yelled to his three servants to pass buckets of water up to me, which I sloshed on to the thatch to keep it damp.

The fire approached at a terrifying speed through the high grass and the occasional trees. I reckoned it was coming at fifty yards a minute. The grass was blazing, and the trees bursting into flames like igniting rockets. Twittering birds were flying, antelope and small deer galloping, snakes large and small came wriggling past. At last Simon came back in his car, with a lot of stark naked, off-duty, laughing soldiers in it and on it, followed by many more on foot: some armed with shovels, some with hastily-improvised brooms for beating out flames. I was still on the roof, roaring out orders to the servants for more water from the well: Simon has been good enough to say that he never heard anybody's Arabic improve so fast in so short a time. The soldiers were too late to save the garage *tukhl*, which went up with a roar; but they were able to beat out the flames threatening the actual house. Thanks to their efforts, these divided like a Y, spared the house, and sped down to leeward: where there was no human habitation, so that we didn't care much what happened. A torrential downpour of rain came half an hour later, and the episode was over.

During those alarming minutes on that combustible thatched roof, I kept wondering which of Simon's and my effects had the highest priority for salvage if Simon and his soldiers did not get back in time, and I had to cut and run for it. I decided rather wildly that it must be the little model of the 4-ton sloop *Garleffan*, so named after the highest hill on Kilkerran; we had taken delivery of her in April 1939, and indeed had been cruising in her up the Solway Firth when the war-clouds closed in during late August. Hurrying home in anticipation of those telegrams of recall which we had been half expecting, we rounded the dreaded Mull of Galloway in the dark, and reached Knockinaam Bay, three miles south of Portpatrick, at eight o'clock of a sunny morning. The little house of Knockinaam, now an hotel, was then the dower-house of Dunskey, and my Uncle Tom Inskip, Minister for the Co-ordination of Defence – a hollow title for a hollow job – and my Aunt Augusta were spending the summer there. Out in the bay, riding to an anchor in a dinghy and fishing, was their son Robin, aged twenty-two, who confirmed that his parents were in the house; so we dropped our hook, and rowed ashore to cadge breakfast. Uncle Tom confirmed that the news was ominous; he had just been summoned back to a Cabinet meeting in London, and was planning to travel south by that night's train from Stranraer, the earliest possible means in those non-flying days. So we hurried on northwards, and ran into the father-and-mother of a gale off Corsewall Point, spending some hours hove to, and some more at anchor in the shelter of Wig Bay, before eventually reaching Girvan, and bidding farewell to *Garleffan* for six long years. One of Simon's brother-officers in Equatoria was a passionate builder of model ships, and had constructed a beauty from the *Garleffan* plans. This, I thought, must have first priority. Now, alas, the model has been lost, and both Garleffans, hill and sloop, have been sold. *Sic transit gloria mundi.*

I did contrive to get in a bit of sailing in all my overseas incarnations, before, during and after the war. In Palestine in 1937 I shared an open boat in Jaffa with Norman Phillips of the 60th Rifles, who in 1940 disappeared mysteriously while trying to escape from Calais, and has never been heard of since. He lived in Bembridge, and was a sailing man from birth. For a part-time paid hand we had a convict called Khamis (meaning 'Thursday', so he was inevitably known as 'Man Thursday',) who was always anxious in case we should get back late, for fear he would be shut out of the jail for the night. When I was in the Palestine Police ten years later, I had another boat based on Acre in the north. Both provided perfect therapy for anxious days.

So did the Cairo Yacht Club, when in 1941 I was at GHQ, first under Wavell and then under Auchinleck. Most people went in for dinghy racing, which I personally found too reminiscent of hard work; I preferred leisurely cruising: up to Ma'adi for the night, perhaps, where I had friends among the New Zealanders. My crew and I would beat slowly upstream after the office shut in the evening, and drop down quickly in the morning with the southerly wind and the strong current behind us. My New Zealand friends included three Maori: Tiwha and Charlie Bennett (sons of the parson, by then the first Maori Bishop), and Bill Ngata, son of Sir Apirana. Later, when they used to come back on leave from the desert, they would visit me in the Black Watch flat, in the Garden City, which I shared with four other staff-bound friends, to make inroads on my whisky and gin, which Maori call *wai piro*, or 'stinking water', and lie wallowing in my bath, exhausting my *wai wera*, or hot water, and chaffing me for never seeing a shot fired.

During the monsoon of 1942, in July, I exacted a week's leave from the Joint Planning Staff at GHQ, New Delhi, and went up by myself to a house-boat I had hired on the Wular Lake in Kashmir, with a small sailing-boat attached. The overnight rail journey to Rawal Pindi was followed by a taxi drive up the winding, climbing road through Baramula to the lake, a few miles short of Srinagar. The Sikh drivers were renowned not only for their speed and skill, but also for scaring the daylights out of their passengers as they rounded the corners with their horns blaring and their dazzling teeth grinning in their black beards. On the lake, I had a week of exquisite peace, all to myself except for the couple (and their flock of children) who cosseted and cooked for me. I sailed, I fished, I read, I wrote some poetry, many letters home, and an article for *Blackwood's Magazine*. I gazed at the huge, silent mountains, and remembered how a few years before my sister, on trek into them with her husband a hundred miles beyond Gulmarg, had contracted smallpox and nearly died of it, despite having been vaccinated a month earlier. I remembered also Wavell's tales of the days when, forty years before and 200 miles farther west, he had commanded the mule train on the Chitral relief expedition through similar country.

In September of the same year, I wangled another week's leave, between leaving GHQ and joining Wingate's force in its training area in the jungles of the Central Provinces. This time I had a companion in the shape of John Bankes, height six foot eight, who had been my fag my last half at Eton, when he had been rather smaller; he was on leave from his staff job in Arakan. We went to Bombay in search of sailing, only to find that, owing to some scare of raids by Japanese midget submarines, sailing had been banned by the naval command. We travelled a few miles north, and found a lodging-house kept by an elderly White Russian woman on an arm of the sea at a place called Marve Malad. From a neighbouring village we hired an open boat with three Mahratta fishermen, and sailed north in her for a day or two, discovering some rather eerie abandoned Portuguese forts and churches, peopled only with ghosts. There was one mysterious exception: a village with an enormous Christian Church, which, to judge by the tombstones in the graveyard, dated from the sixteenth century. It seemed to be ruled by a sinister young priest of very dark complexion in a ragged *soutane*. Hordes of hostile children of all ages up to about sixteen followed us around in a menacing manner; there was no sign of any adult at all. In a remote grove we found a tall stone cross with a Latin inscription on it, to the memory of a Gomez, a Da Silva, a Pereira or some such name, also sixteenth century; and what sent the shivers down our spines was the fact that it was festooned with fresh flowers and wreaths, as though it were the object of some unholy worship. After the war, I wrote for the *Strand Magazine* what was intended to be a creepy story based on this experience. My reward, apart from thirty guineas, was a reproving letter from Robert Henriques, accusing me of prostituting my gifts as a serious writer. It didn't wring my withers much. The *Strand Magazine* ceased publication almost immediately afterwards. I hope this was *post hoc* rather than *propter*.

Some years later, I was on reconnaissance in the jungles of Mysore State, with a view to staging an exercise. I was sitting beside the British driver of a Jeep, and behind me were a staff officer and my faithful soldier servant of fourteen years, Peter Dorans (who still lives near Kilkerran). We were driving along a reasonably good metalled track, when I spotted a grass one running off at right angles to the left. 'Turn up there!' I said to the driver. Five hundred yards along it, I spotted a crowd of men, women and children, all dressed in white, and many of them garlanded. There was no room to turn, so we drove on, until I suddenly realized that we were gate-crashing some religious ceremony. The crowd was gathered round a huge old tree, also garlanded, at the foot of which was a small group of robed men, obviously priests. Everybody's jaw dropped: it was conceivable that in that remote area none had ever seen a motor-vehicle before, let alone such a strange one as a Jeep, with four *sahibs* in it. I spotted another track, leading back in the direction from which we had come: so we drove rapidly round the tree and the crowd, with grinding gears in a cloud of blue exhaust smoke, and down the second track, which mercifully led straight back to the main road. I have often wondered what the priests made of it. I hope they kept their heads, and said to their congregation: 'That was a miracle, that was.'

I have always been awed by the trappings of primitive religions, and never tempted to treat them lightly. There is much that is moving in the humble offerings to the *nats* or spirits in the little baskets at every entrance to Kachin villages in the hills of upper Burma; nor are the Kachins alone in deeming it likely that some sort of *nat* dwells on the summit of every high mountain. The summit of many a New Zealand hill is *tapu* to the Maori; and few of us who have stood at the top of even such minor peaks as Cruachan or the Merrick have been wholly unaware of some sort of presence. It was the same instinct which inspired the Athenians to dedicate an altar 'to the Unknown God', which afforded St Paul so providential a text for a sermon when he was sorely in need of one.

Upper Burma in general, and the country of the Kachins in particular, furnished me with some of the happiest memories of the years of war, as well as with some of the grimmest. The rain forests of Mysore had their attractions, though largely nullified by the demands on us of leeches and mosquitoes. As opposed to Mysore, the chief curse of the Central Provinces, where we did most of our training, was the ubiquitous speargrass, which penetrated your boots, your socks and all your clothing, and set up suppurating sores unless you were quick to deal with your punctures. Speargrass was the first plague; dust and red ants followed hard on its heels; I do not hanker after seeing that thirsty country between Saugor and Jhansi again. But I have twice been back to upper Burma since the war, in 1960 with permission, and in 1961 without; and I hope that some day I may be allowed once again to revisit the people who during the war gave us such unstinted help at the risk of their lives. To lower Burma, and as far north as Mandalay and Maymyo, I have also been back in 1967 and 1972; but that isn't *my* Burma, those districts and sub-districts that I came to love so much despite the sorrows that befell us there.

I remember almost every individual bivouac of the first Wingate expedition of 1943. In one, early on, we stayed for three nights, since my column was made responsible for a supply drop for the whole brigade, the first and last of its kind. In none of the others, however tempting, were we ever able to linger for more than one night: on the way in, because the pressure on us to reach our objectives before the Japanese could guess them was an over-riding urge; on the way out, because we were anxious to reach the line dividing the British and Japanese armies. I had lost my long-range wireless set in a skirmish, when the mule carrying it had been shot and fallen over a cliff, and therefore had no means of summoning a supply drop, or of knowing which way the tides of war were surging, or where the dividing line was. In the event, it proved to be precisely where it had been when we crossed it ten weeks earlier: the line of the River Chindwin. The party with me numbered 31 in all; others brought up the total number of survivors to 95; and 28 prisoners were recovered after the war: this was out of a total of 318 that had crossed the Chindwin with me on the inward march three months earlier.

Some of the bivouacs on the road to Imphal and onwards to the Chindwin are also memorable. So as not to interrupt the work being done on the road, and to keep our venture secret, we marched by night and slept by day. It was during this period that we saw Kohima, soon to be the scene of one of the hardest fought battles of the war. But far more memorable are those behind the Japanese lines, after we had crossed the Chindwin, that formidable river. They were always in jungle: we never slept near villages, except when in the loyal security of the Kachin hills. The Burmese or Shan-Kadus, however much they secretly wished us well, had been terrorized into bearing swift information to the Japanese about our movements, though we found many faithful helpers among them too. Some bivouacs were spread-eagled along high ridges, with water hard to come by. Some were by slow-flowing streams, although normally we avoided camping near water, where, especially in times of drought, we knew the Japanese with their superior numbers would look for us. Some, especially in the Kachin Hills, where we could be sure of ample warning of enemy patrols, we established blatantly by mountain streams. Here, beside pools, we could pull off our dusty, sweat-stained clothes, and soak naked in the water, drying out afterwards in the sun on the grass alongside – though always with our weapons handy, and always with guards mounted up and down stream.

The Western Desert seemed a sensible place to fight in, if fight one must. It was sparsely inhabited, and such inhabitants as there were put up with it philosophically. From our defences in Tobruk, in December 1941, I spotted an Arab caravan, children, flocks and all, heading straight for one of our minefields; and I nipped out through it, by a secret path known only to us the defenders, to warn them that they were moving into danger. Their bearded patriarch told me placidly that they were on their annual journey to Derna; that they always travelled this route, and that no matter what infantile games the Germans, Italians and we might be playing, they would continue on their own, sweet, traditional way. It took a posse of my Jocks with bayonets, and their limited but forceful Palestinian Arabic, to induce them, under protest, to take the long but safe way round.

Not so Burma. The Burmese, for all their theoretical attachment to Buddhism, can be warlike, and even cruel, as everybody knows; and nobody could ever accuse the Kachins (some Christian, some still animists) or the Karens (ditto, but mostly Christian) of not being spirited warriors. The Shans, too, can fight, as history shows; and indeed still shows today, when many of them have not let their swords sleep in their hands for a couple of decades. But the Burmese of upper Burma and the Shans wished, for the most part, that we should go and play our silly games elsewhere; wished us, indeed, 'a plague on both our houses'; and who could blame them? For all their long history of dacoity and internecine feuds, their prosperous villages, fertile paddy-fields, pious pagodas, ample space, and peaceful *poongyikyaungs* or monasteries, where their boys went for religious instruction in the tenets of the Lord Buddha, seemed the embodiment of peace. It is hardly for us Christians to sneer at their lapses from the precepts they profess.

For six weeks in 1944 I established a protectorate, which unfortunately proved short-lived, in the Meza Valley of upper Burma: I thought we were there to stay, but the fortunes of war ruled otherwise. Its 'capital' was the large village of Manhton, just south of the Y formed by the junction of the Meza River proper, and the considerable tributary of the Kalat Chaung that flows into it; and its population comprised a total of a dozen villages and at most two thousand souls. With the help of American bulldozers, flown in by American aircraft and gliders and manned by American engineers, we built an airstrip, on to which were flown some seven hundred sorties, and something like four thousand troops. We set up a shop, stocked with clothing materials and many other commodities which had long been what the economists call 'in short supply'. We employed many local men and women, and paid them handsomely in solid silver Indian rupees. We established a hospital, over which the presiding genius was my Brigade Medical Officer, Major Jimmie Donaldson, who was born and bred half-way between Dunskey and Knockinaam. Here villagers flocked for treatment from miles around, even from far beyond the ill-defined frontiers of my 'protectorate'.

I even appointed a sort of local Governor, in the person of Bill Smythies, a Burma Forest Officer like his father and uncle before him, who had been attached to me – one of the best windfalls I ever had – as a Civil Affairs Officer. He held paternal court in the best tradition: people brought their disputes to him just as they brought their ailments to Jimmie Donaldson, and he adjudicated with the same authority and acceptance. When after Wingate's death I was ordered to evacuate the area, which I only did after vigorous protest, Bill Smythies shed his normal respectful shyness, and stormed at me for being the turncoat and the breaker of promises which, in a great part of my heart, I felt I was. I marched out with my troops; Bill, with my blessing, stayed behind, and took his chance, slender though it was, remaining near his people in the 'protectorate', in a fastness which he carved out for himself in the near-by jungle. He survived, and the wounds between us, such as they were, were healed. Ten years later I spent three days with him in Brunei, where he was Chief Forest Officer, travelling over in a launch from the island of Labuan and up the Brunei River, to his house on stilts on the water; and two years after that he was the guest of my wife and myself in Scotland. He wasn't wrong in his decision; and nor, I hope, was I. In some ways, mine was the more difficult; but his was courageous. He was cloaked in loneliness and integrity, while I had countless companions about me.

It seems wrong, somehow, that those splashing mountain torrents and slow-running streams in sandy beds, that brought us such solace at the time, should all be running to waste, unpatronized; and that waves are still breaking on remote beaches all over the world where I have swum, with nobody there to enjoy them. I have a feeling of guilt, of extravagance, as though I had left innumerable electric lights switched on (as one used to do in Andorra, where nobody bothers to switch off, since electricity is free: I haven't been there for thirty years, and this may no longer be true). But there is nothing whatever that I can do about it, and the thought causes me no sleepless nights.

I got back to Kilkerran in time for Christmas 1944, and right bitterly did I feel the cold in that huge, draughty house after four years in hot climates. Only within a yard of the fire did I feel even moderately warm. My new appointment was as the Military Director of Combined Operations, with a Naval and Air Force opposite number, and my old friend Bob Laycock as our triple-Service Chief. Almost my first duty involved going out into the Bristol Channel in a landing-craft in a January snowstorm: my conducting officer in his mercy cut the trip short, and took me back to Appledore, a roaring fire and a bottle of rare Scotch whisky, because he genuinely thought that I was going to die on him, a view which I shared. I spent twenty months in London, followed by a year with the Palestine Police (about which I have written elsewhere), and then three years commanding the 1st Battalion of my Regiment in Germany, from 1948 to 1951, the first two in the Ruhr and the last in Berlin. For political reasons we were psychologically confined to barracks. Our social contacts with the Germans were minimal, and all that we saw of Germany were barracks and training areas.

But I managed to achieve two journeys to countries which for me were new ground. I was still a bachelor, and the next senior bachelor in the Battalion was Freddy Burnaby-Atkins. He had been my pupil at Sandhurst when the war broke out; had been taken prisoner with the Highland Division before he was nineteen; had done a spectacular escape in Germany, only to be recaptured on the Swiss frontier near Schaffhausen; and after the war had been ADC to the Viceroy of India, first with Wavell and then with Mountbatten. He too had itchy feet, and willingly accompanied me on both journeys, the perfect companion. Both had to be done on the then permitted travel allowance of £25 a head, exclusive of actual rail tickets: which meant, in the coarse but useful phrase, 'travelling hard-arse'.

Trip No. 1 was to Spain. Far from being the suburban playground which it was soon to become, it was then regarded as almost inaccessible. Some stigma still attached to it because of what was regarded as its dubious record in the war. Freddy had learned some rudimentary Spanish in jail, and was keen to air it: so to Spain we went, travelling third-class through Paris and Hendaye. On the train, but travelling *de luxe*, was an American couple who were indeed Innocents Abroad. They had never before been out of the States, and were pitifully grateful for our services as interpreters, respectively, in French and Spanish. They were worried on our behalf that we had taken no steps about hotel reservations in Madrid: they themselves had telegraphed for reservations at the Prado, and were mildly worried that no confirmation had been telegraphed back. They were still more worried when we explained to them that the Prado was not so much an hotel as a picture gallery.

Once arrived in Madrid, we husbanded our money carefully; the rate of exchange was favourable; and we were able to visit Toledo. And then one morning we bumped into the famous, nearly ubiquitous 'Prod': Peter Rodd. Prod was the second of the three Rodd brothers whose father had been for eleven years, before and during the First War, the almost legendary British Ambassador in Rome. When the Rodd brothers as a team were running the Allied Military Government of Occupied Territory (known for short as AMGOT) in Italy during the later stages of the war, they had given rise to the pun: '*Amgötterdämmerung*, or The Twilight of the Rodds.' Prod, who was married, though rather *in absentia*, to Nancy Mitford, is said to be the original of Basil Seal in Evelyn Waugh's novels, and I can well believe it. His knowledge of obscure corners and odd characters all over Europe was proverbial and to find him in Madrid caused me no surprise.

Prod had a car, which we hadn't; but he had no 'potatoes' (as he persisted in calling pesetas), whereas we still had a few left. He suggested that we should pool our resources; and the following morning, though hardly at cock-crow – Prod's habits did not lend themselves to early starts – we set off for Andorra, which was then little known to foreigners, though my enterprising mother had once spent a week there. We spent our first night at Lérida, in a filthy little inn where Prod was well known, and the next, after another late start, in a spotlessly clean one in Andorra la Vieja, where Prod had an enraptured welcome from our host, one Raoul. When the word spread that Prod had arrived, half Andorra flocked to greet him, and the evening was reminiscent of Belloc's lovely verses *Tarantella*:

> The cheers and the jeers of the young muleteers
> Under the vine of the dark verandah.
> Do you remember an Inn, Miranda,
> Do you remember an Inn?

I will bet that that Inn hasn't forgotten Prod.

After an even later reveille, we roused the snoring Prod, and forced him to drive us on to Perpignan, where we stood him a final fill of petrol and abandoned him. We persuaded a reluctant station-master to exchange our return tickets from Hendaye to Paris for substitutes from Perpignan, and returned, bronzed but broke, to the bosom of the battalion.

Our next sortie, the following year, was even more ambitious: to Morocco. That country, too, is now a tourist playground; but in 1950 it was regarded as the back of beyond. We lunched in Paris with General Koenig, beside whom I had fought in Syria in 1941: when he was a lieutenant-colonel, GSO1 to the Free French General le Gentilhomme, and I a maid-of-all-work major as Wavell's liaison officer. He had been attached to my Regiment in Silesia in 1920, ten years before I joined it, when Wavell, although a brevet-colonel, had been a company commander, and had greeted my Red Hackle with enthusiasm. I had met him since in Germany when, as the French High Commissioner, he told me of the horrors of being the guest at dinner of his American opposite number. The main course was a turkey stuffed with oysters, reclining on pineapple chunks, and covered with a coating of icing sugar. '*Mais ceux sont des barbares, ces gens-là!*'

Wherever it was that he entertained us, we lunched far

better than that; and our fellow-guest was General Duval, Commander-in-Chief in Morocco, to whom he commended us: he was about to return there by air, whereas we were travelling by rail across Spain, 'hard-arse' as usual. The one thing, said Koenig, in the hearing of Duval, that we must not do was to fly with him: '*comme pilote il est fort dangereux*'. Being junior to Koenig, Duval was bound to laugh at this sally. I had a fellow-feeling for him: I had noticed the reluctance of my own officers and NCOs to fly with me in my little Auster. But Duval agreed to make us welcome whenever we should arrive in Rabat, and he was as good as his word. He did in fact kill himself flying a year later, and his ADC with him.

Once again, Freddy and I passed through Madrid. The British Military Attaché, with whom we lunched, gave us a personal letter of introduction to the station-master to help us on our way. When we reached the railway-station, we saw two long queues. We flourished our letter at an official, who directed us towards the longer of the two, explaining that that was the queue for people with personal letters of introduction to the station-master.

Far more useful was Freddy's letter to 'Teddy' Dunlop, the wife of the doctor to the British community in Tangier. Harry Dunlop, who hailed from Girvan, eight miles south of Kilkerran, was a splendid man in his own right, apart from being a first-class doctor; but he was to some degree *le mari de madame*. Throughout the war his jolly wife had been far more than a popular hostess: she had master-minded a major intelligence network covering the whole western end of the Mediterranean. Harry and she were such well-known characters that they were for ever getting letters of introduction, brought by such spongers as Freddy and I were, but they never seemed to mind, and provided boundless hospitality. To everybody they were 'Harry' and 'Teddy', and the story went that one of their beneficiaries had written her a bread-and-butter letter beginning: 'Dear Teddy – or may I call you "Mrs Dunlop"?' In later years they moved to Lisbon, where Harry died; and Teddy died, most suitably, while on a visit to her old stamping-ground. She is buried in the British cemetery at Tangier, close to the famous Kaid MacLean, long in the service of the

Sultan of Morocco, in years when Morocco was still closed to most Europeans.

If it had not been for Teddy, our journey would have finished ignominiously in Tangier. We had omitted through ignorance to obtain visas for crossing Spanish Morocco into French, and we were grievously short of 'potatoes': but Teddy advanced us cash to pay for overflying it to Casablanca, and a day later we were in General Duval's office in the beautiful city of Rabat. The French always embellished the capitals of their colonies (witness Damascus, Algiers and Saigon, among others), and the Avenue Lyautey in Rabat, with its generous breadth and its palms, was a worthy memorial to the great Marshal who had first 'pacified' and then built up the country. The view from the old palace across the river to Saleh, out of which the corsairs used to sail, is one of the finest I know. Duval did us splendidly. He advised us on where to go, and lent us a car and an armed escort of two French soldiers to take us there; but it didn't escape our notice that they rang up Rabat each evening to report where we had been, and with whom we had spoken.

We went first to Fez, calling on the way at Meknes, where we spent two hours exploring the ancient *mellah*, or Jewish quarter. Both there and at Fez, we learned that several industries, notably those connected with leather, such as saddlery and tanning, had ground almost to a halt. They had been exclusively in Jewish hands, and the younger Jews had emigrated *en masse* to Israel; although a few had trickled back, having found less milk and honey than they expected. Fez, in its ring of mountains, reminded me slightly of Grenoble. Sixty years before, it had been a forbidden city, almost as inaccessible to Europeans as Mecca or Lhasa, although the indomitable Scottish traveller William Lithgow had managed to spend seventeen days there in 1620 or thereby, reporting on its women as 'damnable libidinous'. The reformed libertine, the French cavalry officer Charles de Foucauld, reached it disguised as a Jew in 1883, being hidden for six weeks in the house of Samuel ben Shimoun in the *mellah*. This house, and the room in which de Foucauld was concealed, we were actually enabled to see.

The British Vice-Consul in Fez turned out to be Adrian de Lavison, who before the war had been the covert organizer of intelligence in south Palestine when I had been the overt one. I had often been his furtive guest in the flat in Jaffa, where he lived with his wife Alethea; with him I had paid my first visit to Beersheba. Both had been born and bred in the Middle East, and were bilingual in Arabic. Adrian was a tough cookie. He had lost a foot in the Air Force in the First War, and the pain which he often suffered was reflected in his quick temper, which frequently involved him in bitter battles with his superiors: battles which he seldom won, but always enjoyed. He extracted Freddy and me by force from the hotel in which we had been installed by General Duval – a fact anxiously reported to Rabat on the telephone by our escort – and put us up in comfort in his Residence just within the native city. It was evident from our interview with the charming, elderly French General Laparra the next morning that our change of abode lacked official approval, and that Adrian was looked upon as a sinister figure. He probably was: intrigue was the breath of life to him.

We forged on southwards in our Army car, through Sefrou and Aznou, where grow the most glorious groves of cedars in the world: those of Lebanon are stunted shrubs by comparison. We had hoped to reach Taman Rasset, where Charles de Foucauld, no longer the profligate cavalry officer, but the revered missionary of the White Fathers, was assassinated by Touaregs in 1916; we had not realized that it was almost eight hundred miles farther on. Our southernmost point was Ksar-es-Souk, where we were accommodated in the Government Rest House, and where the only European population was a small posse of Foreign Legion. We went out for an evening drink to the sole café, where the only other customer at the bar was a morose, silent Légionnaire of uncertain nationality. He drank steadily, with his white *képi* askew, throughout the hour we were there, and failed to respond to our approaches. We decided that he was drinking in order to try to remember what it was that he had joined the Legion to try to forget.

We dismissed our escort at Ouida, on the Algerian frontier,

two days later, buying rail tickets to Oran with almost the last of our potatoes, which had now dwindled to a mere handful of francs. We sat up all night on wooden *bancs*, arriving in Oran soon after dawn, with just enough money left to buy us each a *petit pain* and a modest whang of cheese, to find that the ship in which we were hoping to travel to Marseilles didn't leave for twenty-four hours. We spent a cold and hungry night sleeping fitfully on the beach, and boarded the ship next morning. Here again we were in luck. The ship was a new one, still on trial from its builders, whose representative was on board; and the representative was a Pole, who turned out to have been in the Tobruk siege at the same time as I was. He treated us first to an enormous breakfast, and then bullied the Purser into cashing what was certainly a wholly illegal sterling cheque on my lifelong friends, Messrs Cox & King. About this transaction I feel no qualms of conscience, although perhaps I ought to. Once again, we returned to our point of departure bronzed and broke.

Later that year, 1950, Freddy and I both got married; and three years later did a month's tour of Dalmatia together with our respective wives, to see whether the fun of joint travel would still continue. It did. The most memorable part of the trip was its closing stages. We were working our way slowly north, and were in a small hotel on the island of Korçula, where we had made friends with Dr Arneri, the current representative of a Venetian family which had lived there for 400 years. He was a friend and ally of Fitzroy Maclean, my contemporary at Eton, whose connection with Tito and the liberation of Yugoslavia is too well known for me to rehearse.

About seven o'clock one morning, we were awoken by the sound of singing and shouting. I looked out of our bedroom window, and said to my wife: 'This looks like some sort of local folk-lore occasion: I'll go and investigate.' I donned a shirt and some grey flannel trousers, and rushed out to join in a procession of some hundreds of men which was marching along the street. Soon, although my knowledge of Serbo-Croat was minimal, I realized that they were shouting anti-British and anti-American slogans, and proclaiming that Trieste belonged to Yugoslavia, and not to Italy. I had been only dimly aware that this was a major issue of the moment.

My fellow-marchers soon realized that I hadn't the faintest idea of what it was all about, and gradually became friendly, although laughing at my bewilderment. Soon they turned around, and began marching back. By this time we were all arm in arm, and they were clapping me on the shoulder. I now perceived my brave wife Laura, walking towards us with a set face from the hotel, where a waiter, who, like so many Dalmatians, had spent some years in New Zealand, and spoke good English, had told her that the demonstration was an anti-British one. But by this time good humour was prevailing.

We travelled on by steamer to Rijeka (formerly Fiume), where we had left our car; and there met some very shaken Americans, two married couples, who had had a rough time for the same political reasons, having had paving-stones thrown at their car two days earlier in Skopje. I asked them their plans: to which they replied that they would follow us out of Yugoslavia, 'fender to fender', whichever way we decided to go. I rang up the British Embassy in Belgrade for advice, and got the gloomiest. There was no chance, they said, of getting out to Trieste through the disputed Istria peninsula, which was crowded with mobilized Yugoslav divisions, poised to wage war. They recommended a detour through Austria via Klagenfurt.

This seemed to us a boring prospect, the more so because we had promised ourselves a visit to Venice on our way back. We thought we would at least have a try at driving straight through to Trieste down the main road. Off we set, with the nervous Americans immediately astern of us; and all we saw of the massive Yugoslav divisions were a few soup-kitchens, brewing up what smelt like very indifferent soup. We drove through without any bother at all.

In Trieste, I went to pay my respects to the British General, Jack Winterton, whom I knew, and who received me along with his Chief of Staff, who had been a fellow-student of mine at the Staff College. They asked me how on earth we had managed to 'get through'. I replied modestly that we had merely driven down the main road. 'But how,' they asked, 'did you manage to get past the 1st, and the 21st, and the 31st [or whatever they were] Yugoslav Divisions, who are massed on that front, and ready to move?' 'All we saw was a few soup-kitchens,' I said; and for some reason it wasn't a welcome answer.

We took leave of our Americans, who seemed to think that we had saved their lives. One of the men revealed his identity as the owner of one of the most expensive hotels in Washington, and he cordially invited us to stay in it for free for as long as we liked whenever we liked. The opportunity has not yet come, and I very much fear that after this long lapse of time he may have forgotten.

Chapter Five

JOURNALIST AT LARGE: I

In 1958 I sent in my papers from the Army. Soon after my marriage eight years earlier, we had bought a small property near Ballantrae, in the next valley to Kilkerran, within twenty-five miles of both my brothers. The plan was to live at home and write books; but this is an uncertain way of earning a living, and an Army pension is hardly a diamond-mine. So I induced the *Sunday Times* to take me on as a part-time roving correspondent at a fixed salary for three months in the year; later I switched to the *Daily Telegraph*. The idea was that I should specialize in countries which had lately achieved, or would soon be achieving, their independence. As a job it was ideal, and full of interest for the three years that it lasted. The only snag was having to say goodbye so often to my wife and son.

My last command in the Army had been that of the 29th Infantry Brigade at Dover; my first journalistic assignment was to Algeria, where armed rebellion against the French was raging. It was therefore from Dover that I sailed on 17 November 1958 in the cross-Channel ferry after a bibulous send-off. A cocktail party, about which I had not been warned, had been laid on in one of the ship's lounges. The hosts were British Rail, who owned the ship, the Mayor and Corporation of Dover, and the officers of Brigade Headquarters and the Gordon and Cameron Highlanders. These two Regiments, which I had known all my service, were all that was left of the Brigade, which was being disbanded as part of the ruthless surgery then being practised on the Army. Peter Hunt, the Commanding Officer of the Camerons, and destined to be-

99

come Chief of the General Staff, had stationed his pipe-major
on the end of the Dover breakwater, to pipe me out of the
harbour and out of the Army. I felt quite tearful, not entirely
because of the cocktails.

My first stop was Paris. I had never been to Algeria, and
although I knew a number of French officers serving there on
whose help I could count, I wanted to ensure that I would not
be unwelcome at the top level. So I arranged to lunch at
SHAPE with Admiral Barjot, the naval deputy to the Supreme
Commander. Barjot's own deputy was Rear-Admiral Nigel
Henderson, who had married my second cousin, was my
neighbour in Scotland and had been my fellow-student at the
Imperial Defence College: so we had a convivial luncheon.
Barjot and I had 'clicked' when he was second-in-command
and senior French officer during the Port Said affair in 1956,
and I the Director of Psychological Warfare, with a mixed
French and British staff, the oddest job I ever had in my life.
The Admiral was an uproarious character, with a passion for
Black Velvet: he used to call for a jorum of it at surprising
moments. He was lucky not to have faced a Vichy firing
squad: he fell under Darlan's suspicion quite soon after the
collapse of France in 1940, and not without reason, since he
had been an early clandestine member of a Resistance *réseau*.
They could not pin anything precise on him, and contented
themselves with cashiering him. Somehow he fetched up in
Algiers, and found himself a civilian job as a reporter on Alain
de Sérigny's newspaper *L'Echo d'Alger*; and in that capacity he
reported the dramatic Allied landings there in November
1942. He witnessed the British destroyer HMS *Broke* entering
the harbour under fire, much damaged, at her fourth attempt
at 5.30 a.m., one morning, and the even more spectacular
arrival next day of the Headquarters ship HMS *Bulolo*. *Bulolo*
came alongside at twelve knots: her captain was unaware that
his engine-room telegraphs had been severed by a near miss
from a bomb, and only a providential mudbank by the quay
brought her up all-standing and undamaged.

Barjot had at once been reinstated in the French Navy, and
by the end of the war had risen to high rank. He had a difficult
role at Port Said, playing second fiddle to the British, and the

political ramifications were even more complicated than the military. We had often wined and dined together during that curious period, and I had come to be fond of him as well as to admire him. I now asked him, a little shyly, whether, in my new capacity as a journalist, he felt he could give me a line of introduction to General Salan, the Commander-in-Chief in Algeria, who was reputed to be unapproachable. 'Of course!' he said; and he rattled one off to his stenographer in his office as soon as luncheon was over. It proved to be a godsend.

There was another reason, apart from the rebellion, for going to Algeria at that moment: the impending general elections there. The French were anxious that the elections should not be boycotted, though the probability was that they would be. They had at least aroused enough interest to attract a horde of journalists. There were two principal hotels in Algiers in those days. Up the hill was the St Georges, a good old-fashioned establishment, patronized by successive generations of *Colons* on their way to France and back, whose avuncular hall porter Leblanc was adored by the children as he had been by their parents. Down in the city was the Aletti: excellent in a more modern chromium style, and admittedly better than the St Georges for the more clandestine contacts. My eventual pattern was the St Georges to live in, and to entertain my old French Army friends in, as I gradually traced them, and the Aletti at the cocktail hours. But for the first two days, owing to the influx of other journalists, I could insinuate myself into neither of these two, and was obliged to sleep in some rather *louche* little *pension*. Not till the third night was Leblanc, impressed by some of the introductions I was carrying to *Colon* families far more than any other of my pretensions, able to manoeuvre me into the St Georges.

I found in my brief career as a journalist that one particular frustration always recurred. You arrived in a new place bristling with contacts, who might be friends of your own, or people to whom you had letters of introduction, only to fail to establish any touch during the first day or two. X had left the country, Y was away, Z was dead. Then your contacts proliferated, and by the time you had to leave you were longing for two or three extra days' grace in which to exploit them; but the dateline for your next despatch from somewhere else was already haunting you. Salan's ADC was as elusive as he could be, failing to ring back and playing hard to get: probably I wasn't as pushing as I should have been, and I was finding the life an odd contrast to that of a brigade commander, when what you said happened, and you didn't have to kick your heels in waiting-rooms. If it had not been for the kindness of the Consul-General Roderick Sarell (who finished up as Ambassador to Turkey) and his wife, I would have been even more depressed than I was. They jollied me along, and gave me several useful introductions.

It was forty-eight hours before I at last penetrated to Salan's office. He had four or five staff officers with him; he was more correct than cordial. I think he was suspicious of a soldier turned journalist. He refused my first request, which was to visit General Massu, commanding in the Kabylie area west of Constantine where the fighting was fiercest; I had soldiered with him both in Syria in 1941 and at Port Said. Perhaps Salan was jealous of the publicity Massu was getting, of the popularity he enjoyed, and of his status as a national hero; or was there, as repeatedly alleged in the anti-French lobbies, some policy in Massu's area unsuitable for journalists to witness? Salan was already an embittered man. Like so many other French generals – de Lattre, des Essars – he had lately lost a son fighting. He had already sailed very close to the wind in the events of the preceding May, of which I shall treat later, and it was he who in 1961 was to lead the revolt against de Gaulle which so tragically split the French Army right down the middle. And it was Massu who in that mysterious meeting in Germany in May 1968 struck the bargain with de Gaulle which got Generals Challe and Jouhaud, both of whom I knew, and others out of jail; and Salan, who had found asylum in Spain, off the hook. I fear that a joke which I made at this meeting was ill-timed: it certainly misfired. General Salan asked me how long it was since I had left the Army. Technically, my terminal leave had only ended that morning; and, with what I hoped was a disarming smile, I glanced at my wrist-watch and said: 'About twenty minutes!' The frostiness with which this sally was received would have chilled an Eskimo.

I may also well have made a mistake in reeling off a long list of my friends and acquaintances serving under Salan's command: it may have added to his suspicions that I was sinister. He raised no objections to my going south and west, but he formally forbade me to visit the Kabylie mountains. I might well have done the same in his shoes. It was impossible to control effectively the two hundred mountainous miles that made up the northernmost end of the frontier with Tunisia which the irregular forces confronting Massu were constantly traversing. As the French kept saying, they could have won their war already had it not been for the support the rebels had from across the Tunisian and Moroccan frontiers, from which they played a ceaseless game of Tom Tiddler's Ground. These two countries had been granted their independence within three weeks of each other, in March 1956, and were determined to do all they could to help their Algerian neighbours to achieve the same end. There was little sign then of the clashes of interests and of personalities between them which have developed since.

The French situation in Algeria bore a strong resemblance to that of Rhodesia in the 1970s. The *Colons* or settlers had been established much longer than their Rhodesian counterparts, some of them since as far back as the 1840s; but their situation was similar. When the French, in pursuance of the principle of 'hot pursuit', bombed a rebel training camp at Sakiet Sidi Youssef, just over the Tunisian frontier, there was a world-wide bellow of protest from the United Nations and the anti-colonialist lobbies, just as when Rhodesian security forces raided corresponding camps in Mozambique or Zambia. The French were equally outraged when they found that many of the rebels were armed with British weapons supplied only months before to the Government of Tunisia. I checked this later; I had been indignantly shown some of the arms which had been captured, and noted their registered numbers: obviously, once they had been supplied to Tunisia in all good faith, the British had no further control over them. Yet my sympathies with the French were tempered by recollections of the role they had played from Syria during the Arab troubles in Palestine just before the war: when rebels had been caught with French small arms and mortars, and their wounded were being treated in the French military hospital in Damascus. I had seen and spoken to some of them in 1938. Yet I claim that I managed to remain fairly objective during the month for which my sortie lasted, in Algeria, Morocco and Tunisia. I contrived to meet a reasonable cross-section of most of those involved: *Colons*, French officers (including some of the *Affaires Indigènes*, who have always included some remarkable men, like some of our own Arabists and Indian Political officers) and rebel leaders.

One interesting category was that of the election candidates. Few of those who were standing were overtly anti-French, since the opposition had finally decided on a boycott. A few individuals have stuck in my mind. Robert Abdessalam, the Davis Cup tennis-player, was standing for a constituency just outside Algiers; I attended one of his meetings, and he had a drink with me later at the Aletti. He spoke entirely in French, and I had the impression, especially when it came to the heckling, that he was happier in French than in Arabic. By contrast, Professor Marçais of Algiers University, a second or third generation *pied noir* and the son of a famous father, spoke entirely in Arabic, in which he was obviously bilingual. Him too I met afterwards, and thought he had great potential. A third was the fiery, bearded young reserve parachute lieutenant Lagaillarde, who led the pro-French mob which broke into the Government-General in Algiers on 13 May, six months earlier. That astonishing episode, now largely forgotten, resulted in the formation of a Committee of Public Safety. Its members included Massu, Jouhaud, de Sérigny and Abdessalam, as well as Lagaillarde. Salan put his full authority behind it, and was joined by the much respected Admiral Auboyneau, the naval Commander-in-Chief in the Mediterranean. The prominent Algerian leader Dr Sid-Cara (whose sister was another election candidate) was joint President.

The match that touched off the inflammable situation of early May was the threatened appointment of M. Pflimlin as Minister of Algerian Affairs. He was a dove of doves, and his appointment was seen by the hawks as a penance for the bombing of Sakiet Sidi Youssef. This was more than the partisans of *Algérie Française* could contemplate swallowing. They foresaw, correctly, that it was a calculated step along the path of granting independence to a Muslim Algeria. They were not without justification when they claimed that many Muslims wished the old régime to continue. They pinned their hopes on de Gaulle, then still haughtily aloof at Colombey, believing passionately that if he would only come out on their side all would yet be well. De Sérigny in his *Echo d'Alger* published a ringing article with the headline: '*Parlez, Parlez Vite, Mon Général!*'

And in fact the extraordinary situation, which even the participants could hardly believe was happening, was only resolved when de Gaulle did arrive, after being delayed for two days by heavy rain, on 4 June. He was greeted rapturously by enormous crowds, French and Muslim alike: so much so that it took him more than an hour to drive in to the city from the airfield at Maison Blanche, under countless flags, triumphal arches and showers of confetti. Accompanied by his erring but sorely-tried Generals and other members of the Committee of Public Safety, he laid a wreath at the Monument aux Morts (from which Lagaillarde had led the assault on the Government-General). Then, rising to his full height, which was considerable, he raised his hands with clenched fists towards Heaven, and said: '*Me voilà!*'

That evening he made another speech from the balcony of the Algerian Ministry. He was received with such cheers on his appearance that it was three minutes before he could begin it, which he did with the words: '*Je vous ai compris.*' He went on to say, without hedging or ambiguity, that Algeria was part of France. 'There is only one category of Algerians, and they are all French.' It must have been a great performance, worthy of the occasion; but it was small wonder that Salan and his associates felt so deceived when he reversed his declared position on coming to power. My heart still bleeds for poor General de Larminat, whom I knew in Syria in 1941 and in France ten years later. De Gaulle appointed him to preside over the courts-martial of those luckless Generals who had taken part in the 1961 rising: rather than do so, he took his own life. Meanwhile, in the wake of de Gaulle's visit, the Committee of Public Safety was dissolved, Pflimlin's appointment cancelled, and the normal set-up restored. And de Gaulle himself was back in power.

The roads being vulnerable to ambush, I flew the 150 miles to Tiaret, south-west of Algiers and not far from Sidi-Bel-Abbés, the Foreign Legion Depot whose name is familiar to all readers of *Beau Geste*, to spend three nights with a typical *Colon*, whose daughter I had known in France. His name was Langlois, and his property, the Domaine de Sebaïn, the size of a major Texan ranch or the county of Rutland. His family had ruled it paternally since 1894, endowing it with schools and a well-equipped modern hospital. A rebel leader whom I met in Morocco the following week had actually been one of his schoolmasters; and he said to me with passion that if all the French had been like Langlois there would never have been any trouble. He was less enthusiastic about Langlois's younger brother. Actually, the brother dined with us one night, bringing his young wife, and seemed to me charming. He had been married to her only three days before, in the drawing-room, by Langlois senior in his capacity as *Maire*.

I had the deepest sympathy for Langlois, who was devoted alike to his land and his people. His wife had for years been in a mental home in France, and he was consoling himself with the company of a beautiful and cultured woman, who had lived with him for a decade and was a splendid hostess. Her brother was the farm manager, and these five were the only French people still living on the Domaine: all the others had left it for the safety of Algiers or of Metropolitan France. Langlois was fully aware that the days of their occupancy were numbered, but he was determined to stick it out to the end, largely because of the loyalty still being shown to his family by his workforce. Life was not easy. He had to accommodate a section of troops under a French sergeant in his outhouses for the protection of himself and his people, who were being terrorized in the same fashion as has become familiar in Malaysia, Rhodesia and elsewhere. Two nights before I arrived, the house had been shot up. One of the attackers had been killed, but none of the locals had been able to identify the body, which indicated that he must have been a stranger to the estate: unless, of course, the locals were nervous of reprisals. We had to put up steel shutters over our windows each evening at sundown, which, even in November, made the house intolerably stuffy.

We all lunched one day at near-by Vialar in the Headquarters Mess of the local troops, of which the commander was Colonel Jean Costa de Beauregard. I had known him a long time: he was teaching French at Woolwich during the two years before the war when I was trying, with lesser qualifications, to do likewise at Sandhurst; and throughout my two and a half years at SHAPE he had been interpreter to Field-Marshal Montgomery. Thanks to those two incarnations he was well known to hundreds of British officers. I couldn't help twitting him with having been extracted at last from the fleshpots to do a proper job of soldiering.

On the fourth day, Langlois drove me the 120 miles to Orléansville, now renamed El-Asnam. We went the long way round; the usual road through the hills was dominated by rebels, and a near neighbour of Langlois had been killed on it earlier that week while chancing his arm. I had intended to go by rail, but the line was closed owing to a blown bridge. We made Orléansville in time for luncheon, but Langlois insisted on driving straight home, to be sure of getting back before curfew.

Orléansville was a shanty-town of shacks, having been wrecked in an earthquake four years earlier with the loss of 1200 lives. My host was Réné Morel, late Foreign Legion, Brigadier and second in command of the local military district; and it warmed the cockles of my heart to see him again. He was a swarthy ex-ranker, stocky, broad-shouldered, a bachelor, with almost no neck and a perpetual grin. He held the British DSO and MC, and had something like twelve *palmes* to his Croix de Guerre. He had long lost count of the number of times he had been wounded, and I had myself seen him being carried away on a stretcher, using filthy language, during the fighting before Damascus in June 1941. He had a hard war also in Indo-China, before joining SHAPE soon after me in 1951. He owed nothing whatever to influence (or *piston*, as the French call it), but everything to his own worth. He was one of the few French officers with whom I was on *tutoyer* terms.

'There is one man you must meet,' Morel said; and after luncheon we drove into the fringe of the mountains near Lamartine, to see the Bachagha Boualem. On our way we called in at one or two of Réné's military posts, commanded in one case by a young officer doing his national service and in the other by an Adjutant: it was reminiscent of pre-war Palestine, with pockmarks of recent bullets around their embrasures. The Bachagha, which I gathered was a title of Turkish origin ranking one above a Kaid, was one of the few figures in northern Algeria to retain a measure of feudal influence. He too was a candidate for Parliament. He had been a regular soldier, and wore an impressive chest of medals on his Arab cloak. His fine, thin features indicated breeding, and there was authority in every gesture. He had hit the headlines a year or two before, when he ambushed and killed a young French national service officer called Maillot, a communist, who had gone over to the rebels with the convoy of arms which he was supposed to be escorting. This had obviously made Boualem a prime target for the rebels, but he spoke of them with contempt as he fed us on Arab tea and sweet cakes. As we looked out from his verandah northwards across the rich Cheliff Valley, he talked scathingly of lack of toughness in dealing with the rebels. The view more generally held was that the French were being much more tough than they need be. Atrocity stories are the easiest things in the world to manufacture and circulate, and the hardest to refute, but it is virtually certain that there were some excesses.

Back in Algiers after a comfortable train journey, I found messages from all sorts of friends awaiting me, and had several happy reunions. There was Major Laperroussas, a *pied noir* from Tunisia and a perfect speaker of Arabic, who had been on my staff at Port Said; and General Raymond Coche, former Chasseur Alpin and pre-war explorer of remote corners of the Sahara. He and I had planned in 1939 a joint journey to the Hoggar, the Touareg country where de Foucauld met his death, and about which Coche had already published a book:

our trip was planned for the autumn of 1940, but by that time other events had supervened. There was General André Petit, who had become a close friend when I was the senior British intelligence officer at SHAPE, and he the head of the *Deuxième Bureau*. In Paris I had attended the funeral of his brother, killed in Indo-China, and the marriage of his daughter; and we had spent five weeks together at a NATO Intelligence Conference in the Pentagon in Washington in 1952. He was tall, with a round smiling face and a gentle manner; and over luncheon at the St Georges he measured his words carefully, obviously reminding himself that I was a journalist as well as an old friend. I was to have had a drink with him two nights later, but his ADC rang to say that he was stuck somewhere in the desert by a sandstorm preventing his aircraft from taking off.

When the final bust-up came in Algeria some years later, Petit, by then a lieutenant-general, threw in his lot with Salan, and ended up in jail. By that time I was Governor-General of New Zealand, and it was diplomatically difficult to find any way of helping my old friend in his time of trouble. Through the good offices of the New Zealand Embassy in Paris, I made furtive contact with his priest and confessor, a former officer of the Fusiliers-Marins, the French equivalent of the Royal Marines. Thanks to him, I was able, legitimately but discreetly, to contrive from 12,000 miles away that occasional extra comforts passed through into his prison cell. Owing to his ill health and that of his wife, Petit was eventually released from jail even before Massu's intervention. I still see him from time to time in Paris: deprived of rank and pension, but still erect and full of dignity.

Like so many others involved in that miserable affair, Petit was beyond question a man of integrity and honour. Part of the trouble was that in those years the Mediterranean constituted a psychological as well as a geographical gulf between Algeria and Metropolitan France. Soldiers, civil servants, *Colons* alike were all convinced of the righteousness of their cause, although they probably exaggerated the extent of Muslim sympathy for them; and felt justified in counting on the support of their compatriots in France. They were sure that when it came to the crunch they would get it, and that any appeal for it over the heads of the Government would triumph. They were wholly unaware of the abyss that separated them.

My two maiden articles had received gratifying prominence in the *Sunday Times*. Encouraged by a cable from the Foreign Editor which read 'they stand up well', I flew on to Morocco. I found that country far more difficult to assess than the painful but clear-cut issues in Algeria. The sudden remarriage between French and Spanish Morocco, after so long a divorce, was proving difficult to consummate. The French had been able to shovel a considerable amount of money and investment into their part of the country, whereas the Spanish, what with the Civil War and other distractions, and their less buoyant economy, had been able to do little for theirs. The discrepancy was apparent as soon as you crossed the former border at Larache, whether you judged it by the quality of the roads, the schools, the clothing or the footwear. Even after nearly three years of independence, there was much irritation in the former Spanish half, since most of the new local Governors and officials came from the more sophisticated French half of the country. The one personage who really straddled the gap was the King, Muhammad V, the ablest, strongest and most popular figure in the country. He was shrewd enough to keep in his own hands the key ministries of the Interior and the Security Forces. The day I arrived, Balafrej the Prime Minister resigned, in pique at having failed in an attempt to manoeuvre them out of the King's and into his own. The present King, although only thirty when he succeeded his father in 1961, has so far managed to play the game successfully in the same pattern.

There were still French in Morocco, but they were keeping their heads down. There had never been *Colons* in the Algerian or Tunisian sense: a few ex-servicemen and others had been given grants of land, but they had not been there long enough to take real root, and were quick to go, with only meagre compensation, when the wind began to blow cold for them. The French 'pacification' of Morocco under Lyautey and his successors had not been completed until shortly before the Second War. I myself had met in Syria, in the late 1930s, several Moroccan refugees who had still been resisting 'pacification' in the Rif under Abd-el-Krim shortly before. I was surprised to learn on this journey that Abd-el-Krim, that stout old warrior whom I had thought dead for years, was still alive, aged eighty-eight, and living in Cairo; but the long-standing dynastic feud between his family and the King's was as live as ever. The King had sent a royal commission to investigate the Riffis' grievances: it had been furnished with a list of over a thousand specific items.

I spent a night in Tetuan, in the former Spanish Morocco, a beautiful city. It had a Spanish-type square and some old churches; it smacked of Moorish Andalusia. (My taxi-driver said in Arabic: 'Spain's claim to Gibraltar isn't half as good as ours is to Andalusia!') The poverty was pitiful. Within two years everything had soared in price; the cost of electricity had gone up by 400%; and the seasonal employment over the frontier in Algeria at harvest-time, which had meant salvation to so many families, had dried up with the rebellion. There were beggars by the dozen to be fended off. In the Rif proper, for a hundred miles parallel with the coast, a number of armed Riffis had taken to the hills, setting up roadblocks and exacting tolls from passing cars: fortunately my route to Fez was the safe one through Xauen. Once again, crossing from the former Spanish zone into the French, the difference in the degree of development struck the eye: Fez looked positively blooming with prosperity.

I happened to witness one rather pathetic moment in Rabat, when eight French prisoners, captured in Algeria many months before, were being released into French hands. They were all conscripts, all frightened, all emaciated, and did not give the impression of having had a happy time. But my most rewarding contacts were with Algerian rebels in exile. Some were engaged in political and propaganda activities, others in directly military ones. I met none who looked like thugs. The only one I remember clearly, apart from the former schoolmaster from Sebaïn whom I have already described, was a gentle university lecturer from Algiers, who had led several cross-frontier raids, and who was delighted to have first-hand news of his colleague Professor Marçais. He too said that if all the other Frenchmen in Algeria had been like him, there would have been no trouble. I take leave to doubt this: the desire for independence is always heady wine; champions of any addiction are always proselytizers; moderates always toughen up beyond their own inclination so as not to lose their following. But among the rebel leaders whom I met, both in Morocco and Tunisia, nearly all expressed affection for individual Frenchmen, and not necessarily for radical Frenchmen. This university lecturer was no gangster: his chief anxiety was for the well-being of his wife and six children, whom he had left in Algeria and had not seen for two and a half years.

I spent the final week of my tour in Tunisia. I had been there twice before. The first time was flying home from Palestine in my little aircraft in 1947, visiting *en route* some of the North African and Italian battlefields of my Regiment, to gather material for the war history which Lord Wavell, as Colonel of the Regiment, had required me to write. I had landed in a rain-squall at the oasis of Gabés, and stayed with General Dio, a tough desert soldier who during the war had fought his way north from Chad with Leclerc. Dio had lent me a car, a guide and maps, so that I had been able to visit at leisure the hard-fought fields of Medenine and Mareth, and the Wadi Zigzaou, where a half-circle of burnt-out British tanks still bore witness to the bitter fighting. French officers used to go there regularly to study the battle and to learn its lessons. On that visit, in late October, it rained continuously, and I out-stayed my welcome because the airstrip was unusable for twenty-four hours; but I splashed happily around the extensive Roman remains, and passed the time of day with the locals.

I was carrying a letter of introduction to a family called Roux, third-generation *Colons*, who farmed on a comfortable scale, though more modest than that of the Langlois, between Tunis and Medjez-el-Bab. Their war-time experience deserves a digression. Fernand Roux also owned a town house in Tunis, where he was living with his wife, his children and his mother-in-law when the Allied invasion began. He decided that it would be wise to move them all out to the farm: he can hardly be blamed for not foreseeing that the eventual no-man's-land between the British and Germans would stabilize precisely around that very farm; but so it did. Day after day, there would be fighting – sometimes fierce, sometimes desultory – around 'Peter's Corner', a road junction on the Roux estate, which derived its name from Sir Peter Grant-Lawson, commanding the Derbyshire Yeomanry, and which features in every regimental history of that campaign; night after night, both sides would send out fighting patrols, with the farm, an obvious landmark, as their objective. It had become almost a routine for Fernand and Henriette, Henriette's mother, and the five children to pass half the night sitting in slit trenches in the orchard while bullets whistled to and fro over their heads. They found this life tedious as well as dangerous; and one relatively quiet evening they slipped away and walked back the thirty-five miles to Tunis and the more ordered safety of the Avenue de Lesseps.

After the German surrender, Fernand made his way back on foot to the farm, and found the damage less than he had feared, though there was a lieutenant-colonel of the Royal Fusiliers buried in his orchard; his pictures and his treasured piano were all intact. He began the long trudge back to Tunis, trying to thumb a lift. At last a British Army lorry stopped, and an officer sitting beside the driver signalled him to hop up behind. He did; and found himself a fellow-passenger with his own piano. When they reached Tunis, the officer asked him where he wanted to be dropped, and obligingly took him to the Avenue de Lesseps. Fernand, who spoke no English, indicated by grin and gesture that the piano was his, and the officer obligingly supervised its installation in his town drawing-room as opposed to his country one.

In 1951, with five years still to run before Independence, my wife and I were staying with the Roux; and on their advice we spent a week in Djerba, traditionally the Island of the Lotus-Eaters. It was a two-day sweat in those days to get there from Tunis. The first was in a rail-car, which I have always found a congenial mode of travel in foreign parts: the car has no compartments, and you can improve your knowledge, however meagre, of the local tongue by eavesdropping. We were the only Europeans, and the subject of speculation to our fellow-travellers. I pretended at first to have no Arabic, but when I heard them deciding that we were German it was too much for me: I broke silence, and declared my nationality. The railcar lolloped along, pocketa-pocketa, past famous battlefields of the last war: Enfidaville, where dozens of Black Watch and Maori soldiers are buried side by side in the War Cemetery; Takrouna, that extraordinary outcrop of seemingly impregnable rock which the Maori Battalion did in fact capture by storm – where Ngarimu won his VC and Charlie Bennett his DSO (but lost his foot in fair exchange); Wadi Akarit, which Douglas Wimberley claims was the finest battle fought by the Highland Division in North Africa, and where Lorne Campbell of Airds won *his* VC. It was through history that we were doing pocketa-pocketa, and I longed to pull the communication cord, to give me a little time, however expensive, for a better look at the ground than I had had from my little aircraft four years earlier.

There was no doubt still a French general at Gabés in those days from whom to cadge accommodation; but there was no need: there was one modest little hotel, of the standard of a family *auberge* in France, and there we lodged. They made much of us, and retained places for us next morning on the Arab bus setting out for Djerba: a leisurely journey with many stops for coffee, and the oddest of loads roped on the bus roof, including goats and hens. It was seventy miles through Mareth and Medenine until we reached the ferry over to the island: twenty minutes' chugging to a neat little harbour full of sponge-fishing vessels, and thence in another bus to Houmt Souk, the island capital.

I believe that there is now an airfield and a rash of smart hotels on Djerba, and that one can fly direct from Tunis; but there was then only one cosy little two-storey inn of a dozen rooms, with creepers entwining the verandahs, which we had virtually to ourselves. The inhabitants were partly Berber and partly Jewish, the latter descended from former refugees from Spain: into their synagogue at Houmt Souk was built a stone from the Temple in Jerusalem which had accompanied them on all their wanderings. It was a quiet, untroubled place, remote from all the world; Jews and Berbers lived side by side in amity; and it was not surprising to learn that the hotel had been reserved for senior German officers as a privileged rest-house during the occupation: they had not bothered the Jews. The elderly woman owner was not in evidence; we gathered that the French had deemed her over-hospitable to her war-time guests. There was a mere handful of French about the place, apart from the district officer, the policeman and the priest. We spent most of our time sunbathing on a beach and composing a fanciful romance about the island: which eventually appeared as a novel, was read as a 'book at bed-time' on the BBC, reached paperback status, and more than covered our expenses. Some sucker even paid me lovely dollars for an option on the film rights: he never made the film, but he twice renewed the option, and gave me more dollars. I missed him very much when the flow from this unexpected cornucopia eventually ran dry.

So this was my third visit to Tunisia, and I knew enough of the lie of the land to ferret out material for one reasonable feature article. My principal source was the Algerian rebel leaders, whose little office just off the Avenue Jules Ferry (by then inevitably re-christened the Avenue Bourguiba) was easily found. There among others I met both Boumédienne and Boutéflika; but the Tunis group was much less forthcoming than those I had met in Rabat: I never got a smile out of them, I never felt I had convinced them of my *bona fides*, indeed I was never entirely happy until I was back in the security of the hotel. I had asked their colleagues in Rabat to tell them that I would be getting in touch with them when I reached Tunis, thinking that this would smooth my path. I think an unfavour-able *dossier* must have built up (because there were no flies on their intelligence) about whom I had been seeing during the last three weeks, because they talked to me with much reserve; but they gave me enough stuff for my needs, and one re-markable plum.

The *Colons*, poor devils, were even more cautious: they had every reason. Unlike Algeria, Tunisia was already inde-pendent. They had no hope of disposing of their properties, or of being granted compensation for their loss. The Tunisian Government was accusing them of having salted away in France as much money as they were able (which of course they had had the sense to do so far as they could) and were threatening them with the refusal of exit permits until such monies had been regurgitated. Meanwhile, as I saw on two different estates, their Arab employees were visiting them like Nicodemus by night, beseeching them not to depart. By this time I knew a fair number of *Colon* families, and also a network of retired military people who had settled in the Tunisian equivalents of Camberley or Cheltenham, at Sidi Bou Said and elsewhere. The mere thought of Camberley or Cheltenham as a place of retirement gives me what a naval friend of mine used to call 'the dry heaves'; but to grow old gracefully within a dozen miles of Carthage would have been heaven to that generation of Frenchmen who had served their country well; and who had created such little houses, gardens and vineyards as Horace would have approved of. I could certainly have written about such people and their problems, but I had no wish to publicize them or to put them at risk, which perhaps demonstrates that I was not cut out to be a journalist. I failed to meet Bourguiba, who was sick with 'flu in his native city of Monastir: indeed, I never did meet him until April 1961, when I was invited to join the suite of Queen Elizabeth the Queen Mother for her state visit to Tunisia in the Royal Yacht *Britannia*.

That fortnight in 1961 was a real fairy-tale. We sailed from Portsmouth one sunny afternoon, moving majestically through dozens of loyal little yachts in Spithead and the Solent, and spent a day at Gibraltar. A political cloud was rapidly forming in the North African sky: it looked as though the cloudburst between the Army in Algeria and such political leaders as Jacques Soustelle on the one hand, and Metropolitan France on the other, might coincide with the precise date of our arrival in Tunis, with disastrous effect on the programme. With fingers crossed, we continued the voyage. The British destroyer *Saintes*, acting as escort, was joined off the Algerian coast by the French destroyer *Le Bourdonnais*, arriving with great *élan* from the southward. She took station a cable or so off our port beam; her crew lined her rail; her captain, having first saluted formally, removed his cap and waved it exuberantly round his head, while his crew cheered and Queen Elizabeth acknowledged these compliments with slow, graceful waves of her scarf. The captain made a respectful signal of greeting and humble duty, adding the letters DSC after his name: indicating that he must have served alongside the Royal Navy with the Free French during the war. It was one of the few fine days we had on the voyage: the sea a true Mediterranean azure, and the bow-waves and wakes of the three ships a creamy white as we steamed along in perfect symmetry. But the wireless news from Algiers was heavy with doom. It included the tidings that Salan had taken over, and that André Petit had joined him, and been appointed Governor of Algiers. We were hardly surprised when *Bourdonnais* signalled that she had been recalled to base at Oran, peeled off with a sharp turn and a dip of her ensign, and went off to the southward with a bone in her mouth.

The state visit lasted four days. At the banquet given by President Bourguiba the first evening, I remarked to my neighbour at dinner on the inappropriateness of the name of the only woman Cabinet Minister present: she was very pretty, but she was called Madame Haddad, which is Arabic for 'blacksmith'. '*Vous avez raison,*' he replied; '*il y a très peu de forgeron en Madame Haddad!*'

I rang up the Roux, to tell them that Queen Elizabeth had agreed that I might present them to her at Peter's Corner, on her way to visit the War Graves Cemetery at Medjez-el-Bab. There was a gasp, a long pause, and Fernand said: '*Vous êtes toujours plein de surprises!*' I arrived at the rendezvous a few minutes ahead of the convoy, to find Fernand and Henriette standing uneasily (for all that they were on their own land) in the suspicious glare of a posse of Tunisian police, who knew nothing of the arrangement. They didn't think much of my own credentials, either; and it wasn't until Queen Elizabeth arrived and greeted the Roux with her usual warmth that the *flics* relaxed. As for the Roux, it was perhaps some consolation to be able to greet her on their own acres, from which they were about to be evicted for ever. They were able eventually to carve out a new home in the Dauphiné, where they already had some family footing.

To revert to 1958, I mentioned how one of the Algerian

leaders in Tunis had given me an unexpected plum. He asked me suddenly how the British war in Oman was going. I said with truth that I knew of no such war: he snorted in disbelief, and shortly afterwards showed me the door. Back in London, I went to see a very senior soldier. He admitted that there was indeed such a war; that they were surprised that it hadn't leaked before, but realized that it must soon burst on the world. He was grateful that I hadn't flown a *ballon d'essai*, but had kept my mouth discreetly shut. I had a joint meeting with him, with the appropriate Minister of State, and one or two others concerned. The general idea was that, in the circumstances and as a reward for my discretion, I might be given a few yards' start ahead of other journalists. I would be tipped the wink when to poise myself geographically. I swore my editor to equal secrecy, and went home to wait.

Soon came a tip to preposition myself at Aden, a place I always hated, and I was assured that I would find the authorities both there and in the Gulf all out to be helpful. At Aden they certainly were: a message was awaiting me at the airport to say that a car would fetch me from the hotel to Government House at 7 p.m. in time for an hour's talk with the Governor, Sir William Luce, before dinner. My arrival there coincided with a power cut, and the ADC led me by the hand through the pitch-black house to the verandah overlooking the sea. 'How nice to see you again!' said the invisible Governor. With more truth than tact, I said that I hadn't realized we'd met before. 'Of course we have!' he said. 'I was Private Secretary to Huddleston when you came to Khartoum with Wavell in 1941. And you know Dicky Beaumont, don't you?' I shook hands with another figure whose white dinner-jacket I could dimly see in the dark, and was about to say that I didn't, when the lights went on, and of course I knew them both: Beaumont (afterwards Ambassador in Cairo) had been Vice-Consul in Damascus when I was there in 1938, and I recognized Luce at once.

A happy evening followed of Middle East reminiscence, than which there used to be none better: for until the war the Middle East (a phrase which was itself a war-time misnomer) was a small world, in which everybody knew of everybody, even if they didn't actually know them. It had its full quota of eccentrics, which included some of its famous travellers. One of the most distinguished of these, Adrian van der Meulen, the Dutchman with his neat little beard, was in Aden at that moment, and he and I dined together the following night at The Galleon restaurant, run by a Palestinian friend of mine from Ramallah. But many of the legends tended to hinge on the great public servants who followed in the steps of Cromer and Wingate in Egypt, and of P. Z. Cox and Arnold Wilson in Iraq a little later. These were all before our time, but we knew some of the giants that followed them, especially those who, like Luce himself, had grown up in the Sudan Political Service: Harold MacMichael, Kinahan Cornwallis, Douglas Newbold, John Willie Robertson. The Sudan Political had always re-cruited on personality, record and interview alone – no non-sense with written papers: hence the old jibe, from which envy was not absent, that the Sudan was a country of Blacks ruled by Blues. The Levant Consular Service was another *corps d'élite*, contributing much to the pool (though housing in its time one or two talented oddities like James Elroy Flecker). From that stable came Sir Reader Bullard, the variety of whose career, as recorded in *Who's Who*, still sounds gloriously exotic, with such entries as 'Vice-Consul, Bitlis, 1910; 3rd Dragoman 1911; Acting Consul Trebizond 1912.' He married a daughter of A. L. Smith, Master of Balliol; wrote a splendid auto-biography called *The Camels Must Go*; was followed into the Foreign Service by two of his four sons, and lived to be over ninety. *Bright Levant*, by Sir Laurence Grafftey-Smith, offers another admirable picture of the old Levant Service.

I shall always think of Cornwallis and Bullard, in Baghdad and Tehran respectively, standing as foursquare as the Pillars of Hercules in that crazy summer of 1941, when all around them seemed to be tottering. Bill Luce, though young enough to be their son, came from just the same mould as these other giants. Having risen rapidly within the Sudan, he reached his peak early, but remained on that height, in the Sudan, in Aden and in the Gulf, for twenty-five years without ever showing any sign of becoming stale, and remaining always modest. In September 1977, three days before he and his wife were due to stay with us once again in Ballantrae, he dropped down dead in his garden. It is unlikely that the death of any former British official hereafter will call forth such widespread grief in the Arab world as Bill's did. He was mourned the length and breadth of the Gulf; behind the iron curtain which has so cruelly descended on the scene of his labours in what was the Aden Protectorate; and throughout the Sudan, right down to the frontiers of Equatoria, where he was Deputy Governor nearly fifty years ago.

I found plenty to do to keep me amused while awaiting my next nudge. I visited the Church of Scotland mission at Sheikh Othman, a depressing experience: I don't think they'd ever made a convert, and the missionary's local nickname was 'The Deceiver'. I spent two nights with the Levies on the Yemen frontier, being fed on tinned haggis, hearing a few bullets fly, and rather shaken by the conditions in which the local Sultan incarcerated his enemies, in a medieval fort, each with a ball and chain attached to his ankle. I flew up in an old DC3 to a desert strip, where an oil party was boring, despite the fact that the frontier at that point had not yet been delineated. No aircraft had landed there before, we were homing on a beacon, and I was in the co-pilot's seat. When we got there, a sandstorm was blowing; and the visibility was so limited that although the pilot and I could see the landing-strip, indicated by empty kerosene-tins, on the down-wind leg, we couldn't see it on the up-wind. In the end, we had perforce to land down-wind, with all the risks entailed. As we taxied to the end of the so-called runway, I told the pilot how glad I was to be flying with somebody who had long experience of these conditions. 'Don't you believe it!' he said. 'This is my first-ever flight in Arabia. This time last week I was with Scottish Airlines.'

A signal from London indicated that I should get to Bahrein as quickly as possible. Geographically this might seem rather like a Knight's Move, but Bahrein was the direct channel, both political and military, between London and what was going on in Oman. The Air Marshal gave me a seat in an RAF aircraft, and sent me off; Bill Luce wished me joy; and as we took off from Khormakhsar and headed across the empty desert for Bahrein and eventually for Oman my spirits soared: the more so because the Commander of the Sultan of Oman's forces, David Smiley, was one of my oldest friends, who had been urging me to visit him for years. Everything seemed set fine.

At Bahrein I had a rude awakening. A surly Group-Captain, no less, brushed aside a cloud of subordinates and demanded in person to see my travel documents: all I could do was to refer him to the C-in-C in Aden, and I thought he was going to blow a gasket. Worse happened when I went to call on the Political Resident, in whose diocese lay Oman and all that I had come to see. He was as cold as ice; he went so far as to say: 'We don't want your sort here!'; and he handed me a signal from the Foreign Office to say that in view of the representations made to them from the authorities on the spot they must reluctantly withdraw the facilities they had offered me. He refused to engage in any discussion, and dismissed me, forbidding me to go anywhere near Muscat or Oman.

I too, in my time, have had what seemed to me good reasons for discouraging the incursion of journalists into a sensitive area for which I was responsible; but I am sure that I have always been more civil than that man was. I did achieve one minor stroke of revenge that evening: as I left his office, I was button-holed by a tall, thin Brigadier in uniform, who introduced himself as Ted Tinker, commander of all the troops in the Gulf, and invited me to stay the night. I gratefully accepted. After I had settled in, he said that it was the Political Resident's weekly At Home, for which he kept open house, and would I like to attend? Would I, indeed? The expression on the Political Resident's face as I arrived and embarked on a frontal assault on his stock of whisky did much to reconcile me to my disappointment.

As a consolation prize for Oman, the Brigadier offered me a few days with the Trucial Oman Scouts, whose commander, Colonel Stewart Carter, would be flying back to their headquarters at Sharja from Bahrein the following day. I jumped at this. I had not been to Sharja since my visit with Wavell in 1941, when the only European inhabitant was Adams the Imperial Airways agent. There had not yet been many changes.

The Gulf was still dotted with the sails of dhows, and Sharja Creek, which has now been reclaimed and built on, was thick with them. Indeed, the Scouts had a dhow of their own, which when I arrived was actually loading in the Creek near the officers' mess with stores for an outpost two days' sail down the coast. A lucky young British officer was about to embark in her for the cruise, and I was sorely tempted to ship with him. I accepted instead an invitation from Carter to fly down to the Buraimi Oasis, the ownership of which was hotly disputed between several claimants, though Carter's troops actually held it. A visit to Buraimi at that time was a scoop for any journalist.

On the way to Buraimi, I witnessed the most absurd car collision of all time. Across a vast area of desert, as flat and as clear as a billiard-table, two Land-Rovers, driving in opposite directions, altered course so as to meet, presumably to enable their drivers to have a chat. With all Arabia to manoeuvre in, they crashed into each other. We circled them, but at least the drivers were not badly hurt: they had both jumped out and were engaging in fisticuffs as we resumed our course.

Buraimi was real *Beau Geste*. The garrison lived in a mud castle three storeys high; its only British officer was a major whose company commander I had been at Sandhurst twenty years earlier, and whose spiritual home was obviously the Foreign Legion. I should have been prouder than I was of the enthusiasm which I had evidently instilled in him. He explained to me at length his arcs of fire, his emergency plans, the intricacies of local politics, when all I really wanted was a pink gin; but he had neither pink, nor gin.

What interested me even more than the fort was the villages of the oasis, with their elaborate subterranean water-channels, exactly the same as Persian *quanats*: stone-lined, ingeniously contrived, open every few hundred yards for purposes of access. The water was bright and clear, cool and fresh, far removed from the brackish stuff with which desert-dwellers must often be content. And if one were in any doubt about the potential of irrigation, there was the experimental farm I visited next day, close under the mountains which lie to the eastward of Sharja and Dubai, run by a Canadian couple called Huntingdon.

Carrots, cabbages, onions, lettuces, leeks, almost every vegetable you could name, were growing in abundance in apparent desert.

Sorrowfully I returned to Aden on my homeward way, the object of my visit unaccomplished. To turn the knife in the wound, the aircraft stopped for an hour on the strip at Muscat, where David Smiley met me. I had known him ever since I was Wavell's ADC, and he at Sandhurst with Wavell's son. He had had one of the most exciting wars of anybody I knew, being first parachuted to fight with partisans in Albania, and subsequently to patriots in Thailand. A real glutton for punishment, after years of fighting in Muscat and Oman, he took on the job of adviser to the Royalist cause in Yemen, spending months in every year with them from the home he had established near Alicante in Spain. It was not the sort of campaign from which you could withdraw every few weeks for a spell of hot baths and good dinners in the equivalent of Shepheard's Hotel, such as the boys of the Long Range Desert Group in the war used to make the most of: it was real hard lying. When I was in Oman in 1974, and was being received with my wife by the magnificent-looking Ruler, then in his early thirties, Sultan Qaboos bin Said, I let slip that I had known David for forty years; and I could sense that my prestige went up several notches.

Meanwhile, David and I fumed together, in the shade afforded by the hot little hut that did duty in those days for an air terminal on the Muscat airstrip, at the thwarting of our plans to spend a week or two together witnessing his war. He was suffering from many frustrations, and I think even such a brief period of letting off steam had some therapeutic value; but it was a poor substitute for the fun we would have had. Our last frolic together had been with our wives and children in the totally different environment of Stockholm, sailing in the backwaters north of that city (where he was Military Attaché) in high summer.

A few days later, there appeared in one of the more sensational of British newspapers a highly-coloured report of what was going on in Oman. It was based entirely on hearsay and rumour and was full of inaccuracies, but there was enough substance and mischief in it to be embarrassing to the authoritics. I was sorely tempted to stick my tongue out: it was so obvious that a couple of authoritative articles in a newspaper of the standing of the *Sunday Times* could have done much to spike the guns of potential critics in advance. On only one other occasion, in Jakarta, did I encounter similar obstruction from a British diplomatist; but that time there was some sort of case for the line he adopted.

I must confess that it never occurred to me that the campaign in Oman would drag on for another twenty years, or cost us a continual trickle of sacrifice in lives.

Chapter Six

JOURNALIST AT LARGE: 2

The magic of the names Chimborazo and Cotopaxi never stole my heart away as they did W. J. Turner's, but for me there was always something glamorous about the Irrawaddy. It is a benevolent river, embodying the spirit of Burma as the Nile embodies that of Egypt; and it has become one of many geographical features in the world – rivers, mountains, headlands, bays, valleys – for which I have developed an almost tangible affection. Yet for a period of thirty days in March and April of 1943 the Irrawaddy seemed to assume an evil and hostile personality intent on the destruction of the little force under my command. Nothing could be more ludicrous, but I was under considerable strain at the time, and may perhaps be forgiven for being slightly cuckoo.

My column had crossed the Irrawaddy from west to east on 10 March in a spirit of exhilaration right under the noses of the Japanese, who arrived in time only to fire at our backsides and our final boatloads as we disappeared into the freedom of the far bank in the swiftly falling twilight. But a month later, on 9 April, when we were trying to cross back, the far bank had become a trap, and we were in poor nick. We had had a mere nine days' worth of rations dropped to us, which we had been able to supplement with only meagre local purchase. What with battle casualties, malnutrition, disease and other disasters, my strength was down to under 30% of what it had been on the eastward crossing.

That whole experience was utterly alien to anything I had ever expected might befall me during a life which I had innocently hoped might bring me some excitement: I had never foreseen such an ordeal, both physical and spiritual, as this, nor such agonizing decisions as would come my way, involving the life and death of individuals. Yet even at the very worst moments of the campaign I realized what a hauntingly beautiful country was that particular tract of upper Burma through which we were moving, however painfully; and we were building up, furthermore, a great indebtedness to some of the local people who, at enormous risk to their own lives, were helping us when we were down on our luck and on the run.

I had always longed to revisit the area, and if possible to seek out and thank some of the people who had hidden us and fed us and led us in those dowie days. My first application, immediately after leaving the Army, had been refused, on grounds which were not specified, but which I knew were because of unsettled conditions up country; but my second was granted, and the outcome was one of the happiest months of my life. Harry Hodson, the then editor of the *Sunday Times*, was interested, because a general election in Burma was pending, and anyway he liked the idea of a few articles on the general theme of 'Return of a Chindit'; and Billy Collins, my publisher, also liked the idea of a book on the same theme (or at any rate I persuaded him that he did). So what with the *Sunday Times* paying my own expenses, and the generous House of Collins offering an advance of royalties on the book, I was able to take my wife with me, the only one of my journalistic sorties when this was possible. More than that, I was able to share with her something of what that major experience of my life had meant to me. Half the time she must have been bored stiff, but she behaved impeccably.

It was an idyllic journey, facilitated by the sympathy and imagination of those who had it in their gift to make or mar it. The British Ambassador in Rangoon, Sir Richard Allen, although we had never met, put his whole weight behind our aspiration; pulled every string on our behalf; and 'misappropriated', as the Army would say, the British Council Land-Rover at Mandalay for our use. The Burmese Director of Military Intelligence, Colonel Bo Lwin, who, I had been warned, was the complete master of Yea or Nay concerning our journey, gave us leave to fly by the weekly civilian plane to Myitkyina in the far north, provided that I undertook to abide in every respect by the instructions of Colonel U Saw Myint, the local commander. And Shan Lone, OBE, MC, the representative in Rangoon of the Kachin State, whom I had known slightly during the war and whose name was a legend to all who had served in upper Burma during those years, promised to alert the Kachins that I was on the way: which from him was the equivalent of broaching a bottomless cask of goodwill.

We flew to Myitkyina, and spent a week touring from there to the south and west; descended the Irrawaddy in an Army launch from Bhamo to Katha, which we used as a base for another week's touring of old haunts; and finally dropped down the Irrawaddy by steamer to Mandalay, and back to Rangoon by overnight train: this last being something of an anti-climax. I managed to find a gratifying number of those who had helped us seventeen and eighteen years before, including many of Bill Smythies's old cronies, and the man who had ferried us across the Irrawaddy under fire that evening long ago. Not until now did I learn his name, Tun Sein. I had often wondered whether, and if so how, he had got away with it: he had apparently managed to persuade the Japs that he had acted entirely under duress.

These reunions with war-time comrades are what stick most securely in my memory; but so also do the astonishingly beautiful country scenes. There was our first evening in the Government Rest House at Myitkyina, 700 miles north of Rangoon, when we looked out from the verandah across the Irrawaddy, still modest in size and a mere 300 yards wide, hardly able to believe that we had so far achieved our ambition as to reach square one of our dream. There was the evening in another rest house on the west shore of the Indawgyi, or 'Great Royal Lake', eleven miles long and five miles broad, where the locals had not seen a European since just after the war ended: where we watched the rise of the moon out of the mountains and across the waters. There was the night we spent in Manhton, the 'capital' of the 'protectorate' I mentioned in an earlier chapter, made warmly welcome by my former lieges, and entertained off plates and with spoons made from the aluminium of crashed aircraft. There was the heavenly day on the river between Bhamo and Katha, which involved threading the Second Defile. Above and below the defile the river is wide and shallow; the channel between the shoals and banks is indicated in an amateurish but effective way by little sheets of tin hung on bamboo poles and shimmering in the breeze. As you approach the defile no gap in it is visible. The sluggish, meandering river pulls itself together, and becomes swift, narrow and resolute. In the great barrier of mountain, 3000 feet high, that blocks the way, a tiny chink suddenly becomes visible, into which the river rushes; and you are swept through three miles of narrow, twisting gorge, while the helmsman is hard put to it to prevent the vessel from turning broadside on. I reckoned that at one point on the right bank, judging from my own eye and the contours on the map in my hand, the cliff was not less than one thousand five hundred feet sheer. The jungle came down pretty thick to a certain level above our heads, below which was naked rock: an indication of the different levels of the river at different seasons.

The twenty-four-hour steamer trip from Tigyaing, just below Katha, down to Mandalay was another joy. The cabin staff was thrilled to have European passengers on board again, after a gap of several years; and we were not the only ones: two enterprising Englishwomen from Rangoon had defied the agonized advice of their husbands, flown to Bhamo, booked themselves on the river-steamer, and far from being raped by dacoits were having the time of their lives. The cook and steward, both veterans of the golden age of the Irrawaddy Flotilla Company, vied with each other to produce the traditional menus of that era, including the ubiquitous *crème caramel*. From the snub bow to the dripping stern-wheel, there was real romance in those river-steamers; and romance, too, in the timber rafts, hundreds of yards long, with the little thatched shelters on them for the raftsmen's families, drifting down to the Delta with no thought of time. I was to repeat some of that trip a year later, coming down from Myitkyina to Katha on a succession of goods trains, and repeating the steamer trip to Mandalay. But neither in 1967 nor in 1972 was I allowed north of Mandalay. Little is known of what goes on, except that the country is disturbed; the Government's writ doesn't run, and nor do those enchanting steamers. In 1967, my wife and I were in Burma as guests of the Government, General Ne Win having been kind enough to invite us to spend a week there on our way home from governing New Zealand. We still had one ADC with us, James Osborne of my own Regiment, the last vestige of our fading glory; and the evening we arrived in Mandalay, I made him get into a gharry with me to drive down to the waterfront, promising that he would see a sight he would never forget: river-steamers, sailing craft and rafts all jostling each other. There was nothing whatever to be seen; nor was there when, in 1972, I repeated the experiment with James's younger brother Bruce, also in the Regiment and also acting as ADC, in my capacity as its Colonel. As Pepys wrote of the Thames 300 years earlier: 'Lord, how sad it is to see no boats on the River.'

But in 1967 my wife and I did see, in our privileged status as guests of Government, the famous leg-rowers of the Inle Lake, in the southern Shan Hills. I went there again, without my wife, in 1972, and saw individuals rowing in that manner; but in 1967 the authorities laid on for us a spectacular race between four canoes whose crews must have numbered sixty or seventy each. There were some abductions near there soon after my 1972 visit, and in 1974 my eighteen-year-old son, who had arranged to stay with a friend of mine only twenty miles from Inle, was refused permission to leave the airfield at Heho. But the pendulum is for ever on the swing, and I noticed lately that Inle was once again being advertised as a tourist attraction.

I would have loved him to have had in common with his mother and me memories of that heavenly place and people. The lake is fifteen miles long and five broad, one thousand two hundred feet up, with mountains on either side running up to four or five thousand feet, and with dramatic silhouettes. The canoes peculiar to the lake are all the same shape, whatever their size: a narrow beam, and a long overhang both fore and aft. The nearest I have seen to them have been in Thailand, which is not surprising, since Shans and Thais are of the same stock. Whether or not the canoes are still paddled by leg, or propelled by modern outboard motors, they retain the same shape: both on the Inle and in the Floating Market of Bangkok. When visiting the Inle, you board your boat in a creek which forms the waterfront of a small village; you sit not very comfortably on a log, with your back to a thwart; your gondolier shoves his outboard motor into gear; and you are off at a considerable speed down an avenue of reeds fifteen feet high, which quickly reveals itself as only one of many in a whole labyrinth; you are drenched in spray. Leg-rowers, displaying the same lack of awareness of time as the raftmen of the Irrawaddy, work their craft slowly up your reed-avenue as you speed down it, with their sturdy leg-movement; and one wonders why this particular method of propulsion has never, so far as one knows, been used anywhere else in the world. The six or eight villages dotted about the Lake look more like floats than islands, and are threaded both by streets and waterways. Also about the Lake are little pavilions on stilts, used for fishing; and it was from one of the larger of these that we watched the racing. A lavish picnic had been laid on for us, and as we finished we saw these two huge canoes approaching from opposite directions, propelled at a surprising speed by mixed crews of men and women using the back of the knee, with their paddles bound to their legs. They were in high spirits and full of hilarity as they shouted chaff at each other, before being induced to line up half a mile or so away, so that the finishing line was at our pavilion.

I watched them through binoculars as they took up their positions, chivvied by an umpire in a boat with an outboard motor; and then with a great cheer they were off. The finish had all the thrill one could wish for, one crew winning by what wet-bobs would call a canvas, and the losing crew laughing so much that their canoe toppled slowly over towards us, and dropped the lot in the drink: men, women, boys and girls all together. They pushed the canoe to our platform, hauled it out, drained it, and then staged a second race, at the end of which both sides were splashing each other and laughing their heads off.

*

In 1960, my wife returned to Scotland direct from Rangoon, but I still had other fish to fry. There were the Burmese general elections to be reported for the *Sunday Times*, and although they are old hat now, they were not without interest then. The situation in the country eighteen months before had been so chaotic that U Nu, the *de jure* Prime Minister, had invited General Ne Win the Chief of Staff to step in and restore order. The current contest was between U Nu's faction and his breakaway rivals. I had a long interview with U Nu, which satisfied me that there was much to be said for the widely held view that he was a sanctimonious old humbug. Ne Win was a far more positive chap, and it came as no surprise to me or anybody else when a few years later he showed U Nu the door, and himself took over the reins of government.

I flew to Moulmein to get a slant on the elections from a provincial centre. Apart from a desire to see the place, an invitation had reached me care of the British Embassy in Rangoon. One moonlight night in 1943, I had been involved in a skirmish in a small village called Hintha, on the eastern side of the Irrawaddy. It all began with my walking into the village at about four o'clock in the morning, accompanied by two Karen soldiers to act as interpreters. At the cross-roads in the middle of the village, I saw four men sitting round a fire chatting, and greeted them civilly, before I realized that they were Japanese troops. I pulled the pin out of the grenade I was carrying, put it on to the fire, and ran like hell, with the two Karens keeping up nicely. The events of the rest of that night were fairly confused, and in the course of them I got wounded in the hip. I had never seen or heard of either of the Karens again; but here, suddenly and out of the blue, was a letter from one of them, Colour-Sergeant Po Po Tou, from 99 Dalhousie Street, Moulmein, to say that he had seen in the papers that I was back in Burma, and could I come and stay?

I had a glorious three days with him. He lived in some style, in a two-storey teak house, with a large family and his fine bearded old father, who had long been an employee of one of the British timber firms. Until two years before, he had been out in the jungle with the Karen rebels, but had accepted the amnesty. I insisted during my stay on making my number with the local Army commander, in order to keep my nose clean with the authorities in Rangoon (whom I hadn't told of my proposed visit to Moulmein, in case they might oppose it); and there was a moment of embarrassment when Po Po Tou and the brigade major came face to face: since it was to that same brigade major that Po Po Tou had surrendered. There was a moment of even greater potential embarrassment when, one evening after dark, two emissaries came in from the jungle asking to see me: they were delegates from the Karen rebels still in the field, some of whom were war-time comrades of mine, notably Saw Hunter. Hunter wanted to see me, and to ask my advice. I sadly sent him back a message to say that I felt to some degree a guest of the Burma Government; that I wouldn't see him; and I implored him to make his peace, and to use his influence to ensure that the Karens could play a major part in the new Burma, rather than disrupt it. He was killed, still in the field, a year or two later. Back in Rangoon, another approach was made to me one evening after dark, from the shadows of the Karen resistance; but this too I rejected, though feeling like Judas.

For me, the two ghost towns of Burma are Maymyo and Moulmein. Time was when victorias trotted up and down their streets with British women carrying parasols, and regimental bands played Gilbert and Sullivan from rotundas. Many families who had spent happy lives in Burma had planned to live out the rest of them, with their Karen nannies and Mugh cooks, in those spacious, comfortable teak houses: so warm in winter, so cool in summer. Now not a single European lives in either. Po Po Tou drove me up the Ridge, to see the sunset: according to him, it had been a ritual for the British in old days, and I could see why. The waters of the Salween, the 'dark river', here pour out into the Gulf of Martaban after their long journey from Tibet; and there were ten minutes at sundown when the black islands and the rosy sea made a fleeting contrast of brilliant colour.

Prompted by Po Po Tou, I paid a formal call on a poor old retired Burmese ex-Civil Servant: he had been up at Cambridge before the First War, and the great moment of his life was when he had been presented to Queen Mary at a Buckingham Palace Garden Party in the 1920s: he repeated to me, several times over, the two bromides she had addressed to him. He had dressed up for my visit in a grey frock-coat of Edwardian vintage. He was very frail, very sad, very lonely; he hated the new Burma and everything about it.

I met an even odder character two weeks later, when I drove down the road from Imphal to the Burma border at Moreh in an Indian police jeep. He must have been in his seventies; he wore a gold-rimmed monocle on a black cord, and produced a visiting-card the size of a postcard, inscribed 'His Highness Lieutenant-Colonel Dr . . .' followed by no fewer than six names. He claimed to be the son of a dethroned Raja; to have been sent down from Oxford; to have acquired medical degrees from Edinburgh, Trinity Dublin and Genoa; to have served as an MO with the Canadian forces and in Salonica in the First War; to have published a book on philosophy in Italian; and to have been sent to jail for nine months for throwing acid in his chauffeur's face. He told me that he worshipped different gods every day of the week ('Jesus on Fridays'), using incantations written by himself in English verse in a school exercise-book, of which he read me several. One evening prayer, addressed to Morpheus the God of Sleep, ended up:

> Send me tonight the best of pleasant dreams,
> And tomorrow let there be no dreadful screams.

He gave me an excruciating drink distilled by himself from ginger, and begged me, with all the earnestness of Ben Gunn in *Treasure Island*, to send him some cheese from Calcutta, which I did.

The last time I had been on that road was on the way out of Burma in 1943, when I was driven up it in an ambulance by virtue of my wounded hip. I felt a bit bogus, as a month had passed since I had been hit, and I had covered well over two hundred miles in the interim; but having been marching non-stop with a pack on my back for more than four months, I was in no mood to refuse a good offer. It was nostalgic to see again the road which I had first known when it was under construction, a few months after so many refugees had died on it in the tragic evacuation of Burma in 1942. Now, thanks to the authorities in Imphal, I was also allowed to travel down the Tiddim Road, made famous by the hard fighting of General 'Punch' Cowan's 17th Indian Division. My host was a Manipuri official (one of the few: as a matter of policy most of the key jobs had been filled by Indians); and he took me to lunch at Moirang, where the village headman, a shrewd man with considerable education, had during the war joined the Indian National Army, to fight for the Japs against the British. He made no bones about it: this had been an error: the INA officers had been a third-rate, gutless lot, and the Japs were crooks. What was more, he added, his people had had a damn sight better deal from Imphal when the British ran the place than now, when the Indians did. As the two principal Indian officials had been especially kind to me – I remain in touch with both to this day – I was mildly embarrassed.

After luncheon, I drove on south for an hour or two, marvelling at how the 17th Division, and the Chin Levies under their indefatigable leaders, had kept up the pressure on the Japs in that almost vertical country. I was rewarded also by finding a bilingual stone by the roadside in memory of some local Kuki chief, of which the English inscription ended:

In 1945 he became a Christian, and now he lies with the Lord.
Erected by his beloved children at the cost of 300 Rupees and
      One Pig.

I rank this high in my collection of public notices which I have seen with my own eyes, rating it equal top with three others:

From a lavatory in a Nigerian officers' mess: 'Please do not flourish: Toilet is licking.'

From Mandalay: 'Please be kind to animals by not eating them.'

From Bethlehem: 'Dr Suleiman Said, Specialist in Internal Women.'

That journey of early 1960, apart from a few days in Delhi, ended with a short visit to Sikkim, the small mountain state sandwiched between India and Tibet. The flood of Tibetan refugees fleeing before the Chinese invasion was down to the merest trickle, which I wanted to witness. The journey involved a one-hour flight from Calcutta to Bagdogra, and then a taxi-drive up into the hills at Kalimpong. On the way I made a small diversion to visit the site of a war-time camp at Siliguri, where Younghusband had his base for his march to Lhasa in 1904; and where forty years later I had run a couple of courses in jungle warfare, lasting two weeks each, mostly for young officers newly out from home.

The drive up to Kalimpong and on up the Tista valley to Gangtok, the capital of Sikkim, is as dramatic as you could wish. I spent a night in Kalimpong, in the Himalayan Hotel, run by old Macdonald and his three daughters. He was in his late eighties, half Highland and half Lepcha, and had been with Younghusband on his march to Lhasa. To be the guest of him and his daughters was more like staying in an old-fashioned Victorian house than in an hotel. At Gangtok, 50 miles further on and 5000 feet higher up, and looking across an astonishingly deep valley to the terraced and cultivated mountains on the other side, I stayed in the *dak* bungalow, which had few creature comforts to offer.

Sikkim was a Tibetan state, in that the royal house was Tibetan; but the majority of the population was Nepalese, and the Indians had already encroached greatly on the Maharaja's powers: since then they have virtually dethroned him. The Political Officer in 1960 was A. B. Pant, one of the ablest officers in the Indian Foreign Service: he had already been five years in the appointment, and was probably better informed about what was going on in Tibet than any other man. This was my first meeting with him, but I met him several times subsequently, when he was representing India in Jakarta and in London, and I always found him impressive. He allowed me, with one of his juniors as chaperon, to drive in a Land-Rover fifteen miles out along the Lhasa road, upon which many Tibetan refugees were working. The road climbed higher and higher, until we were up to 10,000 feet, only

4000 feet below, and almost within sight of, the Jelap La, the actual pass into Tibet. At this point the official, who was coy about answering questions, decided that we had gone far enough; and we returned to the *dak* bungalow and to supper.

I discovered two other Europeans in Gangtok; or, to be precise, they discovered me. The first was Martha Hamilton, the Edinburgh girl who was running the school there. In my youth, I had known old Miss Mary Hepburne-Scott, sister of Lord Polwarth, who was vaguely reputed to have done great things as a deaconess-missionary of the Church of Scotland in Marco Polo country, so to speak: only now did I learn that what she had in fact done was to found and run this school beyond the settled bounds of India, in a period when scant protection could be afforded her. I was ashamed to recall how my generation had giggled at the old lady's eccentricities when she came to retire in Scotland; and it was Martha Hamilton, now for some years Headmistress of St Leonards in St Andrews, who was responsible for my enlightenment.

The other was an English lawyer representing the International Society of Jurists, based in Geneva, which was deeply concerned with the apparent authenticity of reports on atrocities, amounting almost to genocide, emanating from Tibetan refugees. With the help of a young English-speaking Tibetan official, Namgyal Taring, from the staff of the Dalai Lama (who was at this time being housed by the Government of India, with some embarrassment, in the hill station of Mussoorie), the lawyer was interrogating some of the most recent arrivals. By now, these were few and far between: all the obvious passes such as the Jelap La, or the Kangra La (the 17,000-foot one used by Younghusband on his first Tibetan venture), had long been closed by the Chinese. Only the occasional group, with desperation as their spur, still came out by what Peter Fleming describes in his book *Bayonets to Lhasa* as 'unsuspected cracks in the mountains'.

I found this series of interrogations one of the most haunting experiences of my life: the refugees were so simple, so unsophisticated, so puzzled, so totally unable to understand what had happened to them, and why. The Chinese had arrived, and taken away all their children, saying that they were sending them to school; all the monasteries had been closed, and the lamas sent packing; and on themselves Chinese doctors had carried out mysterious and painful operations which, all too obviously, had in fact been sterilization. Kalimpong, Darjeeling, and many other hill stations were full of Tibetans, deprived of their children, with no trade to follow and no means of earning a living. I have no idea to what degree they have been absorbed during the twenty years that have since passed.

In Delhi I managed to get an interview with Nehru, the chilliest conversation I have ever had with anybody: I couldn't get even the most wintry smile out of him, though I coaxed him into saying a few things about the world at large which rated the front page of the paper. It was the more sad because his house was the one which used to be Lord Wavell's, as Commander-in-Chief, in which I had often stayed, and which was full of jovial or frivolous memories. The actual room in which Nehru received me had in old days been the ADCs' office, and the scene of many a convivial occasion, but Nehru didn't offer me so much as a *nimbu pani*. When I last saw that familiar house, a few years ago, it had been converted into a Nehru Museum; and my former bedroom had suffered the humiliation of being metamorphosed into a lift-shaft.

In Delhi also I bumped into Wilfred Burchett, the Australian journalist, whom I hadn't seen since he was the *Daily Express* correspondent in Burma during the war, when he had written a book about the Chindits. In 1945 he had become a fanatical Communist, had made his home in Russia, and had turned up in Korea as a war correspondent on the Chinese side. Somebody in the British High Commission rang me up and asked me out to luncheon; and when I said I couldn't, as I was lunching with Wilfred Burchett, there was a gasp, and my friend said: 'You can't lunch with *him*!' I said that *he* couldn't, but I could; and I did. I found him curiously mixed-up. His object in coming to Delhi had been to make contact with the Australian diplomatic authorities, to get Australian passports for his two children, born in Russia; my recollection is that he had had a brush-off. I remembered him as a brave, brash, efficient, self-confident man: now he seemed to me confused, lonely and wistful, like a man trying to remember what he had lost, not unlike the Légionnaire at Ksar-es-Souk. But he did tell me one startling thing, which I took to be a *coup*. At that time, Russia and China were thought to be closely in cahoots; and a few weeks before, Burchett had flown down from Moscow to Peking with Khrushchev in his personal aircraft for a visit to Chou En Lai. Not only had Chou En Lai not been on the airport to meet Khrushchev, but he had been represented by only a very Third Eleven team. According to Burchett, Khrushchev had been expecting the full VIP treatment, and was livid; and Burchett prophesied that this would prove to be the first crack in the ice. As soon as I was free from the luncheon table, trying hard not to appear too interested in this revelation, I composed a hasty despatch in my hotel room, and buzzed it off eagerly to the paper. They didn't believe it, and it never appeared. I think that if I had been a real professional journalist I would probably have died of a broken heart.

But my days as a professional journalist were numbered: for the most surprising of reasons. I had done two years with the *Sunday Times* and three months with the *Daily Telegraph*, making six or seven foreign tours in all. I was breakfasting one morning in the New Club in Edinburgh, when I was told that I was wanted on the telephone. I told the waiter to take a note of the number, and that I would ring back when I had finished my bacon-and-eggs; but when he said that it was Buckingham Palace, I decided that my bacon-and-eggs had better wait. The voice on the other end of the line, with whose owner I had been at school, said that it had a slight shock for me, which was no more than the truth: would I be interested, if invited, in following in the footsteps of my father and grand-fathers as Governor-General of New Zealand?* The voice said that this was in no sense an offer, only a tentative approach from 'an honest broker'; but if I were interested, would I go to London and have a talk with the New Zealand Prime Minister, who was staying at the Savoy? I was given to understand that he was compiling a list of possible runners.

---

* To be strictly accurate, my grandfathers had been Governor. The office was elevated to that of Governor-General in 1917.

For several excellent reasons, it was three months before the thing went firm; but by the beginning of July 1961, it had been decided that in November 1962 I should succeed Lord Cobham as Governor-General. We had been at school together; he was a cousin of my wife's; the whole thing was as cosy as could be. But how could I go on earning my living as a journalist once the fact was known that I was Governor-General-designate of New Zealand? I couldn't. So everybody was sworn to secrecy, and the plan was to announce it after Christmas. I had two brothers and a sister, my wife two brothers and four sisters; and we didn't tell any of them.

One month later, a certain peer, who had been in his day a Secretary of State, sent a postcard in all innocence to my mother-in-law, saying: 'Wouldn't it be fun if Bernard and Laura were to succeed Charles and Elizabeth Cobham in New Zealand?' She sent it on to my wife, adding: 'Wouldn't it?' I did my best to put a candle-snuffer on both, telling them that they had stumbled on the truth and swearing them to secrecy: though wondering whether it wouldn't be wiser to leave it all alone. But in planning my next and last journalistic journey, I did have in mind the opportunity it offered for a good look at countries and problems in which New Zealand would be involved. Nobody would know why I was wandering in those parts; they would speak to me freely; I might learn a lot.

My new boss, the Editor of the *Daily Telegraph*, was Colin Coote: a shrewd man. When he spotted how eager I was for my next sortie to be a sweeping one over a wide swathe of south-east Asia, he asked me point-blank why. So I admitted him also to the small circle of those who knew my future. He rose to the occasion, and agreed to play ball: indeed, he entered into the spirit of the thing, and discussed constructively what would be useful to me as well as to the paper. We decided that I should revisit Burma, Singapore and Malaysia, renewing my contacts with Ne Win, Lee Kuan Yew and the Tunku, and then have a look at Indonesia and Netherlands New Guinea, both of which would be new to me. Netherlands New Guinea was the only remaining toehold of the Dutch out of all their East Indian empire, and the Indonesians under Sukarno were already sharpening their carving-knife and saying grace before meat as they looked at it. On this and other counts, it was obvious that Indonesia was going to make trouble before the world was much older; and both as a journalist and as one about to be bound up with the fortunes of New Zealand, it was an obvious place for me to visit. So hugging my secret to my bosom, I set off on a tour which I planned to last some two and a half months.

I had previously found Singapore a good jumping-off place for that part of the world, and the office of the Commissioner-General for South-East Asia (now defunct), which was housed there in Eden Park, the ideal source for local briefings. From there I flew to Kuala Lumpur, where I sustained a shock. I had arranged to stay with Charlie Bennett, who was then the New Zealand High Commissioner there, and very close personally to the Tunku, with whom he used to play golf (despite being minus a foot) every morning at 7 a.m. He had warned me that I would be arriving before he and his wife Betty had got back from a visit to Penang; and when they walked in I was enjoying a dram of whisky provided by their solicitous Malay butler. I thought there was something constrained about their manner. After a few minutes, Charlie said: 'Haven't you got some news for us?' 'No,' I said, genuinely puzzled. His face fell; and then he said: 'We'd heard that you were going to be our new Governor-General.' I ought to have said that it was the first I'd heard of it, but instead I sprang to my feet, and said: 'Who the hell told you that?' 'Open up that champagne, Betty!' he said; and, damn it, they already had some on ice, in anticipation. It was the first leak, and it shook me to the boots, as this was still more than three months before the agreed date for the revelation to be made, and I knew that even Lord Selkirk, the Commissioner-General in Singapore, didn't know. I traced the indiscretion to a British official in New Zealand who should have known better: he had told a British visitor in strict confidence, who had leaked it to Charlie a week before on his way home through K.L. I cabled him a snorter back in London; but Charlie and Betty had told nobody, and they kept it nobly to themselves until the announcement was made.

Meanwhile, I had learned that my Chindit brother-officer

Bob Thompson had gone up to Vietnam, on the recommendation of the Tunku, as adviser on internal security to President Diem. It is difficult to telescope Bob's career into a few sentences, but briefly it was this. Having learned to fly as an undergraduate at Cambridge, he had joined both the RAFVR and the Malay Civil Service; and when the Japanese war broke out he was learning Chinese in Hong Kong. He had resumed uniform, and raised an irregular force to harass the Japs on the mainland as they attacked Hong Kong. When Hong Kong collapsed, he had made his way overland to Kunming, whence he had been flown to India. There he joined Wingate's Special Force as one of its RAF officers, and, apart from displaying outstanding gallantry in the ground fighting, had been the principal architect both of the air supply system which revolutionized the whole Burma war, and of the direct air support by bombers and fighters of troops on the ground. He had won the MC on our first expedition, and the DSO on the second. Returning to the Malay Civil Service after the war, he had risen rapidly within it; had become Secretary of Defence at a relatively tender age; and had been one of the few senior British officials to be retained by the Tunku for a few years after independence. I did not resist his invitation to fly up and see him in Saigon.

On the aircraft, I found as fellow-passengers two distinguished South-East Asian statesmen, one a Malay, the other a Singapore Chinese, with both of whom I had a slight acquaintance; and we whiled away the time by drinking gin-and-tonic and playing Liar Dice. When, later on, I boasted to Lew Kuan Yew that I had taken quite a few dollars off them, his comment was: 'I'm not surprised: they're both very stupid men!' This, my first visit to Saigon, lasted only three days: I got a cable from Colin Coote to say that I was trespassing on another correspondent's territory, and should get on to Jakarta as soon as possible.

For Indonesia and for Dutch New Guinea, I had taken the precaution of being briefed by the Foreign Office before leaving London, and thought I had their blessing; but the Oman experience repeated itself. When I arrived at Jakarta late one afternoon, and went to pay my respects at the British

Embassy, hoping for some encouragement, I got the very reverse. The Ambassador was away up-country, and I was received by his Counsellor, a nice but embarrassed man. He had orders, he said, to tell me that I was not a welcome visitor, and was not to be afforded any facilities by the Embassy; and went on to add, with even more embarrassment, that the Embassy staff had been instructed that I was not to be offered hospitality or help of any kind. I withdrew, humbly, hungrily and thirstily, and went in search of an hotel, knowing no Dutch and no Malay, and having hoped at least for some advice. I failed to find one, and spent an uncomfortable night sleeping on the floor of the airport restaurant, defying the attempts of the staff to eject me, sleeping in my clothes, and using my briefcase as a pillow.

On the second day, when I was in near despair at being able to make no contact with anybody, I happened to meet the British Naval Attaché, who was so appalled at my story that he put me up for a night in defiance of the Ambassador's embargo, and invited the Military Attaché to meet me. The two of them marched me in to the Ambassador the following morning, and I had a session with him: not a friendly one. He was worried by what he had heard from the Foreign Office: that after travelling in Indonesia I was going on to Dutch New Guinea. He had deduced, not unreasonably, that any articles I might write from there would come down in sympathy with the Dutch, thereby making his task in Indonesia more difficult than it already was. He might have said so in person, rather than treat me as a pariah. All my instincts, all my past, inclined me to support those in authority, not to make mischief. The *comble* was when I met him years later, at a diplomatic reception at Buckingham Palace, and he greeted me with the words: 'We haven't met since you were our guest in Jakarta!'

The relaxed atmosphere enabled me to travel over the hills to Bandoeng, where I met a General, through the good offices of the Military Attaché, who was frank with me about the present and future of Sukarno, the Communists, and other influences in Indonesia, which enabled me to publish some worthwhile stuff in the *Daily Telegraph*: he was a forceful man, independent and unafraid, who in post-Sukarno years served as Ambassador in London.

I had intended to spend a full month in Indonesia, but I came to the conclusion that such a long period with few contacts and no knowledge of Malay would not be rewarding; and after the leak in Kuala Lumpur I felt I should speed up my programme. I had concealed from the Indonesians my intention of visiting Dutch New Guinea; and before leaving London I had made a special trip to The Hague to arrange that my visa for New Guinea could be issued in Singapore after my Indonesian trip, so that my destination would not be betrayed by my passport. The Dutch Consul-General in Singapore was expecting me, and all went smoothly.

New Guinea from end to end is 1200 miles long, and the wholly artificial frontier from north to south along the 141st meridian of longitude splits it almost precisely in half. The Dutch capital of Hollandia was on the northern coast, close to the Papuan frontier, and not easy to reach; but the QUANTAS flight from Singapore to Darwin called at the Dutch island of Biak, at the western end of New Guinea proper. Eyebrows were raised among cabin crew and fellow-passengers when I left the aircraft there: it was apparently as rare for anybody to get off at Biak as it is at Anchorage or Gander. I was viewed with suspicion also by the chief Dutch authority on Biak, a naval captain with an Irish wife, until he got on to the authorities at Hollandia by radio, and found that I was expected. He and his wife entertained me to dinner in the throbbing heat – Biak is at sea level, and only 4° south of the Equator – and I spent two nights in the tolerable airport rest house, awaiting the twice-weekly plane to Hollandia. I tried to pass the time swimming, but what with coral and sea-urchins the bathing wasn't of the best.

The eventual flight, at breast-stroke speed in an elderly DC3, along the coast to Hollandia revealed high mountains to the south, from which foothills, covered with thick jungle, and threaded by broad, sluggish rivers, sloped northward to the sea. Hollandia was a pleasant, unpretentious little town at the head of a small harbour, with red-roofed houses stretching up the hill to the Governor's two-storeyed residence. I lodged in the Government hotel: there was no alternative, but I found it comfortable and well-run. Also living there was de Groot the Chief Justice, who took me up to call on Dr Plateel the Governor. Both were men of dedication and charm, but under no illusion that anywhere in the world was there any sympathy for the Dutch over their problem.

The only plausible part of the Indonesian claim on West Irian, as they called it, was their position as heirs to the Dutch empire; there was no ethnic link whatever with the population. The coastal Papuans bore no resemblance to Malays: they looked to me more like Melanesians. They loathed the Indonesians, some of whom had served there as junior officials in pre-war days. One evening in a lakeside beershop, I had a long talk through a Dutch interpreter with a man called Kaisiepo, a modest little former civil servant whose pretty daughter was the cashier in the hotel: he had found himself to his own surprise the acknowledged figurehead of Papuan aspirations. Kaisiepo's theme was that his people needed time to learn to rule themselves: he used the phrase: 'We are a fruit being shaken off the tree before it is ripe.' His deputy-leader was a young man called Womsiwor who as a boy of fifteen had fought with the Americans during the liberation; the beaches around Hollandia were still strewn with the wreckage of landing-craft from the seaborne assault. Womsiwor had been adopted as a mascot by his American unit, and smuggled first to Japan and then to the States in the kitbag of a Negro soldier. He had returned to New Guinea with a self-acquired American education. Kaisiepo and he, plus a couple of Dutch missionaries, appeared to be the dominant figures in the newly-established New Guinea Council, an elected body of twenty-eight members which the Dutch had just set up. There was only one of their number who was thought to be in favour of Indonesia; and he only because he had a wife and children held as hostages in Jakarta.

Another evening, in my capacity as a journalist – and the Dutch told me that I was the first British or American journalist they remembered coming there since the war ended – I went up to Government House to hear Kaisiepo and his colleagues lay before Dr Plateel their request to be granted a National Flag and a National Anthem. They unfurled the one and sang

Following the bier at the funeral of Queen Salote

Landing at Rakahanga, borne ceremoniously on a converted bed

Arrival at Raoul Island
(Peter Fleming is photographing the scene from the boat below)

the other: both were hideous, and I gave Dr Plateel full marks for not wincing more than he did. He undertook to forward both to Queen Juliana for her consideration. There was a sequel to this incident, which I have sometimes quoted as a prime example of unscrupulous propaganda. When, two or three weeks later, I returned to the outside world, I boarded a west-bound QUANTAS aircraft at Biak, and was provided with the previous day's Australian newspapers. In them was a report date-lined Jakarta, of how the brutal Dutch had tried to impose a new flag and anthem on the hapless Papuans in Hollandia, and had ordered marines to fire on the crowd when they refused to comply. I fear that my report for Colin Coote was pedestrian stuff compared with this.

I managed to spend four days in the Baliem Valley: it was meant to be two, but I got marooned by weather. The Baliem is unique, and even now few Europeans have been there. In 1938, an American called Richard Archbold was flying a float-plane across New Guinea from north to south, when he suddenly spotted, in the high mountains running up to over ten thousand feet, a long, fertile and totally unrecorded valley, with a muddy, serpentine river running through it, crowded with villages and intensive cultivation. With considerable courage, he put down his plane on the river, and found himself in the Stone Age. On the river banks were hundreds of stark-naked savages brandishing spears. Sensibly, he risked neither himself nor his passengers among them, but took off again.

The distractions of the war years prevented any follow-up, but the legend of Archbold's discovery was not forgotten; and after the Australian-American recapture of New Guinea from the Japanese, it became the subject of renewed interest. There were several factors which enabled the Baliem to remain almost as difficult to find as the Holy Grail. One was the virtual impossibility of reaching it on foot: the river pours out of it in a gorge which is simply not negotiable; but it had been reached on foot shortly before my own visit, by a party going in from the Wissel Lakes, which are themselves at the back of beyond. The journey took them twelve weeks from their starting-point. Another spell which keeps the Baliem almost as inviolate as the Sleeping Beauty is the veil of mist that creeps over it every day soon after dawn, and shrouds it until nightfall: so that the door is open sometimes only for minutes. Occasionally in 1944 and 1945, after the recapture, the Americans flew a recreational flight, taking off in time to capture the dawn moment before the mist closed in, to enable their passengers to peer down at the valley which only Archbold had visited; but a stop was put to this after such an aircraft crashed, with the death of all on board, including several Service women.

It was fifteen years after Archbold's brief landing on the water before anybody actually set foot in the valley. In 1953, Dutch Roman Catholic missionaries established themselves, quickly followed by Australians and Americans of strongly evangelical leanings, flying their own light aircraft. (It is of one of the Australian missions in Papua New Guinea that the tale is told of how they tried to ban smoking among their converts: to be confronted by banners reading: 'No Tobacco, No Hallelujahs!') In 1957, four years before my visit, the Dutch put in a District Officer. The current one lived with his wife and two children in a prefabricated tin hut, at Wamena, the twin of the one in which I was myself accommodated.

We had flown first over swamp, then over jungle, then over a succession of tree-clad ranges, mounting higher and higher like steps. The pilot called me forward, to lean over his shoulder as we approached a narrow slit in the mountains, and suddenly the valley opened out below us. My first impression was of an outsize English park tucked in a crevice among these fabulous mountains: with patches of woodland of alternating shades of light and dark green; many straight lines to indicate cultivation; and the muddy corkscrew of the river, running eastward as far as the eye could see, apparently straight into the barrier of the mountains. As we circled down, I could see the myriad villages: wooden houses, some rectangular, some round, all with brown thatched roofs. A swarm of minute black figures scattered from the strip as we approached, the burdens on their backs making them look like so many ants.

The valley is sixty miles long, and for all its narrowness is estimated to have forty thousand inhabitants, whose collective name is 'Dani'. They are well-built, and much taller than the coastal Papuans, to whom they bear no sort of resemblance;

but they disfigure themselves by a curious stance and gait which amount almost to a deformity: they stalk along sticking out their backsides, while at the same time they brace their shoulders back like Guardsmen. The women wear grass skirts, the men only phallo-crypts, a technical word which I refrain from translating. They smear their faces with black grease, stick feathers coquettishly in their ringleted hair, and thrust bones or other articles through their ears and noses. I have a coloured photograph of one with the lobe of his ear decorated by an Ever-Ready torch battery; and of another whose nose was burnt off by a jealous husband for trespassing on his matrimonial preserves.

They have no iron: their natural implement is a stone axe-head, whipped with bark-string to a piece of wood the shape of a wishbone. They have bows and arrows, pigs and dogs, ginger, bananas, sugar-cane, sweet potatoes, and salt, but curiously no fish: either in the river, its tributaries or the numerous lakes. They fight with each other at the drop of a hat. I was taken for two hours up-river in a metal boat with an outboard motor, and on either bank there were Dani with obviously excellent appetites beckoning me to come ashore.

For two days running the early morning gap in the mist withheld its benediction, and the aircraft could not get in. But at last it did; and I got back to Hollandia, back to Biak, back to Singapore, back to London, back to Ballantrae, and back to all the clishmaclaver, when my appointment to New Zealand was at last announced between Christmas and the New Year.

Chapter Seven

SOUTH PACIFIC: 1

New Zealand is so much in my bones that I could never bring myself to write of it as though it were a scene of foreign travel. There are still many families in Britain and New Zealand who feel equally at home in both, and for whose progeny it is a toss-up in which they live or die. Cadet branches of both my father's family and my mother's, Fergussons and Boyles, settled in New Zealand in the last century; and although both names have died out there, plenty – some might say too many – of their descendants through the female line still infest the country. The present head of the Boyle family, Lord Glasgow, spent part of his boyhood in New Zealand; one of his sisters was born there; and there are Fergussons and Hunter Blairs in this country with New Zealand blood. There are Studholmes, Cliffords, Elworthys, Williamses, Rhodeses, Neilsons, Russells and many others who straddle both countries impartially. A few years ago, within the decade in which I write, and all at the same moment, the British Chief of the Defence Staff, the Dean of St Paul's, the Governor of Northern Ireland, the principal dancer at the Royal Ballet, the leading conductor and two of the principal singers at Covent Garden were all New Zealand born, and the last three all had Maori blood.

One of the leading pioneer farming families in the Province of Canterbury was that of Deans. Canterbury was largely settled through the efforts from 1848 onwards of the Canterbury Association, of which the presiding genius and chairman was the Lord Lyttelton of the day: the mutual great-grandfather of Lord Cobham, my predecessor as Governor-General (who was also Lord Lyttelton), and of my wife. It was primarily and proudly an Anglican body, and what its members aspired to establish was something not far short of a theocracy, with the Cathedral, the public school on the English model which is now Christ's College, and the University, all at the heart both of the city of Christchurch and of the community as a whole. But their Anglican settlement had been anticipated by a handful of Scottish families, Deanses, Hays, Sinclairs – Presbyterians of the blackest dye like myself, and all still prominent in the Province: at this moment of writing, a Hay is Mayor of Christchurch. The original Deanses were two brothers, William and John, from Riccarton, near Kilmarnock in Ayrshire, who transported to Canterbury not only their skills as farmers, but also many local place-names, including that of their local river, the Avon. Christchurch boasts of being the most English of New Zealand cities, and people are consequently quick to assume that the Avon derives its name from Stratford: they are wrong.

William was tragically drowned before he had time to marry, in the wreck of a ship in which he was bringing some fresh stock from Australia; but John married a McIlwraith from Auchenflower in Ballantrae parish, two miles from the house in which I write, and it is from these two that the dynasty of Deans is descended. At least five other families in Ballantrae have kin in New Zealand, most of whom send pilgrims from time to time to visit the rock whence they were hewn; and the first Presbyterian minister in Dunedin, the Rev. Thomas Burns, nephew of the poet, was Minister of Ballantrae from 1826 until 1830.

So when my wife and I and our son, then aged seven, arrived in New Zealand in November 1962, we did not come entirely as strangers; and we were made to feel at home from the moment of arrival until the morning of our departure, five years later. The only discordant note that first day was when we were driving to Government House after I had been sworn in by the Chief Justice on the steps of Parliament Buildings, and a man on the pavement, pointing to my eyeglass, shouted: 'Take it out, Claude!' From then on, it was accepted as a harmless eccentricity.

The life was busy, but enormously happy; one woke up to each new day looking forward to what it would bring. When Parliament was sitting, which in those days was from the beginning of June until shortly before Christmas, one had to be in Wellington for Wednesday of each week, to preside over the Executive Council, which in fact was the Cabinet in another role: otherwise one was free to tour and to carry the Queen's greetings to every corner of the country. From before Christmas until the beginning of February was a holiday period; from the second week in February until the opening of Parliament, we would base ourselves on Auckland, in the old and gracious original Government House, which dated from the 1860s, and which my father, my mother and I had all known as children: it has now become the property of Auckland University. (Government House, Wellington, a large, comfortable building, also entirely of wood, dates only from 1912, when it was built on the site of a former lunatic asylum: a circumstance which was recalled much too often for my liking.) From Auckland, without the weekly commitment on Wednesdays hanging over our heads, we were able to embark on more extensive tours; and it was my fancy that our very first from there should follow the same route as that on which I had accompanied my parents through the Bay of Plenty to the East Coast in 1926.

Except for our first summer, when we had only been in the country for two months, and neither needed a holiday nor knew the ropes, we spent our Christmas and our January in the Bay of Islands, which Anthony Eden once described to me in a letter as the most beautiful place on earth: he had spent some months recuperating there on the island of Urupukapuka after his severe illness in 1956. It was from Urupukapuka that Zane Grey used in my boyhood to indulge in big game fishing, and to fly an enormous flag from his masthead when returning from the fishing grounds after a successful sortie. This is now normal practice, but was regarded in those days as bad taste; and there was a great belly-laugh when a young Auckland businessman, Marsden Caughey, having caught a very small *mako* shark, circled Grey's huge gin-palace of a yacht flying a pair of pyjama trousers.

Like Anthony Eden, I have been fortunate in the number of beautiful places that I have seen; but I am not tempted to challenge his pronouncement that the Bay of Islands is the most beautiful of all. When in the fullness of time I was made a life peer, and had to attach a territorial designation to my new title, I cabled the New Zealand Government to ask whether I might call myself 'of the Bay of Islands', and they gracefully agreed within twenty-four hours. Captain Cook was the first European to sight it, in 1769, and it was he who gave it that inspired name. Twelve miles across at the entrance, sixteen deep, and more than twenty wide, it includes 150 islands and islets, and a mass of creeks and inlets, most of which we managed to explore during the total of eighteen weeks that we spent there over the years. A timely legacy to my wife enabled us to buy a speedboat of shallow draught, with an ample cabin and cockpit, which could fish, tow water-skiers, penetrate shallow creeks or run up on a beach with equal facility. We called her *Te Aaka*, which is Maori for *The Ark*, and she became well-known in every nook and cranny of the Bay. There were two Maori villages in particular, up the Mangonui inlet, to which there was no access by road: we called on them every year, sure of a warm welcome, as on other friends, both Maori and European, at Te Rawhiti ('The East') and elsewhere.

Only once did *Te Aaka* let us down. It was on the eve of Waitangi Day, the anniversary of the signing of the Treaty of Waitangi between Captain Hobson, the first Governor of New Zealand, and the Maori people, on 5 February 1840. Waitangi is on the western side of the bay, and the site was bought and given to New Zealand through the generosity of Lord Bledisloe, who succeeded my father as Governor-General in 1930. Apart from a sizeable chunk of land, the gift included the restored 'Treaty House', and the open ground, or *marae*, in front of it which was the actual scene of the event. The anniversary is celebrated every year on the spot, in the presence of the Governor-General, the Prime Minister and a vast gathering of Maori and Europeans alike; the Queen has twice attended in person (as indeed she did my first year). As Captain Hobson was a naval officer, and the Royal Navy made the arrangements for the original occasion, the Royal New Zealand Navy runs the show, always impeccably, and is represented in force.

On this particular afternoon, we were fishing in *Te Aaka*,

far out near the mouth of the Bay. We had as guests Sir John and Lady Grandy: he was then Commander-in-Chief of the British Forces in the Far East; he was subsequently to be Chief of the Air Staff and Governor of Gibraltar, and is now Governor and Constable of Windsor Castle. When the time came to go home, the engine wouldn't start (water in the petrol, according to the post-mortem). We managed to get a tow from another boat which was on the way home from the same fishing-grounds, and it never occurred to me that the cruiser HMNZS *Royalist* or the two frigates lying off Waitangi in anticipation of the morrow's events would recognize *Te Aaka*. But an alert officer of the watch, Collins, who had been our shipmate in *Lachlan*, did just that. I suddenly realized that honours were being paid us as we were being towed ignominiously past, and that John Grandy and I were attired only in bathing-trunks and yachting-caps: adequate for the activities that we had been engaged in, but hardly for the attentions of *Royalist* and the two frigates. Never have I donned a shirt faster.

Another Waitangi Day Eve was a Sunday, and we attended Divine Service on board HMNZS *Lachlan*, the Navy's survey vessel. I was in white tropical uniform, and wearing white buckskin shoes. I suddenly became aware that these latter were wet, and that the whole deck was awash with swirling water. It stopped and started again, stopped and started again, to the detriment of our devotions. The mystery became clear when we realized that the official photographer – no seadog, he – had sat himself down on a convenient wheel, which was in fact a hydrant, and every time he swivelled round to take a photograph he was inadvertently flushing the deck.

I will conjure up only one more of my many memories of the Bay: the 150th anniversary of the first Christian sermon ever preached in New Zealand. On Christmas Day 1814, the Rev. Samuel Marsden, who had landed from New South Wales two days before in the company and under the protection of a local chief, Ruatara, addressed a gathering of Maori in the hollow above the bay of Oihu, close under the lee of the western headland enclosing the main Bay. He chose as his text: 'Behold, I bring you glad tidings of great joy', and spoke through an interpreter. On Christmas Day 1964, we reenacted the same scene on the same spot in the presence of a large crowd, half Maori, half European. There was still no road to it, and the people had assembled partly on foot overland, partly by sea: it is the only time in my life that I have seen four Bishops wading ashore, with their breeks rolled above their knees and carrying their robes and mitres in suitcases.

The congregation was gathered around the hollow, which made a natural sounding-board for their voices, especially for the deeper pitch of the Maori. We said the familiar prayers in our respective tongues. The Maori language being restricted in its vocabulary, these take slightly longer in Maori than in English; and the final, sonorous phrases of the Lord's Prayer, for instance, ending *Aké, Aké, Aminé* ('For ever and ever, Amen'), echoed around the hollow long after the European voices had ceased, above the calling of the gulls and the sounding of the sea. I read in Maori the story of the birth of Christ from the Gospel of Luke; and the sermon was preached, from the same text as Marsden had chosen, by his own great-great-grandson, the Vicar of Pendeen in Cornwall, who had come to New Zealand for the occasion. He was accompanied by several members of his family, including his son, another Samuel, now also in Holy Orders; and some collateral descendants of Ruatara – his direct line had died out – were present. The gathering was somehow reminiscent of the Feeding of the Five Thousand, and of earlier scenes on the shores of the Sea of Galilee. On the same day, a Maori Anglican Clergyman, Canon Samuel Rangiihu of the Tuhoe tribe, was preaching by arrangement at Pendeen. It fell to him also to preach in St Paul's Cathedral on the Sunday that Sir Winston Churchill died; and he was inspired, before he began, to offer a minute or two of *tangi*, or traditional Maori mourning chant, from the pulpit. My sister was present, and heard it: she testified that nobody thought it incongruous, or anything but deeply moving.

There were certain occasions when the Governor-General was required to disappear. One was when the Sovereign came. Since the Governor-General represents the Sovereign, there is no place for him when she herself is present: he greets her when she arrives, and takes leave of her when she departs. She came in February 1963, when I had been only two months in office: we greeted her at Waitangi, where she arrived, and bade her farewell at Christchurch two weeks later, when she left. We did entertain her and Prince Philip for luncheon and dinner one day in Wellington half-way through her visit, but spent the rest of the time in anonymous fishing. They were using the royal yacht as a base, so no question arose concerning accommodation. When the Queen Mother came in 1966, also in *Britannia*, we again made ourselves scarce; but we did meet her at Bluff, at the extreme south of the South Island, and took passage with her in the yacht on the short overnight voyage round to Dunedin. We also shared two short fishing breaks, each of thirty-six hours, in her arduous tour: one at Lake Wanaka in Otago, glorious in its autumn colours; the other at Taupo. Otherwise we kept our heads well down.

The other period when tradition demands that the Governor-General should keep out of the public eye is during the run-up to a General Election: not because he might be suspected of exerting influence, but because during such a period there are distractions enough already. New Zealand holds General Elections every three years, so there were two during my five-year tenure. For both, I was able to borrow the survey vessel *Lachlan* which I have already mentioned. *Tutanekai*, of blessed memory, had been replaced in 1930 by a new vessel *Matai*, designed to carry out as before the twin functions of tender to the Lighthouse Service and, on occasion, yacht to the Governor-General; and I had been greatly looking forward before my appointment to exploiting her to the full. But during the war she had been converted, at great expense, to more martial uses; and after the war, there had never been quite the same requirement for her. With the advent of radio to ships, there was no longer the likelihood of castaways on distant islands, or the need to maintain caches for them; and it was considered cheaper to maintain beacons and lighthouses by local contract. Anyway, *Matai* was disposed of, I think to Hong Kong, on the very day that I disembarked at Wellington in 1962; and I was deprived – and rightly – of that admittedly extravagant perquisite.

But discreet enquiries elicited the fact that there was a

lot of surveying still to be done in the Sounds, especially in the approaches to the head of Doubtful Sound, where there was a good deal of maritime activity in connection with the hydro-electric work at the head of Deep Cove. It proved fairly easy to bring the dates together, and to enable the survey to coincide with my period of enforced inactivity. We therefore boarded *Lachlan* after dinner one evening in Wellington in November 1963, for a leisurely cruise through the Sounds and to Stewart Island which lasted ten days: leisurely, because we had plenty of time, while the ship's boats were engaged in their surveying tasks, to idle away the odd day in the waters I had known as a boy. Unlike *Tutanekai* or *Matai*, *Lachlan*, although 1400 tons as opposed to *Tutanekai*'s 800, had little accommodation; and our party was restricted to my wife, myself and one ADC, my second cousin Timothy Usher in my own Regiment.

Heavy rain and limited visibility, which are endemic in the Sounds, restricted our activities; but we were able to discharge the survey duties required of us in Doubtful Sound and to meet the tunnellers, drawn from a multiplicity of nations, working under American direction at Deep Cove. They were housed in a former trans-Tasman liner, the *Wanganella*, which had once featured in a dramatic shipwreck near the mouth of Wellington Harbour in 1957, but had been successfully salvaged: she was now in use as a hostel-cum-hulk; we visited the men, a cheerful lot, on their mess-decks, and dined on board, before dropping down the Sound after dark for an anchorage suitable for the next day's surveying. The morning dawned bleak and boisterous, with roaring winds, driving rain and bad radio reception, made worse by the towering cliffs on either side of us. The survey boats went out, with their crews cocooned in oilskins; but we cancelled our intention of fishing, and settled down snugly to our books, thanking our stars that we personally were under no obligation to go surveying.

Soon after 11 a.m. (or six bells, if you insist), a mutilated radio signal was brought to me in the shape of an order from Naval Headquarters in Wellington to *Lachlan* to half-mast her flag. Every sort of horror flashed through my mind, of which the chief was: had something appalling happened to the Queen?

I told the captain not to comply until we could get more details, and his radio-operators strained every nerve to raise Wellington more clearly. Half an hour later, Timothy Usher came into my cabin with a slip of paper in his hand, saying: 'I should fasten your lap-strap if I were you, sir, before you read this.' It was a signal, still corrupt, from an undetectable origin asking whether I was prepared to make a public statement on the death of President Kennedy. I had no notion whether it was from an official source or from some other. In the event, we recalled the survey boats from their tasks, and steamed back up the Sound to Deep Cove, where *Wanganella* was berthed, where radio reception was better, and where, in any event, there were telephone lines. During that hour or so of steaming, we speculated whether the President might have been killed in an air crash, or possibly assassinated.

At Deep Cove, where the American engineers were white with shock, we were able to establish the truth, so far as it was known. The request for a statement proved to have come, not from the Government, but from an enterprising press agency, and I was able to ignore it; but I could and did issue through Wellington an official statement, and sent messages of condolence to the appropriate people. Four days later, some miles to the eastward of Stewart Island, at the approximate time of the President's funeral, we stopped *Lachlan*'s engines and observed two minutes' silence. I didn't know then that the Pipes and Drums of my own Regiment, which had played before the President and his family at the White House a few days before his death, were taking part at that moment, at the special request of Mrs Kennedy, in his funeral procession.

The following year, in April and May of 1964, we made the traditional visit to the islands of the South Pacific which are administered by New Zealand, and to some of their neighbours. My parents did it in *Tutanekai*, as my mother had done it with her parents in the 1890s in *Hinemoa*, both mere cockleshells as compared with the majestic cruiser *Royalist*, in which we embarked from the naval base of Devonport in Auckland, one April morning shortly before midday. As we left Government House, Auckland, for the base, Naulls the Senior Orderly said, the tears on his cheeks: 'May I, as a last privilege, shut the door of Your Excellency's car?' He was about to retire; he had been the Junior Orderly in my boyhood when the Senior Orderly had been Barwell, who in his turn had been Junior Orderly in my mother's girlhood. So close were the family links.

Royalist at 5600 tons was a huge ship compared with *Lachlan* or *Tutanekai*, but her cabin-space was not designed to accommodate a Vice-Regal party, comprising a Governor-General and his wife, their nine-year-old son, two ADCs, a lady-in-waiting, and a guest: Peter Fleming, with whom I had shared many adventures in the past, and with whom I particularly wanted to share this one. All ranks, descending in strict order from Captain Brian Turner, had to shift one down so far as accommodation was concerned. The midshipmen finished up in a hovel, bunk over bunk over bunk, which they nicknamed 'The Kasbah': and when I saw it I was not surprised. *Royalist* was old and without air-conditioning, within four years of being scrapped; her living conditions in the tropics were barely tolerable. As for our son Geordie, who was supposed to share a cabin with Peter Fleming, he found even the first night intolerable, before we had cleared the moderate climate of New Zealand: he was driven out by the fumes of Peter's pipe – not the first victim of that horror – and for the rest of the voyage slept on a mattress on the deck of the captain's cabin, which was occupied by my wife; I was in the commander's. Already mercenary at the tender age of nine, he charged Peter a penny a night for the exclusive use of the cabin. I once asked Peter what on earth was the tobacco he smoked; and he replied: 'The remains of the beard that I wore in the Secret Service.'

We sailed in state from the naval base in Auckland Harbour, with ships sounding their sirens and dipping their flags, and a twenty-one-gun salute being fired from a shore battery; with people waving from the North Shore, and yachts escorting us. The only thing that went wrong was when the Band-Sergeant, an old friend of us all, conducting with an excess of zeal on the quarter-deck, knocked off his cap with his baton. This received full and cruel coverage on television, and he was never allowed to forget it.

Our first port of call, two days out from Auckland, was

Raoul Island in the Kermadecs: a group well off the beaten track, which few people have been privileged to visit. My mother used to swank that she had: her sisters and she had accompanied their father Lord Glasgow on a brief visit in *Hinemoa* on their way back from the Cook Islands in 1894, when the Bell family were living there. The Kermadecs are named after the Breton captain of one of the ships of D'Entrecasteaux's French naval squadron, which called there in 1785, and they seem to me to bear a sinister character: no wonder that they show no trace of ever being inhabited – though they may have been visited – for any length of time by Polynesians. They lie, a line of dots on the same ridge, running roughly north and south, as the much more numerous islands farther north that comprise the Kingdom of Tonga. Raoul, the highest, is 1750 feet. Fifty miles east, strictly parallel the whole way, lies one of the deepest ocean trenches known, 8000 fathoms down on the floor of the Pacific. With such a ridge and such a trench running side by side for 1400 miles, it is hardly surprising that seismically this is one of the least stable areas in all the world, and that Raoul, though dormant when we were there, has a long history of eruptions. And the fault runs on, right down into New Zealand, volcanic all the way. Although it is quiescent for some six hundred miles south of the Kermadecs, it bobs up again in White Island in the Bay of Plenty, thirty miles short of the New Zealand mainland. White Island blew up without warning in 1914, killing twelve men who were engaged in mining its sulphur.

The fault continues into New Zealand, still in a straight line, through Rotorua and Tarawera (where the 1886 eruption killed 153 people) and the active volcanoes of Ngauruhoe and Ruapehu, and down into the South Island, where the earthquake near Murchison in 1929 would have killed many more than the seventeen people it did if the district had been more highly populated. My parents visited the scene of the disaster, to give encouragement to the survivors and the rescue workers, on horseback: the only feasible means of travel, since the roads and bridges had been destroyed. Government House in Wellington stands squarely on the fault, a fact clearly illustrated by a well-known air photograph. One of my ADCs, Andrew

Parker-Bowles in the Blues and Royals, whom I had engaged as a replacement at an interview in London during my mid-term leave, was shown this photograph soon after he arrived, and said ruefully: 'I don't remember any mention of *this* in the Hyde Park Hotel.' Being made of wood, as I have already said, the house used to give only a gentle shoogle (to use a Scotticism) during earth tremors, whereas a more solid building would probably have suffered damage.

The Bell family were not the first to make their home on Raoul Island, but their effort lasted longest. Tom Bell was a veteran of the Maori Wars, and his wife Frederica an English immigrant. After two ill-fated ventures in New Zealand, and a third running an hotel in Samoa, they landed on Raoul with their six young children in 1878, hoping to make a living out of raising vegetables and pork, and selling them to visiting whalers. They survived thirty-six years of recurring disasters, but were eventually defeated by the decline of the whaling trade and the dwindling of their always rare customers. On the outbreak of war in 1914, they were evacuated against their will by the New Zealand Government; and poor Bell, then aged seventy-five, embarked on a long and fruitless lawsuit against the New Zealand Government for compensation. He spent his last years as a nightwatchman for a boat-building firm, and died, still yearning for Raoul, shortly before his ninetieth birthday.

When we dropped our anchor in thirteen fathoms off Raoul at 7.30 that April morning in 1964, the only inhabitants were the crew of a weather-forecasting station, some ten strong, which had been established a few years earlier. We were put ashore in a heavy swell in a motor-whaler, superbly handled by the Maori coxswain, Petty-Officer Hiki. We made fast to a couple of buoys specially laid for us by the shore people, just off the stone jetty, and clambered three by three into a large basket lowered into the whaler by a crane: it was reminiscent of boarding the *Wainui* with my pregnant sister thirty-eight years before. Inevitably, the press representatives were given first priority, so that they could photograph and report the second load, which comprised my wife, my son and myself, as we were hoisted spinning into the air, and then deposited on the jetty with a bump. We climbed a steep path for 300 feet up the cliff, to be greeted near the top with a painted notice which read: 'If you're just about "blanked", you're just about there!' I hoped, probably vainly, that the word which I have rendered as 'blanked' was the first time that our son, who had hitherto led a sheltered life, had encountered it. Another fifteen breathless feet brought us on to the plateau. Here we were confronted with a parking-meter, which our hosts later confessed to having stolen from an Auckland street the night before they sailed, to remind them of home during their year on Raoul. Eight out of the ten were New Zealanders, one of whom I had previously met in the Antarctic and was later to meet in Vietnam; the ninth was an Australian, and the tenth a Jerseyman, who exchanged outlandish greetings in Jersiais with my naval ADC, Peter Gibaut, who was another such.

Two of them were doing their second tour on Raoul. Their hostel, as they called it, was surprisingly comfortable, and they took great pride in their vegetable garden, their mown lawn, and all the other activities on which they spent their leisure. Raoul, its 'Blue Lake' and its neighbouring islands, all un-inhabited, was a paradise for ornithologists and for people with similar interests; but over it all hung the threat of its explosive history, like the island in that enchanting novel *The Violins of St Jacques*, and the ill luck which had bedevilled so many of its earlier settlers. At Denham Bay, on the far side of the island from where we had landed, was a cemetery in which were buried, among others, Fleetwood Denham, the sixteen-year-old son of Captain Denham of HMS *Herald*, who had died from fever when his father's ship was visiting the island to survey its approaches in 1854, and a number of Tokelau Islanders, marooned there in 1860 by an unscrupulous black-birding skipper. He had been transporting them for sale to Callao, in Peru, when he discovered among them what he (probably inaccurately) described as 'plague': he put them ashore and left them to die. It is known that an American called Halstead was living on Denham Bay at the time, with two Samoan wives and an unrecorded bevy of children: presumably it was he who buried them.

In 1968, soon after I left New Zealand, Raoul blew its top

At the South Pole

Visiting New Zealand
troops in Sarawak

The author in his library
at home in Ayrshire

yet again, in a major eruption. A frigate of the Royal New Zealand Navy was hastily despatched, and in the nick of time evacuated both the current staff of the weather station and a scientific expedition which had been put ashore only a few days earlier. We, by contrast, departed from Raoul after a single happy day with as much dignity as one can contrive when being lowered by basket from a crane into a bobbing whaler which is rising and falling fifteen feet on every swell. Peter Fleming subsequently wrote an amusing account of the whole trip for an American magazine, and ended his story of this particular day as follows:

> When it was time to leave, we said goodbye to them with regret, and they gave us a pig. Though hardly what might be called a keen student of Imperial protocol, I felt, as I shared an airborne laundry-basket with the headless carcass of the pig and Laura Fergusson's lady-in-waiting, that I was breaking fresh ground in this specialized field.

Two days later, at nine in the morning, we dropped our hook off Nuku'alofa, a beautiful little town, the capital of Tonga, in full view of the red-roofed palace. In no way do I mean it patronizingly when I say that the palace was somehow reminiscent of that in the Babar books. There is a natural dignity about the sovereignty and the Royal Family of Tonga that I have nowhere seen surpassed; and I shall always remember Queen Salote with affection, as well as with immense admiration and respect. When we entered her audience chamber, she was standing erect and imposing at the far end, fully two inches taller than I am (and I am two inches over six foot): royal indeed, but welcoming and gracious; with a deep, melodious voice. Almost the first thing she said was to express her sorrow that she had been ill and unable to receive my parents when they called at Tonga in 1926, when she was already Queen: her husband and consort, Prince Tungi, had done the honours instead. She had had an emergency operation the day before they arrived. She said that she regretted it the more because she knew how beloved they had been in New Zealand, and in all the islands they had visited. I am not sure how widely it is known that 'Salote' is the Polynesian version of 'Charlotte', and that her great-great-grandfather and his first wife had taken the names of George and Charlotte after the then King and Queen of Britain.

After our audience, we changed out of full dress tropical uniform, which was beginning to wilt in the heat, into civilian clothes, and were taken for a drive before luncheon. We made the acquaintance of the ancient tortoise, known as Tu'i Malila, who was presented to the Queen's ancestors by Captain Cook. The long grass of the Queen's garden, where he was skulking, was surrounded by a low wall, which we could have stepped over as easily as Remus stepped over Romulus's, had it not been rendered sacred by a *tapu*. But the *tapu* did not make it improper for the British Consul's Tongan driver to call across the wall to a gardener to search out Tu'i Malila and bring him over to see us. We watched the gardener scuffing the grass with his feet and looking around him, until he suddenly pounced, picked up the tortoise, upside down and kicking wildly, and brought him over to the wall like a baby in arms. The poor old beast was blind and battered and blackened, having suffered every conceivable mishap during the last few years. First he had been run over by a Land-Rover, and then he had been caught in the long grass when a gardener was burning it off, and been half roasted. The horror-stricken gardener had rescued him just in time, and rushed him off to hospital, where he had literally been put to bed, until he recovered, and was returned to his grass. I had the feeling that, if he had not been blind, he would have given us a dirty look at being disturbed. He has since died.

The Queen received us for luncheon *al fresco*, in a large shelter, especially built, of upright palm stems dug into the ground, swathed with palm fronds, and decorated with drooping garlands of flowers. We were offered sherry, tomato juice and cigarettes, and after ten minutes adjourned to a similar shelter near by, where we sat on cushions, set on a mountain of blossoms, with our feet under a low table to enjoy a cold collation of such proportions that the table itself was invisible. It was piled high with 'a quarter of a mile of sucking-pig' (to quote Peter Fleming again), and with mutton, turkey, ham, lobsters, crays, cucumbers, yams, breadfruit, bananas, pears, papaya and raw marinated fish. Of this last, the Queen said: 'That is raw fish: it is very good.' The first half of her statement was in my view more accurate than the second. For drinks, all served in coconuts, there was beer, fruit juice and coconut milk, which we had been warned not to spill on one's clothes: it stains in perpetuity. We ate with our fingers, which we dabbled afterwards in basins of water brought round to us with flowers floating in them. The Queen and we and her immediate entourage sat at the top table in the shelter; some two hundred other guests sat on the ground at two tables projecting at right angles out into the hot sun.

After luncheon we adjourned to the original shelter, to watch dancing. It began with five hundred girls from the High School, ranged in five rows of a hundred each, who had been personally coached by the Queen at their last two rehearsals: their precision was faultless. They were dressed in red, white and blue: white dresses with blue tunics such as schoolgirls wear the world over, and red headbands and red cloth bracelets two inches wide on their wrists, the three colours contrasting with their brown faces, arms and bare feet. A huge grey-haired drummer sounded off for some minutes on three skin drums, each with a different note, mounted on a table: hitting them with a rhythm which was to become familiar to us during the next few weeks, swinging round and round, and every now and then hitting the bench he was sitting on, for good measure. '*He's* enjoying himself, anyway!' murmured the Queen in my ear, with her little tinkling laugh. Then the girls started up, and kept going for half an hour: swinging this way and that, turning right and left, reaching up and down: so that what you saw, in addition to their lovely movements, was a constant kaleidoscope of their four contrasting colours. They were followed by three teams of dancers from different tribes, each of about fifty men and fifty women, with the same drummer carrying on tirelessly. They were encouraged by the plaudits of the vast crowd on the fringes of the *malae* (the Tongan and Samoan variant of the Maori word *marae*) shouting what sounded to me like *Malié!* which I took to be the equivalent of *Bravo!*

In the afternoon, my wife, my son and I were driven round

part of the island by the Crown Prince Tungi, now the King, who showed us some of the sights, including the flying-foxes and the standing stones, the Tongan equivalent of Stonehenge, known as the Trilithon. One thing I had never seen before, nor indeed since, was the spectacle of domestic pigs of the long-nosed variety having a leisurely bathe in the sea. We finished our tour with tea at his house; and the day ended with the Queen, the Crown Prince and his younger brother, Prince John Tu'ipelehake, and ourselves dining with the British Consul. The Queen was much relaxed after the ceremonial of the day, and spoke freely of the many problems of her kingdom, past, present and future. She talked at length of the controversial Methodist missionary Shirley Baker, who had established such an ascendancy over the kingdom during the latter part of the nineteenth century: scaring the life out of everyone alike with threats of hell-fire, and of foreign plots to annex Tonga; fining women ten dollars who wouldn't wear a pinafore, and men a similar amount if they exposed their torsos; banning all the traditional dances, running a puritanical dictatorship based on fear, and lining his pockets the while. He had actually been Prime Minister, self-appointed, for some years, before a British man-of-war arrived and removed him. She spoke also, with non-Victorian frankness, of the problems occasioned by the stationing of American troops in Tonga during the war, and of the obvious aftermath. At the appropriate moment, towards the end of dinner, she proposed our own Queen's health with the simple words 'The Queen', without qualification. She was especially kind to our son throughout the visit; and when we set off next morning in the launch for *Royalist* from the British Consul's house, where we had been staying, she was down at the water's edge at the end of her lawn, blowing kisses to him from the end of her long brown arm.

She had a house in Auckland, to which she used to repair for a few weeks each year to escape the hottest of the Tongan weather; she made it available to Tongan students in Auckland, of whom there were many, when she was not using it. She would come and see us in Auckland from time to time; for her alone, except for other Royalty, we used the front door:

normally we used the side one. It was always a joy to see her, and I remember especially an occasion when our elderly neighbour from Ayrshire, Admiral Sir Frederick Dalrymple-Hamilton of Bargany, whose family and mine had been friends and neighbours for centuries, was staying with us, and Queen Salote came to tea. He bowed profoundly when she arrived; but, by the time she left, what was going on closely resembled a flirtation. It was one of the most successful tea-parties for which I have ever been responsible.

The Admiral, incidentally, had been serving as a young officer in the Royal Yacht at Portsmouth when my parents sailed for New Zealand in 1924, and had gone up to South-ampton to see them off. He set his mind on doing the same thing for my wife and me when we sailed from Tilbury to take up the same office thirty-eight years later. He was then aged seventy-two, and there were thirty-one years of age between us; but nothing would deter him, not even the prospect of two uncomfortable nights in the train from Scotland. He came on board and drank our health; and his was one of the last handkerchiefs that we discerned waving from the dock, as *Rangitane* cast off and began slowly moving down-river.

I once discovered from Queen Salote quite by chance that she had never seen the coloured film *The Flight of the White Heron* which described our own Queen's extended Common-wealth tour of 1953, in which the visit to Tonga and Queen Salote herself figured so prominently. I appealed to the BBC to lend me a copy to show her, and they flew one out to me within the week. A projector was rigged in the Auckland Government House, Queen Salote came up to tea, and after-wards we all settled down to see the film. The Tonga part of it ended with her bidding farewell to the Queen and Prince Philip, as they set off in their launch for *Britannia,* and the final shot showed her pulling out a hanky and mopping her eyes. When she saw this on our screen, she laughed, and said: 'Why not? It was a wonderful visit, and that was how I felt.' She asked if she could borrow the film for showing in Tonga: I said: 'Yes, of course!' and I hope the BBC duly got it back.

The sad day arrived when I was told in confidence that her expectation of life was not more than six months, and that she might suffer greatly during the intervening period. I reported this to the proper quarter. Soon I was told that another more rapid illness was mercifully supervening. During the interval she was created GCMG, so far the only woman ever to be so. The news reached her on her death-bed; the insignia, sadly, too late. We were about to go on holiday to the Bay of Islands when she died in Auckland just before Christmas 1965; and we made arrangements for her to lie in state in the drawing-room of the Auckland Government House. An officer stood guard at each of the four corners of her catafalque, and many of the considerable Tongan population of New Zealand were able to file past in homage. Thereafter, she was flown to Nuku'alofa in an aircraft of the Royal New Zealand Air Force; and my wife and I, the New Zealand Prime Minister and other New Zealand dignitaries followed a day later for the funeral. I took with me the insignia of the Order of Saint Michael and Saint George, which had arrived only that morning; and within an hour of my arrival, in the presence of the new King, I laid them on her coffin in the palace chapel.

An extraordinary hush lay on the town and island: not a child spoke, not a dog barked. Within the palace garden after nightfall, beyond the *tapu* wall, there sprang up more than a hundred tiny fires each with four or five men sitting round it. Each group represented a different community from the myriad islands of Tonga, stretching north and south for 200 miles. All night the men kept their vigil in utter silence. With dawn they were gone; and I noticed that there was no trace of any fires on the grass: they had all been kindled on trays of sand, so that the grass should not suffer.

Next morning at ten the funeral procession set off in slow time for the royal mausoleum. It was led by a Guard of Honour of the Royal Guards, followed by the Police Band, playing alternately, and quite beautifully, the Dead March from *Saul* and the Funeral March of Chopin. Then came the clergy, and then the Royal Bier, a huge affair with a black canopy ten feet high, carried on poles by more than a hundred men. The new Crown Prince and his first cousin followed, carrying on cushions Queen Salote's insignia of the newly conferred GCMG and the GBE; the King and Queen, and behind them his brother and sister and the rest of the Royal Family; then my wife and I, the Head of State of Samoa, and the Governors of Fiji and American Samoa; then leading figures from most of the Pacific countries, including the Prime Minister and Leader of the Opposition of New Zealand, and Queen Salote's kinsman from Fiji (of which he is now Governor-General), Ratu Sir George Cakobau. The vast crowds lining the route, with traditional black mourning mats around their waists, sat with bowed heads, their eyes on the ground, as the bier was borne past: only the occasional child ventured to look up.

The mausoleum is a huge, terraced block, enclosing vaults which have been used for royal burials for the last three generations. When the procession reached it, after a hot march which took the best part of an hour, the bier was laid beside the vault in which the Queen's consort, the late Prince Tungi, was buried in 1941. As the service ended the hereditary undertakers took over, surrounded by a continuous curtain of *tapa* cloth. This was raised above their heads by something like two hundred women, so as to obscure from us all what was going on behind it. They held it aloft with arms uplifted for an hour and twenty minutes without a pause, a remarkable feat of endurance, while we heard the sound of hammers, first chipping away at the concrete, then knocking it back into place. At last the women lowered the *tapa* cloth, the royal undertakers reappeared, and the funeral was over.

If I were to compile a list of the dozen most impressive people I have known in my life, I would be bound to include Queen Salote. She combined sincerity and shrewdness, simplicity and sagacity, to an extraordinary degree. She was deeply religious, but no prude; as a ruler she was both tender and strict. Under the law and constitution, she possessed and exercised powers of life and death, and of corporal punishment, for the latter of which the instrument was an old-fashioned cat-o'-nine-tails, used chiefly for such crimes as robbery with violence; but she employed them all sparingly. There was no question of the love in which her people held her, and even the young were not impatient with her firm, matriarchal, old-fashioned sway.

She was without question a great personage, sadly conscious that she represented the end of an era. Her death, at the early age of sixty-five, cast a shadow over the whole Pacific, and beyond. The affection she inspired was not limited to her own people, and she radiated it outwards as well. She had a high regard for A. C. Reid, a devoted Scotsman who served two terms as the British representative in Tonga under a succession of different titles – Agent, Commissioner, Consul, Deputy High Commissioner (though *de facto* High Commissioner) – who came back for his second term at her special request, and who enjoyed her full trust: for him, her death was like a family bereavement. To the end of her days, she remained surprised and touched by the extent to which she had won the hearts of the people of Britain at the time of the Queen's Coronation; and I shall certainly remember her until the end of mine.

Chapter Eight

SOUTH PACIFIC: 2

From Tonga we sailed for Niue, twenty-four hours' steaming to the north-east. Throughout the cruise, I used to enjoy standing on the bridge beside Captain Brian Turner – I don't suppose I was very welcome – as we approached each island, to see whether or not it would duly come up over the horizon; and so it did, every time, right under our bow: 'every time a coconut', as you might say. One was always aware of its loom before one actually saw it, a slight discoloration in the blue Pacific sky; but it was nevertheless a fresh thrill each time. These coral islands thrust themselves up out of the sea on vertical stalks, usually ringed by a reef forming a lagoon; and in the reef there are only a few gaps, sometimes no more than one, kept open by the inflow and outflow of the tide. The opening was rarely wide enough to allow *Royalist* to enter, and we would land in boats while she cruised off-shore, sometimes out of sight of land, since the water was too deep for her to anchor.

Niue is one of those islands that has no lagoon; it wears its encircling coral reef on its person like Humpty Dumpty's cravat in *Alice in Wonderland*, so that the reef constitutes the actual shore. Here and there it has been blasted, so as to afford landing places. At Niue, unlike most other islands, *Royalist* was able to anchor two cables off-shore, where a northerly set prevented her from swinging dangerously; but she could not lie there overnight, partly because a shift of wind might put her at risk, but also because of the rhinoceros-beetle, the scourge of Niue. This is a wicked insect one and a half inches long, which bores with its proboscis into the tops of young coconut palms and ultimately kills them. It sleeps by day and flies by night, so that visiting ships are forbidden to stay within its range after dark in case the beetles fly off, stow away, and become unwelcome illegal immigrants to other islands where it has not yet become established.

From seaward, Niue – oval in shape and five miles across – looks as though it had been pushed up from the bottom of the sea by two different upheavals: you can distinctly see its 'waist' running round the island at a constant height about one hundred feet up, roughly half-way to the top, which constitutes a rim to the saucer-shaped plateau. Alofi (meaning 'Love'), the principal village out of a dozen, lies on the 'waist' on the western side, above a rough jetty made of coral. The 5000 inhabitants are Polynesian, and akin to both Tongans and Samoans. Most of them seemed to be present when we landed. I was briefed to respond to the traditional challenge with the words: 'Spare me!' in Niuean, which no doubt I did beautifully, and the welcoming speaker was a police sergeant, with First War medals and the BEM. He made kindly reference to my parents, who had spent three days here; and I kept to myself the fact recorded in their respective diaries that they had been unfavourably impressed by the then resident Methodist missionary of the London Missionary Society, whom my father described as a trouble-maker. There had been a sad incident ten years before our visit, when three convicts had broken out of jail and murdered the Resident Commissioner as he lay in bed with his wife; she and their three children had been left unmolested. It was in that same bedroom that my wife and I were accommodated. The Niue people were black ashamed of this blot on their traditional hospitality, having long since lived down the name of 'Savage Island' which Cook had chosen because of his reception by their ancestors; the recent murderers were still serving life sentences in New Zealand.

Niue lies on the edge of the hurricane belt, and is vulnerable to this hazard every few years. In 1960 and 1961 there had been two hurricanes in succession, one of which destroyed the War Memorial which my father had unveiled in 1926. It fell to me to do the same service for its replacement, and I was impressed by the number and bearing of the ex-soldiers, all proudly wearing their campaign medals: in both wars, Niueans joined the Colours in numbers out of all proportion to the population. This was followed by a feast, and a drive round the island; but the villages were empty except for the very old and the very young: all the rest had flocked to Alofi for the morning's junketings.

The rest of the afternoon was free, and we celebrated our liberty with a swim in one of the most delightful bathing-pools I have ever known, near a village a couple of miles north of Alofi. There was some sort of fault in the coral, which yielded a natural pool shaped like a figure-of-eight close under the cliff. We donned our 'togs', as bathing-trunks are called in New Zealand, in the Pastor's house, and walked to the pool across the village green through a vast crowd: it was the most public swim in which I have ever indulged. Two young men guided us – we had been warned to wear shoes – across fifty yards of coral to the point of entry, and came in with us. Small blue fish called *papa'ou*, about four inches long, darted to and fro among us in the clear water, above the coral gravel that made up the bottom, and we revelled in our freedom for all of an hour. Not till we got back to the Residency did we find that my wife had lost one of her tiny pearl and diamond ear-rings.

A cocktail party in the evening was followed by a buffet dinner-party. The American Mormon Mission had been invited to send one representative, but the whole bunch turned up: four crew-cut, earnest young men, for whom at least it can be said that they made no inroads on the Resident Commissioner's stock of liquor, Mormons being more total than teetotallers: they do not even drink tea. Peter Fleming confided in them that he had long been considering embracing their faith, and across the room I could see him nodding sagely at them as they expounded it. An hour after they had taken their leave, he returned to the billet which he was sharing with Timothy Usher, and found them awaiting him with stacks of pamphlets and a copy of the Book of Mormon, plus an extra one for Timothy, and a flood of proselytizing which they continued into the small hours, until he told them that he had to be up early to attend Divine Service with me, the next day being Sunday.

Divine Service was at 7.45, after breakfast; but such was the loyalty of Peter and Timothy to my wife that they suggested that, with great reluctance, they ought to forgo the delights of worship, and return instead to the bathing-pool in search of her missing ear-ring. Touched by this devotion to duty, I gave their mission my blessing, to the envy of the other Peter, Peter Gibaut, who loved swimming, but whose turn it was to be in waiting. By fortunate chance, and despite the sea-bottom of coral gravel, Timothy spotted the ear-ring in six inches of water a mere yard in, and the two of them brought it back in triumph, though not until after another prolonged swim.

Shortly before we sailed, a grubby envelope was put into my hand. It contained what purported to be an illiterate letter from a group of Niueans, saying that they hoped I wouldn't forget that it was they who had found my wife's missing ear-ring. It didn't take me long to recognize the dastardly hand of Fleming.

We sailed at 9.30 a.m., with a tremendous send-off: our son Geordie enriched with the gift of a full-sized one-man catamaran, in which he immediately sat, although on dry land, and went through the motions of paddling, to the delight of the populace. He continued to do so for much of the next twenty-four hours, on *Royalist*'s foredeck, and eventually, three years later, brought her home to Ballantrae. We ourselves were loaded down with presents of every kind; and Peter Fleming staggered on board burdened with enough extra copies of the Book of Mormon for pretty well every one of his fellow-members of the Garrick Club. The jetty was lined on one side by 400 members of the Boys' Brigade, and on the other by a similar number of Girl Guides. Tears were shed; and the crowds were still waving as we climbed the ladder of *Royalist*, anchored once more two cables out to sea; as her anchor churned on board; and for as long as the eye could discern them. From start to finish of our visit, as in all the other islands, there were constant enquiries after the health of the Queen, and assurances of loyalty to her: although none had ever seen her, and few had any expectation of ever doing so.

It may be of interest, not least to those who are given to accusing the British of greedily mopping up unprotected territories to gratify an imperialist appetite, that Niue applied three times – in 1887, 1898 and 1899 – to be taken under

British protection before it was finally accorded in 1900. At different times in the nineteenth century, Hawaii, Tahiti and Samoa all made similar requests. In February 1843, an impulsive captain in the Royal Navy, Lord George Paulet of HMS *Carysfort*, at the instigation of the British Consul, actually declared Hawaii a British protectorate; but this was quickly disavowed, and in July his superior officer, the Rear-Admiral commanding the Pacific station, formally saluted the Hawaiian flag, negotiating instead an agreement for special privileges for British subjects. Before the end of that year, France and Britain signed an agreement that neither would annex Hawaii, nor establish a protectorate over it. But in that same year of 1843 the French did declare a protectorate over Tahiti, while the Tahitians were still hoping for British intervention. As for Hawaii, it was eventually annexed, *de facto* if not *de jure*, by America in 1899, eventually becoming the fiftieth State of the Union in 1959, the same year as Alaska.

On Samoa, where there were British, Australian and French missionaries in the 1830s and 1840s, and where an enterprising German firm from Hamburg was established in 1857, various covetous eyes were cast. In 1872 the Americans signed a treaty with the chief of Tutuila, the principal island of what is now American Samoa, which gave them exclusive rights to the establishment of a naval base on the magnificent harbour of Pago Pago (pronounced Panga Panga). The chief had previously twice offered it to Britain, probably from fear either of the Germans or of a powerful and hostile tribe on the larger island of Upolu to the west of him. Encouraged by this success at Pago Pago, and urged on by American commercial interests, who produced what purported to be a petition from the chiefs of western Samoa asking for protection, President Grant despatched in August 1873 an envoy to take soundings. He was so well received, and with such high honours, that the mild anxiety which already existed among other nations turned to something like alarm.

Already in 1871 the German Consul in Apia had alerted his Government and hinted that the Americans should be forestalled; and the New Zealand Government had suggested point-blank to the British that either a protectorate should be-established, or the islands annexed as a colony. In October 1873, at the urgent suggestion of his Prime Minister Julius Vogel, my grandfather Sir James Fergusson as Governor made a strong plea to the Imperial Government that something on these lines should be done. In his despatch he weighed the respective merits of the islands coming under New Zealand or coming directly under Britain: he would prefer the former solution but for the fact that New Zealand had embarked on a heavy and expensive domestic development programme, and would be unable for the time being to find enough money to meet the needs of such a commitment. He got a brush-off from the Gladstone Government, but made another attempt five months later with a slightly different scheme, also the brain-child of Vogel: to float a company on the lines of the East India Company, or of Rhodes's British South Africa Company of fifteen years later, which would encourage the simultaneous growth of both economic and political ascendancy. This plan fared no better. Possibly if he had tried again later that year, when Disraeli had replaced Gladstone, it might have had a warmer reception; but for some reason the matter was allowed to drop, and he resigned as Governor for personal reasons early in the following year.

The idea was not yet entirely dead. The Americans had cooled off, rejecting the favourable terms brought back by their envoy. In 1877 a party of representative chiefs visited Sir Arthur Gordon (then Governor of Fiji, and later of New Zealand) to discuss the possibility of a protectorate; and in 1883 a slightly suspect petition for annexation by New Zealand was produced by an Irish trader in Samoa. Finally, in 1900, after years of shilly-shallying, an agreement was signed between Britain, America and Germany which caused dismay in Australia, and even more in New Zealand, but which did at least herald fourteen years of stability. America was confirmed in her rights in eastern, and Germany in her claims on western, Samoa; Germany withdrew, in favour of Britain, some shadowy claims she had on Tonga (which remained independent, but with a measure of British protection) and on Niue; Britain gave up all claims on western Samoa, in return for which Germany ceded to Britain her possessions in the Solomon

Islands. How far the indigenous populations were consulted I do not pretend to know. In August 1914, Western Samoa was occupied bloodlessly by an expeditionary force from New Zealand, and after the war came under New Zealand mandate; it finally achieved full independence in 1962.

The inhabited Cook Islands number twelve (not counting Niue, which I regard as an island apart), and are scattered over a rectangle 900 miles by 600, with a population of 20,000: nearly as many again have settled or been born in New Zealand during the last thirty years. Some of the islands have close ties of kinship; others, such as Pukapuka, feel, and seem, communities all on their own. There are considerable differences in language. In some I found New Zealand Maori was fully understood; in others, including Pukapuka, the tongue sounded more like Samoan. The Maori, in their migration to New Zealand in the fourteenth century, passed through the Cook Islands, shedding some of their people on the way; the Ngatiporou of the east coast, in particular, seem to have some affinity with the people of Aitutaki. Some of the more northerly islands were discovered by the Spaniards long ago: Pukapuka in 1595, Rakahanga eleven years later. Six more were found by Cook in 1773, and Bligh visited Rarotonga in *Bounty* in 1789.

The Cook Islanders were therefore not a politically cohesive group; but collectively they became more and more worried by the advance of the French, especially when they saw what had happened in Tahiti, where Queen Pomaré's dynasty had been overwhelmed and dethroned. In 1881, the Rarotonga people were frightened out of their wits when a French man-of-war arrived, and her captain, instead of first paying a courtesy call on the Ruler, a majestic woman called Makéa, picked the brains of the traders on the foreshore before proceeding casually to her modest palace. Makéa rejected with dignity the present that he offered, and took counsel with other chiefs: her own consort was Ngamaru, the chief of the neighbouring island of Atiu. Some years later, she and Ngamaru visited New Zealand, and cautiously asked about the possibility of some measure of protection, though making it clear that she had neither the desire nor the right to abrogate any of her sovereignty before consulting her subordinate chiefs and her people. That was in

1885; and in 1888 her request was accorded to some degree: in that Captain Bourke of HMS *Hyacinth* sailed round six of the southern islands, including Rarotonga and Aitutaki, hoisting the Union Jack, and giving each chief a letter, wholly without authority, saying that his island had 'become part of the British dominions', confirming him in his position, assuring him that his rule would not be interfered with, and enjoining him to exercise it with moderation, care and justice. Within two or three years, other islands were given similar protection on equally flimsy authority by equally carefree naval officers, who must have had great fun doing it. It reminds me of my own performances in 1943 and 1944, when I was cheerfully granting five or ten years' remission of taxation to villages in Burma, whose inhabitants had been helping us in one way or another. Incidentally, when Pukapuka was taken under protection by HMS *Curaçoa*, one of the junior officers on board was my Uncle Patrick, then Lord Kelburn, who was to succeed as Lord Glasgow in 1915; he died just short of his ninetieth birthday during my first year as Governor-General.

In 1890, the New Zealand Government appointed as Resident and Government Agent one F. J. Moss, a former New Zealand MP with considerable experience of the Pacific, who did all he could to encourage the islands to draw closer together. He had no powers other than persuasion, but he induced five of the southern islands to send representatives to a pseudo-Parliament at Avarua, the capital of Rarotonga – the principal island – in 1891, over which he sensibly refused an invitation to preside: the chief native judge of Rarotonga took the chair, and by common consent Makéa was elected its head. Moss was still Resident when Lord Glasgow visited the island, arriving on 30 March 1894: 'a day', he recorded in his diary, 'that we shall all remember to the end of our lives – the day of our arrival at Rarotonga'. He and his wife, my mother and her sisters, were travelling in *Hinemoa*, with the future Captain Bollons still her Second Officer; and when we were children, long before we knew that our family was to be linked with New Zealand for two more generations, my mother used to regale us with tales of that unforgettable voyage, to Rarotonga and to two other Cook Islands, and to sing some of the songs she heard there. I still remember one of them from my childhood, extolling in a single verse the undying friendship between Makéa, Ngamaru, my grandparents and *Paratané*, or Britain. If this book had a sound-track, I would record it without a moment's hesitation.

Lord Glasgow visited only Rarotonga, Mangaia and Aitutaki, but it is evident from his diary that he fell deeply in love with both places and people.

The time arrived when we had to take leave of our kind hosts, and it was really quite affecting. Makéa gave way, and cried without any attempt at concealing it . . . They all flocked down to the landing-place to see us off, and cheered us. We got into our boats, and returned to the *Hinemoa* with real sorrow that one of the most delightful weeks of our lives had come to an end, and that we were taking leave of people at once so amiable, happy and captivating.

Nevertheless, although he was as strong an imperialist as his first cousin, my other grandfather, who was his senior by only a year, he did not share his expansionist ideas. (I remember him as an old man of eighty-two, with a long spade beard, shortly before his death, sitting in a lug chair in the dower-house of his family home of Kelburn, at the other end of Ayrshire from Kilkerran, with his ear cupped in his hand, while my grandmother, born Dora Hunter Blair of Blairquhan, read the family prayers which he was no longer capable of doing.) Unlike Sir James Fergusson, with his long political experience, he had spent all his career in the Royal Navy, which he had joined at the age of twelve, and into which his son and grandson followed him. My reading of him, from his diaries, from family tradition and from New Zealand archives, is that he was basically a bluff, simple sailor; shrewd and sensible, but distrustful of politicians, and determined not to be taken for a ride. Shortly before he became Governor, his predecessor, Lord Onslow, had been asked by the Liberal Prime Minister to create enough new members of the Upper House to give the Government a majority; and Lord Onslow had been unkind enough to say that he must bequeathe this problem to his successor, my unfortunate grandfather. It was a situation analogous to that which confronted King George V when he came to the throne in 1910. Lord Glasgow refused; the Prime Minister appealed over his head to London; and Glasgow was overruled, and obliged to comply.

A new Prime Minister, the great R. J. Seddon, was now in office; and although also a Liberal, he was paradoxically also an expansionist; his solution to the problem presented by the Cook Islands was to annex them. Glasgow was distrustful of his motives. He wrote to the Imperial Government that he thought that, if annexed, the islands would be 'consciously or unconsciously governed in the interests of the Colony, and not of their inhabitants'. He thought further that annexation might encourage ambitious politicians 'who believe that New Zealand's mission is to be the ruler of the Pacific'. If they must be annexed, he said, it would be better if they were to come either directly under Great Britain, or to be administered from Fiji. It is impossible to assess, after almost a century, whether he was right or wrong at that particular moment, or what precisely was in his mind. Perhaps he simply distrusted Seddon. Perhaps he thought that the timeless, Utopian, simple life of the islanders, which had appealed so much to him, might somehow be preserved and protected from the inexorable march of the imminent twentieth century. For the time being, at any rate, his view prevailed in Britain; but his successor, Lord Ranfurly, either thought otherwise, or was more easily persuaded, or was more amenable to the political advice tendered by his Government. Whichever was the major influence, Ranfurly came down strongly on the side of annexation by New Zealand after a visit to the Cooks in 1899; and within a year it was an accomplished fact. Certain problems have resulted; but by and large the marriage has been happy.

It is time to resume our voyage of 1964. Having had to steam up and down so much without anchoring, *Royalist* by now was thirsty for fuel. It had therefore been arranged that we should put in at Pago Pago for twenty-four hours for a combined courtesy call and refuelling stop. The island of Tutuila proved to be twenty-five miles long and five across, with a central

spine running up to one thousand seven hundred feet, and
Pago Pago in the middle of the south coast. After threading a
gap in the reef three-quarters of a mile offshore, we passed a
point, turned sharply to port, and found ourselves in the
splendid harbour, a mile long and half a mile across, berthing
at a quay at 9 a.m. in a short, sharp, heavy downpour of
tropical rain, which drenched the unhappy 'Honor Guard' of
policemen in white shirts, red hats and cummerbunds and blue
lava-lava or kilts. When the rain stopped, the Governor and his
wife came on board, a friendly, rather earnest couple: he had
the disconcerting habit of addressing his wife alternately as
'Mrs Lee' or 'Mummy'. He had a good reputation and a more
or less free hand in the spending of $24,000,000 a year.

For a quarter of an hour, we witnessed from *Royalist's*
quarter-deck a spectacular display of dancing on the quay by
boys of the High School, stripped to the waist and barefooted,
wearing a sort of blue *dhoti*: it cannot be easy in the best of
conditions to leap in the air slapping breast, tummy, thigh,
calf, and even by extraordinary contortions the soles of one's
feet, and with all the puddles it must have been still more
difficult. The chief soloist wielded two three-foot torches, with
petrol-soaked rags, giving off a ten-inch flame: he tossed them
in the air and caught them again, sometimes changing hands;
over his shoulder, between his legs, lying down, rolling over,
all to the rhythm of drums.

We moved up to an oval, thatched, ceremonial shelter
without walls in the grounds of Government House, for a long
and elaborate *kava* ceremony with the leading *Faipule* or chiefs.
I have now drunk *kava* many times, the first occasion being at
the Dunedin Exhibition in 1925, and still don't like it any
better. Somebody who has often had to partake of it once
described it to me – and I concur – as tasting like other people's
dirty tooth-water. *Kava* is a root which, in former days, was
prepared by girls chewing it and spitting the resulting pulp into
a large wooden bowl, to which water was added; it was then
stirred and kneaded, a sponge of coconut fibre was dipped into
it, and the liquid squeezed out into a half-coconut, from which
one drinks. Nowadays one is spared the chewing part, but the
rest is as before. You accept your half-coconut, pour a small

libation on the ground, saying: '*Manuia!*' and swallow it like a man. If the potion is strong, the inside of your mouth then feels like the outside of a walnut. It doesn't intoxicate the head; but I am told that if through excess of zeal or an over-dose of good manners you drink an undue amount, it plays merry hell both with your legs and your equilibrium.

I had carefully mugged up a few sentences in ceremonial Samoan with which to reply to the speeches of welcome, by listening repeatedly to a tape-recording prepared for me in Wellington; and I couldn't make out why a look of dismay appeared on the faces of the Governor and the Chief Justice as I delivered them, in contrast to the expressions of pleasure which creased those of the *Faipule*. I discovered afterwards that it was American policy never to use the language, and to discourage their officials from learning it, though I could not fathom the reason; the Chief Justice had been twenty-four years in the country, and spoke not a word of it. Until ten years earlier, the island had been under naval administration: one odd by-product of this was that the Samoans, instead of saying 'Yes', said 'Aye, Aye, sir!'

There seemed to be two reasons why the inhabitants of American Samoa had no wish to unite with those of Western. The chiefs of Tutuila, although of ancient lineage, ranked below the three great chiefly families of the west, and had no wish to play second fiddle to them. Secondly, the Americans were pouring money into the country, building hospitals, schools, new housing on a generous scale, and introducing sophisticated methods of education, with television aids and so on. There was a legislative assembly of chiefs, but the Governor had full powers of veto: so that although the ad-ministration was generous and benevolent, it was far from democratic, and in that respect exactly the sort of admini-stration that the Americans have always blamed us for having. Governor Lee was a career civil servant, and conscientious beyond question; but his deputy was a smooth young man who was said to owe his appointment to nepotism in Washington: we certainly couldn't discern any other qualification. It seemed to us also that the local population was sitting pretty, and knew it. When we sailed next morning after a delightful evening barbecue on a beach, at which we were entertained by youths with guitars and ukeleles, Peter Fleming composed some rather ungrateful verses, beginning:

> More in sorrow than in anger,
> We depart from Pago Pago . . .

There could not have been a greater contrast than that between Pago Pago and Pukapuka, our next port of call, which was as primitive as Pago Pago was sophisticated. There are three islands, of which only the main one is inhabited, by 700 people; the other two are cultivated from the main one; there was once a fourth, but a hurricane in the last century stripped it of trees and soil, and it is now no more than a shoal. We were the first ship to call for six months, and they had long since run out of everything other than what they could produce themselves: they had had no tobacco or tea or potatoes for eight or nine weeks. We gave them some to carry on with from our own stores, and signalled Wellington to report their plight.

There is 130 fathoms of water right up to the reef, so we stopped our engines and waited for the Resident Agent, a charming Aitutakian called Tapuia Tiro, to come off. This he did in a boat rowed by four oarsmen plus a stern oarsman steering, who was enveloped every few seconds by the flapping of an outsize New Zealand flag flying from a jackstaff in the sternsheets. Not even through binoculars could I spot an opening in the reef, but the stern oarsman conned her carefully through; and out she came, followed by eight outriggers with some crews of three and some of six paddlers. As we took our places in Tapuia's boat, these paddlers 'tossed their oars' in a style which recalled the Procession of Boats on the Fourth of June at Eton. There was no real gap in the reef, only a place where it was lower than elsewhere: had it been high water we could have rowed through, but as the tide was dead low the crew had to get out and haul us over the coral. Fifty yards short of the beach, an egregious figure wearing an enormous round hat of coconut fibre with red flowers in it began a chant of welcome, which was translated into English from a crib held in his hand by the young headmaster of the school. After thanking Tangaroa, the god of the sea, for bringing us safely to Pukapuka, he finished by saying: 'I will lift you up on my shoulders: I will carry you through our paths to our *marae*, where we will bid you welcome as the representative of Her Majesty the Queen, whom we all love.'

This was the cue for twelve young men to wade into the water, bearing a litter of three long poles, across which was stretched a platform and a sofa. Geordie sat in the middle, my wife on the left, I on the right. They raised us on their shoulders, as promised by the orator, and bore us ashore, up the beach, up to the village and *marae*, where the whole population awaited us, with speeches, dances, and an abundance of presents: mats, hats, model out-riggers, pestles and mortars, and heaven knows what else. One of the dances was by five-year-old boys, under a splendid little hero whose word of command would have been the envy of a Grenadier RSM. Another tiny little chap in the front rank was having continual trouble with his shorts, which was all they wore: if the dancing had lasted ten seconds longer he would certainly have lost them.

There were two Europeans on the island: one a young man seconded from the Ministry of Works in Wellington, who was supervising the erection of some new buildings – school, hospital, houses for the Agent and the Medical Officer; the other a Dutch Catholic priest. The three principal religious denominations in the Cooks, as in many other Pacific islands, are the Methodists, the Seventh Day Adventists, and the Catholics: most of the Catholic missionaries are Dutch and of high quality, though on some of the islands their flock was so minute that it seemed, to my parsimonious Presbyterian mind, a waste of manpower to allot them a whole-time priest. These two were not complaining, but they were deeply grateful for the tea and tobacco we were able to slip them. I was impressed also by the doctor, the only Pukapukan ever to have qualified in medicine, and his part-European Rarotongan wife, who were pleasant and devoted people: both had dark complexions, but the European streak in the wife had come out strongly in their three children, who were almost pure white.

All the islands had their different character, and I recall

each one individually; but it would be tedious to rehearse them all in detail, and the programme on each followed much the same pattern: the challenge; often being carried ashore on a litter or *tango-tango* (once it was an old Victorian double-bed); the speeches, the feasts, the dancing. The bigger islands had European Resident Agents, sometimes with local wives: they were mostly New Zealanders, though one was a Gaelic-speaking Highlander from Lewis, with a Ngatiporou wife from New Zealand. Some of the smaller ones were administered by Cook Islanders. With one exception, who came from Britain – and he came unstuck shortly after, though not because of, my visit – they struck me as being all of high quality: though it was difficult to recruit replacements for those due to retire, since the prospect of autonomy was well this side of the horizon, and one could not blame young men of talent for not enlisting in a service whose days were obviously numbered.

The dancing on each island differed from that of its neigh-bours, though the band that accompanied it was much the same. There would be a sharkskin drum, which afforded a deep and glorious boom, and a big tin, which had originally held either kerosene or biscuits. The other instruments were pieces of wood two feet long, hollowed out like a dugout canoe, which gave a different note according to where it was hit by the drumstick. The rhythms were fast and varied, and we marvelled at the speed of the dancers, and at how long they kept it up. The young men were stripped to the waist, wearing what the Maori call *piupiu*, or flaxen kilts, with garlands of flowers round their necks and bouncing on their chests; the girls, similarly garlanded, wore the equivalent of bikinis. Each new measure was called out by a leader, usually male – only on Niue, I think, was it a woman – dancing outside the ranks of the others; and on they danced, with sweat pouring down them, until one longed to beg them to stop for a breather. If one gave rein to the imagination, one could see why the prudish missionaries had tried to ban it: the movements were as suggestive as they were graceful, and one had to remind one's self that, to the pure, all things are pure: *honi soit qui mal y pense*, and all that. But when from time to time we run through

our projector the coloured films taken by our devoted entourage (because as honoured guests we could hardly take
them ourselves) and at the same time play our tape recordings
of the drumming, our hearts and memories go back to those
lovely scenes and beautiful young people, whether in blazing
sun or the cool light of evening: all is innocent and Arcadian.

On the tiny island of Rakahanga, the ship's company of
Royalist was challenged to a cricket match, and we accepted:
although as a former wet-bob of no distinction I declined
myself to take part. The pitch was a surprisingly smooth piece
of grass roughly parallel with the beach, with palm-trees at
either end. The Rakahangan team lost the toss, and I, as non-
playing captain, opted that our team should bat first. Our
opening batsman strolled out to the wicket resplendent in the
colours of the Eton Ramblers, asked for middle-and-leg,
surveyed the lay-out of the field in a professional manner, and
took his stance. The Rakahangan opening bowler, after a
mere two and a half paces, bowled a ball so fast that I never
saw it; nor did the batsman. Nor did he see the second ball,
which took out his middle stump as clean as a whistle. It took
some time to find the ball among the palm-trees, since the
wicket-keeper hadn't seen it either. *Royalist* was all out for
twenty-two (top score Captain Turner with eleven, run out
through an error of judgement by Peter Fleming), and
Rakahanga won by eight wickets.

Another memorable island was Palmerston, where the
population of something like eighty souls, many others having
emigrated, is all descended from an English seaman called
William Marsters, who settled there in 1862, aged forty-one,
with three wives from Penrhyn Island (one of the remoter
Cooks which we also visited), two of them sisters. They have
been much written up, having often been called on by yachts-
men cruising in the Pacific, attracted by their romantic origins
and history. I am afraid I saw no reason to dissent from the
warning given to my parents by Captain Bollons before they
called there in *Tutanekai* in 1926 that they were 'an avaricious
and grasping lot', a view that my parents both confirmed in
their respective diaries after their visit. From the moment that
they came off in their boats to greet us until we left, they were

begging all the time. I gave old Ned Marsters, their chief and the grandson of the original William, two 50 lb bags of flour, a 70 lb bag of sugar and 4 lbs of cigarette tobacco and papers: he not only failed to offer a word of thanks, but asked for more: he even asked to be given a new out-board engine. While ashore, we were taken to see the grave of the old rascal who had bred this parasitic community, and saw the inscription on his gravestone: '*Blessed are they who die in the Lord.*' They all got drunk on some sort of home-brew during the course of our short visit; and when we returned to the ship some of them clambered on board, and tried to raid the canteen. One of them was so plastered with liquor that he fell overboard, and we watched him swim with difficulty ashore, half fearing – and perhaps half hoping – that he might be taken by a shark on the way. He wasn't.

The most interesting thing about them, apart from their curious history, was their dialect. Among themselves they speak what I am told is Penrhynese, but to us they spoke Dickensian English, the English of Sam Weller and his father, substituting W for V. 'Werry, werry good to see you,' they said; 'werry, werry nice.' There was evidence of jealousy between the three clans, the descendants of the three original wives, although they were obviously 'werry, werry' in-bred, despite the introduction of some new wives from Mangaia and elsewhere. Two of them took Peter Gibaut aside, and told him that they didn't trust old Ned (who was Government Agent, Pastor and everything else, the complete Pooh-Bah) to share out fairly the stores we had given him. Peter coped with this fast ball by falling in as many as he could muster, and reading out the full list in the presence of Ned, who looked daggers at him the while. 'Evidently not a very happy community, I think,' wrote my father in his diary, a judgement which seemed to me still valid thirty-eight years later. I heard afterwards that Ned Marsters was putting it about that it was I, and not he, who had got drunk on his home-brew. I did have a mouthful of it, and I would sooner have had *kava*, any day.

Rarotonga was great fun. There were many people there who remembered my parents; there were even a few who remembered the Glasgow visit in 1894. Although there was not yet a Premier, there was an elected temporary head of government with the cumbrous style of 'Leader of Government Business', half Scots and half Mangaian, whose mother had met my mother (as recorded in my mother's diaries) on Mangaia in both 1894 and 1926. There was also the granddaughter of Makéa and Ngamaru, also called Makéa, still ranking as the principal *Ariki* or high chief – the title is still also in use, although sparingly, among the New Zealand Maori – in the Cook Islands, to whose local honours had been added the CBE: a majestic personage like her forebears.

Rarotonga is a beautiful island, which I was to visit twice again during my tenure as Governor-General: once to confer on it its new autonomy, and once to bid farewell at the end of my tour of office. It was metropolitan in atmosphere compared with the other Cook Islands, but still in those days fairly primitive, with only one modest hotel on the waterfront. It is symmetrically round, with one high peak of 1700 feet, which once again Peter Fleming thought it his bounden duty to climb on Sunday morning, rather than accompany us to Divine Service: he reported the last few hundred feet as hairraising, which they certainly looked from sea-level. After church, which was packed, we relaxed on a beach on the other side of the island, at Titikaveka, where the Commissioner had a hut; and happy we were, with a generous picnic, and plenty of scope for swimming inside the reef, with nothing to fear from sharks.

At this moment, in 1964, the question of autonomy for the Cooks loomed large. New Zealand was anxious – in my personal view prematurely anxious, though her anxiety did her credit – not to be labelled as a colonial power, and was keen to confer autonomy on all her dependent territories as soon as possible. It was decided to hold a plebiscite in the Cooks, not an unreasonable idea. The United Nations Committee of Twenty-Four, which was concerned with the abolition of colonialism, declared its intention of sending a commission to 'supervise' the voting. I objected to this phrase: I could not see what right they had to 'supervise' something which the New Zealand Government had mounted, with the full agreement of the Cook Islanders, of their own volition, but suggested to the New Zealand authorities that they might instead be allowed to send 'observers'. This alternative wording was accepted; and in fairness I think that the original expression was proposed out of sheer ignorance of the *nuances* of the English language. The Commission of three duly arrived, headed by a pleasant Sudanese, who came up to call on me at Government House. I dredged up from my fading memory such Arabic courtesies as I could recall, and we got on like a house on fire.

The plebiscite went well, and turned out as we had all expected: agreement for complete autonomy, except for Defence and Foreign Affairs. In 1965, on my way back to New Zealand from mid-term leave, I spent two or three days in New York, where I was told that the Committee of Twenty-Four was about to debate the Cook Islands plebiscite, and that I could sit in and hear it if I wished. I stipulated that if I were to attend it must be *incognito*, for I knew my place as a strictly constitutional Governor-General; and it was arranged that I should have an anonymous seat in the gallery. But in the corridor I met my friendly Sudanese chum, who smelt strongly of garlic as he embraced me. He must have sneaked: for, as I took my obscure seat, the chairman smote his table with his gavel, and said: 'I bid welcome to His Excellency the Governor-General of New Zealand!' I wondered how on earth I was going to explain this to the Prime Minister when I got back to New Zealand: fortunately he never called on me to do so. Meanwhile, I listened to my Sudanese friend paying tribute to the way in which the plebiscite had been conducted, and to the faultless record of the New Zealand administration of the Cook Islands over the last sixty-odd years. He proceeded to move that his Commission's report should be adopted. To my astonishment, there were three dissentients: if I remember rightly, they were the representatives of Iran, of Bulgaria and of Tunisia. Of the last I am sure, for he was a man I had met in Tunis; and I tackled him in the corridor afterwards, and asked him why he had voted as he had. He looked sheepish, and said that he had done so on instructions from Tunis. What the blazes did those three countries know about the Cook Islands? This is only one of several experiences I have had which make me sceptical about United Nations committees.

Mangaia was of special interest to me, since the people's memories of my parents and grandparents were unexpectedly vivid. One old lady of eighty-six described Lord Glasgow's beard, and repeatedly illustrated its length with her hand whenever she caught my eye. I was shown a black ebony walking-stick with a silver top, suitably inscribed, which my father had given in 1926 to John Ariki, a famous character who had ruled the island with a firm hand for many years, and who was still very much present in spirit. His great-niece Louisa had just been elected Ariki to follow John's son, her uncle, who had died the previous month. The spirit of Queen Victoria was also much in evidence: they flew a special flag, which had last been flown during my parents' visit: a Union Jack surrounded by a broad white border, on which was painted, near the hoist, a portrait of Queen Victoria with a Maori complexion; and the island's sole pillar-box still bore the letters VR. As usual we were showered with presents. When we got back to the ship, I counted as I took them off the number of shell necklaces hanging round my neck: there were 79 in all, and they weighed 9 lbs. There were floods of tears when we left at sundown: we let the ship drift for an hour or so, flood-lit, and then fired off half a dozen star-shells as well as our saluting-guns as a means, however inadequate, of expressing thanks. We were rewarded by cheers and singing from the people massed on the beach in the dark.

At Mauké we had difficulty in getting ashore. There was a heavy swell; *Royalist* was rolling 15°, and the surf-boat into which we had to jump from the accommodation-ladder – no easy acrobatic feat when you are wearing a cocked hat and a sword – was rising and falling eight feet each time. One of *Royalist*'s motor-whalers towed us as far as the boat-passage through the reef, which was close to the shore without any lagoon; two men swam off from the reef to take our bow-ropes, one on each side, with which they swam back, handing them over to teams of men on the reef, who hauled us in sharply on the first suitable wave. (My parents recorded in their diaries that they had to wait fifteen waves before getting a good one.) Not surprisingly, we did broach-to slightly, and Brian Turner and I both got thoroughly drenched. We then clambered on to the usual *tango-tango* or litter, and were borne triumphantly up to the village on sixteen brawny brown shoulders.

Tamuera (Samuel) Ariki the chief, a small, sprightly, wizened man of eighty-seven, treated me at first with some reserve: apparently he had been expecting my father, whom he had received all those years before, and it took some persuading by the Agent, a bilingual Irishman born on Rarotonga, before he accepted that I was not an impostor. Later, despite his years, he joined in the dancing for a minute or two, gyrating and sinking on his heels like everybody else. As we were leaving, he begged for a photograph of my parents, which I duly sent him from Wellington after our return. This time we had to wait in the boats for twenty-five minutes before a suitable wave carried us over the reef; the ship's band, which to the delight especially of the children always accompanied us ashore, got bored with waiting, dug out their instruments, and struck up *The Eton Boating Song* to while away the time.

That day we 'did' two islands: Mauké in the morning, and Mitiaro, thirty-three miles distant, in the afternoon. At Mitiaro, my parents, having had difficulty in extricating themselves from the hospitality of Mauké, had arrived so late in the evening that they had been prevailed on by their hosts to spend the night ashore. Willie Tou Ariki the chief had been a baby in arms at the time, but he knew all about it; and the older people regaled us with reminiscences of what my parents had done and said, and showed us precisely where their beds had been made up. They had planned to persuade us to follow that precedent, but we hardened our hearts, and returned on board.

Next day, my fifty-third birthday, we landed on Atiu. They went one better than Mauké, in that our *tango-tango* was carried by twenty-four men instead of sixteen. It was here that the Agent was the Hebridean MacAulay, with the Maori wife, and he told us that the people had been up all night, preparing the succession of triumphal arches along the three-mile track to the main village. The final one made the most of my unfortunate initials: it was inscribed in huge letters 'WELCOME, B.F.!' I had thought that my birthday was an intimate family secret; but when we reached the village green, the ship's band, which had landed before us, having first played the National Anthem, continued without drawing breath into *Happy Birthday To You!* in which the whole population joined, having obviously been briefed. I could not feel that this was in strict accordance with protocol. MacAulay had had the imagination to leave time in the programme for a bathe in the pools of the reef during the afternoon, and very welcome it was: memorable, too, with every shade of blue, green and white in the huge combers as they broke over the coral.

That evening, our final night aboard *Royalist*, I 'cleared lower deck', as the Navy says, and standing on a capstan thanked the whole ship's company for the twenty-five unforgettable days that the cruise had lasted. It hadn't been much fun for them, in the intolerable heat and without air-conditioning; and because we hadn't been alongside anywhere except at Pago Pago and at Papaeete in Tahiti (where we had also paid a courtesy and refuelling call, and where we already knew the French Governor Grimald, who had entertained us on our way to New Zealand two years earlier), it had been difficult to give them a run ashore, owing to the scarcity of ship's boats and the brevity of each programme. We held a succession of short parties: for the Master-at-Arms, the Band-Sergeant (still being chaffed about the loss of his cap), and the CPOs, and for the cooks and stewards who had ministered to us; then we had drinks in the ward-room; and finally entertained the Captain and Commander to dinner. And so to bed, after a long day, and with the prospect of Reveille at 5.30 a.m.

Next morning came the last Cook Island, Aitutaki: the second of the group in terms of population, and the home of the Henry family. Old Geoffrey Henry, the half-caste who had been my parents' interpreter throughout their tour all these years before, and whose son, now Sir Albert Henry, was destined to become the first Premier after autonomy, was present at the welcoming ceremony: very frail, and deeply touched at meeting our son, the fourth generation of our mingled families that he had known. The Aitutaki dancers had the reputation of being the best in the Pacific, though how one reaches that verdict is anybody's guess; but they had been adjudged so at a competition held in Tahiti the previous year, to celebrate the 150th anniversary of the Fall of the Bastille, which I would have thought irrelevant to Polynesian dancing. Their leader was a stocky little man with remarkable muscles, who indicated each change of measure by whistling with two fingers in his mouth like a Scotch shepherd, and who contrived astonishing contortions while leaping in the air.

Aitutaki has a large lagoon, five miles by five. During the war it was an American flying-boat base, and the Americans had blasted an entrance through the reef wide enough and deep enough to enable *Royalist* to enter and anchor in comfort and safety. Two RNZAF flying-boats were awaiting us now, to convey us on the next stages of our journey; and after our three-hour visit we set off to board them in *Royalist*'s barge, with Captain Turner in attendance as his last duty. We were accompanied by a launch towing a double canoe, with a platform stretched across the two of them, and on the platform Aitutakian musicians and some of their fabled dancers, playing and dancing like mad. The ADCs so far forgot their dignity and duty as to blow kisses at them all the way to the flying-boats, and I hadn't the heart to restrain them. I clambered on board the first one, took my seat where the co-pilot should have been, and thus had a privileged view of the Aitutaki people as we swooped low over the crowd, and of the ship's company of *Royalist*, no longer in their spotless whites but stripped to the waist as they enjoyed the sun: waving up at us as we zoomed over at 100 feet before shaping our course for Apia in western Samoa where we were to spend the night.

Our visit to western Samoa, which was divided into two by a two-day excursion to the Tokelau Islands, was as happy as could be, though it had in it the seeds of potential embarrassment. The history of the first twelve years of the Mandate, from 1918 onwards, was not happy. There were ancient rivalries between the three great families of Tamasese, Malietoa and Mata'afa; between them and the Administration; and between the Administration and certain agitators. These last were businessmen of various origins – mostly of mixed blood, part Samoan, part German or Scandinavian – who resented Government intervention to prevent exploitation by middle-men of the labours of the cultivators. The intrigues and in-fighting of those years are too tangled to recount here; but my father, whose executive powers in those days were still con-siderable, backed the tough line taken by the Administrator, as opposed to the more placatory policy favoured by his Government. The Administrator was a rugged Englishman, Sir George Richardson, who had joined the Royal Artillery as a boy soldier, had arrived in New Zealand at the age of twenty-three as a sergeant-instructor of gunnery, and had finished the First War in command of the New Zealand Division. He was a man after my father's heart, whom he backed to the full: acquiescing in Richardson's recommend-ation that the trouble-makers should either be put under house-arrest or deported, according to their status. I was therefore both delighted and relieved, as our evening wore on and became more relaxed, when both our hosts, the Head of State and the Prime Minister, whose respective fathers had been involved in those events, introduced the subject off their own bat, and volunteered that my father and General Richard-son had been right, and that the traders had been the villains of the piece.

The top appointments in western Samoa tend to rotate between the three great chiefs, and at the time of our visit the Head of State was Malietoa and the Prime Minister Mata'afa; Mata'afa and his wife (who had beaten me soundly in a single at tennis) had already been our guests in Wellington. We were housed in Vailima, the former home of Robert Louis Stevenson, where my Uncle Patrick had dined with him several times in 1893, the year before his death, as a midshipman in *Curaçoa*. It is a beautiful two-storey house with large, airy rooms: much the same as it was in Stevenson's time, except for an extra wing added when it became Government House. We were entertained to a State Dinner there that evening, but Malietoa let us off lightly: our flight from Aitutaki had been long, and we were due to leave for Atafi, the northernmost of the Tokelau Islands, at 7.45 in the morning. After a 'light' breakfast of no more than five courses, we were duly airborne.

The easternmost Tokelau, Swain's Island, belongs to the United States; the other three, with a total population of 2000, have come under New Zealand since 1925, and constitute something of a problem. They are far from New Zealand, only 8° south of the Equator; they have no material value, no viable economy and no wish for political independence. Still less have they any desire for the alternatives that New Zealand was then offering them: joining the Cook Islands, with whom they have nothing, not even language, in common; or joining western Samoa, who they feared would treat them as poor relations. Two of the islands are Protestant, and the third, Nukunono, Catholic: it was on Nukunono that we spent our one night ashore, billeted according to sex with the New Zealand priest and the American Mother. Far more remote and less developed than any of the other islands we had seen, the Tokelaus represented the Ultima Thule of our travels.

Back at Apia, before a day of ceremonies, a party of us struggled up the hill to pay pilgrimage to Robert Louis Stevenson's grave. We started at the first flush of dawn, hoping by so doing to dodge the heat; but the path is nearly vertical, there had been a downpour of rain during the night, and by the time we reached the top, having slithered and slipped all the way up, it had taken us thirty-five minutes, the sun was high in the heavens, and we were all in a muck sweat and whacked. On the tomb, there is a schoolboy howler in the inscription of the famous epitaph. Instead of reading: 'Home is the sailor, home from sea', an intrusive 'the' has crept in between 'from' and 'sea'. I heard that my predecessor Charles Cobham had given £50 to have it recut correctly: I don't know what happened to the £50, but the howler still cries out, for all to see who have the energy to undertake that daunting climb. I said to Mata'afa that I imagined that he'd done it often. 'Never in my life,' he replied; 'I'm waiting until we have a helicopter!'

Peter Fleming and the ADCs stopped at the foot of the hill, two hundred yards short of Vailima, to swim in the stream before breakfast; but the rest of us carried on to prepare for the day's doings. Once again it was Sunday, so there were not too many public engagements; we had had the *kava* ceremony the evening of our arrival. Church at 9.30 with His Highness, with some very fine singing; buffet luncheon for fifty with the New Zealand High Commissioner, followed by an hour's talk with him; a short siesta; an hour on 'boxes' – paper-work which had arrived from New Zealand; writing letters of thanks and letters home. In the evening there was a buffet supper for 200 people, given by Mata'afa the Prime Minister and attended by Malietoa the Head of State, ending up with a moving half-hour of family prayers.

Next morning Peter Fleming took leave of us, to fly home *via* Pago Pago and the United States: he had been the best of company throughout the month, and we were sad to see him go. When he lunched with my wife and Geordie and me one Sunday at Ballantrae seven years later, on his way north for his annual grouse-shooting on the family moor at Blackmount near Glencoe, we reminisced at length about this journey, and the many others we had in common. Three days later, just as his party had started to walk the hill, he opened his season characteristically with a right-and-left. The keeper had just retrieved his birds and resumed his place in the line, when Peter dropped down dead. So ended a life which had been packed with adventure, and of which he had never wasted a moment.

Our party, less Peter, took off for Fiji: an exhausting nine hours' flight, for with all their virtues flying-boats are noisy, and their vibration seems to set a-quiver the very marrow of your bones. I had been looking forward to a siesta when we arrived at Government House in Suva, but instead there was first a parade and then a cocktail party at the New Zealand Air Force flying-boat base at Lauthala Bay. By the time the Governor's dinner-party assembled, with both George and Edward Cacobau (pronounced Thakombau) and many other distinguished people, I was half asleep, and I regret to confess that by the time we reached the coffee stage I was having to prod myself with a surreptitious fork in order to keep awake.

We returned by land plane, as opposed to flying-boat, to Wellington: a shivery, wintry Wellington, where the weather was so bad that we were diverted to the RNZAF air station at Ohakea, two hours' long drive away, as opposed to ten minutes; we didn't reach Government House until just before dinner. Next day we attended the opening of the new Anglican Cathedral, opened the new Law Society buildings, and attended an ecumenical conference; on the next I had four interviews in the forenoon, and in the afternoon three more (including two hours with the Prime Minister) and a meeting of the Council of the Duke of Edinburgh's Award. It was a happy treadmill to be back on, but something of a treadmill all the same. Our hearts were still full of the islands and the welcome we had had there; of the sounds and sights and smells and colours; of the exciting landfalls; of the constant breaking of the long rollers on the reefs; of the dancers and the rhythm of the drums; of the garlands of flowers which some wore round their hats like Beefeaters, and others round their hair like Nero, and all round their shoulders; the smell of frangipani and the taste of coconut juice were still with us. Those five weeks had something of the quality of a dream; but far from leaving not a rack behind, they have lingered with us ever since.

Chapter Nine

SOUTH POLE AND SOUTHERN CROSS

It was difficult to find any corner of New Zealand or of her dependencies where my parents had not forestalled me with a visit, but I 'huffed' them on two. One was the Tokelaus, already described; the other was Antarctica, which no Governor-General in his senses would have essayed to visit in my father's day, when there were no facilities and nobody to see. In my time it had become disgracefully easy, and I would never have forgiven myself if I hadn't gone there. By the Antarctic Treaty of 1959, no country claims sovereignty over any part of Antarctica, but its administration is divided into seven sectors, like segments of a cheese, each converging on the South Pole itself. Two of the sectors come under Australia, making up by far the biggest holding, 110° out of the 360: they are divided by the smallest sector of all, the 5° allotted to France and known as Adélie Land. The other four come under the United States, Norway, Britain (known variously as the Falkland Islands Dependencies or the British Antarctic Territory) and New Zealand (the Ross Dependency). These last two cover respectively 60° and 50° of longitude; and the Ross Dependency was allotted to New Zealand by a British Order in Council in 1923.

The Ross Dependency derives its names from Sir James Clark Ross, who was born in 1800 in Stranraer, sixteen miles south of Ballantrae, in a house which still exists as an hotel. At the age of eighteen, he had accompanied his uncle Sir John Ross, the son of the minister of Inch, two miles east of Stranraer, on the first of several Arctic voyages; and while sailing with Parry had been the first man to reach the North Magnetic

Pole in 1831. In 1839 he was selected to command an expedition of two ships, *Terror* and *Erebus*, both under 400 tons, to investigate the phenomonon of 'territorial magnetism' in the high latitudes of the southern hemisphere. Among his officers were McMurdo, Hallett, Crozier and others whose names now feature prominently on the maps and charts of the Dependency. They spent the summer of 1840 discovering and recording much that had never been seen before, and penetrated farther south, to 78°4′, than anybody had ever previously been. After wintering in the Bay of Islands, they went back for a second season; and finally returned to Britain by way of the Falkland Islands in 1842, rich in new knowledge.

Of the British Antarctic explorers in the early years of the present century, Shackleton went south from the Falkland Islands, and Scott from New Zealand, where his name is still venerated perhaps even more than in Britain. On his first voyage Scott sailed from Lyttelton; on his last, the one from which he never returned, from Port Chalmers, where he is commemorated by a memorial on a hill above the harbour. Three veterans of that voyage were still living in and around Lyttelton or Christchurch when I went back to New Zealand as Governor-General; and Sir Raymond Priestley, who served with both Shackleton and Scott, came out to New Zealand for a final visit, aged eighty, though looking far younger, while I was there, and was flown down to 'the ice'.

The International Geophysical year of 1957–8, during which Fuchs from the British and Hillary from the New Zealand side and their companions did their heroic journeys across the Pole, led to a new burst of activity, and to the establishment of various bases in each of the sectors. By agreement with New Zealand the Americans set up their main base on Ross Island in McMurdo Sound, calling it 'McMurdo', and the New Zealanders theirs, which they christened 'Scott Base', two miles away. I don't know about now; but in 1963 when I was there McMurdo housed about eight hundred and fifty men during the summer and fifty in winter; the comparable figures for Scott Base were forty-four and twelve. At McMurdo the scientists were privileged citizens, who took no hand in the daily chores. At Scott, the Drake tradition maintained, whereby 'the gentlemen must haul with the mariners', and the scientists took their turn with everybody else as 'house mouse': helping to carve the day's supply of ice for melting down into drinking water, and to give decent burial to the day's output of excreta in its icy grave an appropriate distance away.

I took off from Christchurch for Antarctica at 10 a.m. on 6 November 1963, from the same airfield as that from which I had taken off, aged fourteen, for my first-ever flight in November 1925. Then, I was a passenger in an ancient Bristol, of which the fuselage consisted largely of canvas. In my excitement, I forgot the pilot's instructions not to move my feet from the wooden lath on which they were resting; and when I did, there was a loud *zip*, a long flapping tear, and a splendid view of the blue waters of the Pacific beneath me. This time I was in a huge United States Navy C 130, or Hercules, laden with heaven knows how many tons of stores and equipment. McMurdo and Scott were maintained logistically by a squadron of these, based on Christchurch, and by the RNZN Antarctic Support Ship bearing the historic name of *Endeavour*. A month earlier, I had sailed for an hour in *Endeavour* as she set out from Wellington on her first trip of the season, as far as the Heads, where I was taken off by the pilot cutter; I would have liked to do the whole voyage in her, if only I could have spared the time.

My host was Rear-Admiral James R. Reedy, United States Navy, the over-all commander of Operation Deep Freeze, as the Antarctic enterprise was called. He and his wife became close friends of ours, as of everybody they had dealings with in New Zealand; they stayed with us more than once at Government House, and in later years at Ballantrae. The US Navy abbreviation for Rear-Admiral is 'R.Adm'; Jean Reedy was inevitably known as 'Madam Radam', and she shared with my wife a fierce resentment that women, no matter how exalted the rank of their husbands, were not allowed down to 'the ice'. She threatened to found a protest society called SQUAW, meaning 'Society for Querying the Unavailability of the Antarctic for Women', with my wife as President and her as Vice, but it availed her nothing.

The Admiral and I travelled in comfort on the flight deck,

where there were a couple of bunks just abaft the flight crew, and a galley for cooking. The only snag was that the flight deck was grossly over-heated, at a temperature which could be reduced only at the risk of converting the rest of the passengers, travelling somewhere in the bowels of the aircraft, into a collection of icicles. At 1 p.m. we were served with a sumptuous hot meal of steak, coffee and apple-juice; and at 5 p.m. we saw the 10,000 foot bulk of Cape Adair (so called by Ross after his patron Lord Adair) shove its snout up above the cloud, fifteen miles to starboard: our first glimpse of the Antarctic continent. An hour later we touched down on the ice of McMurdo Sound, to be met by Russell Rawle, the leader of that year's New Zealand party: an excellent man with much experience of climbing in the Himalayas. He was accompanied by the whole of his team except for the cook and for those absent on other duties: two at the Pole itself, three at the joint NZ/US Cape Hallett station, and two parties of four each who were out on prolonged dog-sleigh expeditions, engaged in survey. The absence off parade of the cook was accounted for by two reasons which became apparent when we reached Scott Base, five miles and twenty minutes away across the ice, to which we were carried in a large, internally-heated Canadian caterpillar vehicle called a Nodwell; he was partly engaged in cooking an enormous dinner, and partly in standing by to run up my standard on the flagpole as I arrived. He was a versatile man, like all sailors, seconded from the Royal New Zealand Navy for his second or third tour on the ice; and his long red beard interfered with neither of these duties. He neither got it involved with the flag halliards, nor introduced strands of it into the soup. The Admiral and several of his officers from McMurdo came to dinner.

Scott Base is on Ross Island, near Hut Point, where Scott wintered in *Discovery* on his first expedition. Behind it looms Mount Erebus, rising to 13,000 feet. The Base consisted of half a dozen separate huts, each electrically heated, plus a garage and workshops, linked by a corridor of which the floor is 'permafrost' – ground which is permanently frozen – and roofed with corrugated iron. The corridor itself is not heated, so you have to dress up in full rig whenever you brave it, even to go to the ablutions or lavatory. I forgot how many layers of clothing one wore, but they were numerous, including both gloves and gauntlets. Once – I think it was at Byrd Station – I forgot all the warnings, and incautiously put my hand, which I had bared for a moment to take a photograph, on to a metal rail; and the intense cold of it tore a strip of skin off my palm as though it were Elastoplast. On top of all one wore a bright red anorak with a wolverine hood to pull over one's head. Everybody and everything, from men to helicopters, with a commitment to be out in the open, wore or was painted red, so as to be more easily spotted, whether from the air or on the ground. My first impression, as I clambered down from the aircraft on to the ice, was how cruel the New Zealand authorities had been to have made up the expedition from such dear old gentlemen: they all had white hair, white beards and moustaches, white eyebrows. It was a minute or two before I found that my own moustache had turned to ice from the warm breath of my nostrils, and that I too was looking as venerable as anybody.

The base complex is thirty feet above the frozen sea, and about a hundred yards from the shore. Since the sun never sets throughout the summer months, an artificial routine is imposed. At what ought to be bed-time, circular blocks of wood are inserted in the portholes of each hut, and the lights are turned off, for all except those whose turn it is to be on watch, and to check instruments, outside thermometers and so on during the night. I was given the privilege of quarters to myself in the little sick-bay, and slept the sleep of the just until somebody came to open up my porthole and allow the bright sun to stream in. I spent the first forenoon inspecting the base: garage, workshops, science laboratories and dog lines. Most of the Greenland huskies were out with the survey team, but about twenty were in camp. For all that they look so friendly, except when in harness they fight like hell if they can get within snapping distance of each other: so they have to be shackled on to individual chains, which in turn are shackled on to one great circular chain dug into the ice. For rations they are given a chunk of sealmeat every other evening.

Apart from surveying, the scientific activities cover a wide range: geophysics, auroral studies, meteorology, geology, biology and several other -ologies. In my ignorance, I had not even realized the significance of the word 'Pole', nor the fact that the magnetic poles are indeed just that: that the world is continually bombarded by electrons, which fall sparsely at the Equator, but in increasing numbers as the latitudes get higher. Later in the week I was to see at Byrd Station, in the American sector 800 miles away (where the local commander was incongruously a Hawaiian lieutenant in the US Navy and the senior scientist a Japanese with a black beard), what looked like a marble table which recorded the bewildering rate of bombardment, far beyond my comprehension.

From my porthole at Scott Base, I could see White Island, out on the ice of the Sound. It looked two miles away, but was in fact fifteen. Scott records how two of his men made the same error, owing to the extraordinary thinness of the atmosphere: they tried to walk round it, only to find that they never seemed to get any nearer. Similarly a range of hills which looked to me to be fifteen miles away was actually well over a hundred. I could also see the 'pressure ridge', a jagged irregular wall of ice 600 yards out from the shore. Here two converging currents meet, each carrying its load of ice: the pressure is such that both loads are thrust up into the air and take astonishing shapes. Captain Bridge, who, poor chap, had been made responsible for my safety, took me round some of it that first afternoon, following a course he had marked out with flags. There were caves and caverns, ridges and hollows of all shapes and sizes: the shapes varied from spikes to humps, from whorls to overhangs like a breaking sea; the colours from straight white to sea green to Eton blue. From time to time one had to use an ice-axe to help one's self up and down. Bridge also took us into an ice-cave, where we were introduced through a three-foot opening into a long, high underground chamber: beautiful indeed, but claustrophobic.

The next day we tried to fly to Cape Hallett, a joint New Zealand-American station; but when we got there we found a 45 mph cross-wind on the ice runway: we had to content ourselves with over-flying it, and chatting to the New Zealand leader on the ground by radio. We turned westward, to drop supplies on the New Zealand 'northern' sledge party under Bob Miller*: a real glutton for Antarctic punishment, who had accompanied Ed Hillary on his crossing and had spent more time on 'the ice' than any other New Zealander; he was now breaking completely new ground. We spotted his party of two dog-sledges and four men in a waste of ice punctuated by jagged outcrops of rock 700 feet high. I included in the drop a bottle of Whigham, Fergusson & Cunningham's whisky (the Fergusson, long dead, had been a relation), and heard from them on the radio that it had arrived intact. For this trivial act I (or perhaps the whisky) was to be rewarded with immortality: 'Fergusson Glacier' on the map marks the spot to this day.

I remember that flight with especial clarity because of the variety of the ice we flew over. It comes in every colour and every degree of consistency. Sometimes, when it is breaking up, it looks like a jigsaw puzzle on a table which somebody has jogged: you can see where all the pieces used to fit. Sometimes on a flat ice table you see icebergs of any size up to a mile or two long, ready to be liberated and to float out to sea as the summer approaches its height and the flat ice melts: they look like chips off the top of a birthday cake. Sometimes you see in the pack ice a 'lead' of open water, startlingly blue. And over vast areas the ice is discoloured and brown: it reminded me of flying over the Libyan desert towards Kufra, or of southern Iraq over Ctesiphon. We saw also the Emperor Penguin colonies on the west side of Coulman Island, like stains on the ice: we didn't fly below 1500 feet for fear of disturbing them.

I wasn't told until afterwards that owing to the unexpected headwinds we had run things rather tight in the matter of fuel, and that after a ten-hour flight we had under five minutes' worth left when we landed. I was glad that I hadn't been told.

Another morning we flew by helicopter to Cape Evans and Cape Royds, respectively ten and fifteen miles north of Scott Base. At Cape Evans, Scott's men had their hut in 1910–13. After the Second War, it was visited several times by both American and New Zealand parties, who found it full of ice.

---

* Knighted in the New Year Honours of 1979.

In 1960–1, when Captain Bridge was leader at Scott Base, a party of seven men, working over seven weeks each side of Christmas, excavated both huts. From Scott's they dug out an estimated two hundred and fifty cubic yards of ice and snow, and restored it with scrupulous care. They discovered many relics of its occupation, including tattered and much-read copies of books by Conan Doyle, Kipling and W. W. Jacobs, and magazines such as the *Strand*, the *Windsor* and the *Bystander*. Most of these have been reverently left there. We saw magazines, cooking-gear, blankets, home-made sealskin clothing, Worcester sauce, potatoes, tinned milk, dog-food and hay maize. A few of these last were taken away to see whether they would germinate and grow after half a century: they did. One striking feature was the blackening of the walls and ceiling, from the fumes of the seal-blubber, which for much of their stay was all they had for fuel.

Shackleton's hut at Cape Royds was occupied in 1908–9, and again later. For some reason it was less iced-up, and except for some tinned food-stuffs there were fewer relics. I was much moved to see the bunk which used to be occupied by my old friend Sir Jameson Adams, universally known as 'The Mate', from his habit of addressing everybody as 'Mate'. He cared not a brass farthing what he said to anybody, but he was one of those rare people so nice that everybody went around saying how nice he was; I can see him now greeting me at my wedding reception with the words: 'Wotcher, Mate!' I would have loved telling him how I had seen the bunk which had housed him as a young RNR officer with Shackleton at the age of twenty-eight; but alas he had died aged eighty-two the year before.

There had been two tragedies from that hut. Lieutenant Aeneas Mackintosh, Royal Navy, and V. G. Hayward had perished in a blizzard on the sea ice some time in May 1916, and the Rev. A. P. Spencer-Smith had died two months earlier. A rough wooden cross to their memory stood firmly anchored with wire hawsers to a cairn on a knoll just above the hut; and I was asked to unveil a new plaque attached to the cairn 'to the Glory of God and in pious memory' of the three of them. I did so with a sense of something approaching sacrilege. When you contrasted the hardships which all these pioneers had endured with the comfort in which we were travelling and living, you felt very small indeed.

That feeling was reinforced on the day we flew to the Pole itself. 'Great God, this is a dreadful place!' wrote Scott in his journal, and in the depths of his disappointment at finding himself forestalled by Amundsen; and so I thought it. It was 750 miles from McMurdo, and when we were 125 miles short of it the Pole station warned us by radio that there was a cross wind, and that visibility was down to half a mile with every threat of a 'white-out'. The Admiral decided to press on in case of a lucky break, and we managed to get down in a fairly shaky landing, yawing considerably on the ice strip with its edges marked by empty barrels, such as are familiar on improvised strips all the world over.

It was a dreadful place indeed, with not a feature so far as the eye could see, except for the flagstaff which marked the actual Pole as confirmed by the most meticulous scientific instruments, and the radio mast. We were 9000 feet above sea-level; seismological evidence showed that 8950 feet of ice were supported far below us by 50 feet of rock holding us up like Atlas. On the Admiral's advice, I took a few whiffs of oxygen before stepping out, but I was short of breath all the time I was there. The temperature was 34° below Zero Fahrenheit (37° below Zero Centigrade), in other words 66° of frost; there was also a bitter wind driving stinging ice particles before it. We trudged a few hundred yards to a ramp leading underground: it was heavy going in our protective clothing, in which we felt like Michelin men as we sank over our ankles in drift. My moustache had once again frozen solid within three seconds. By contrast, the underground quarters, which one reached through heavy double doors like those below deck in a ship, were of extreme comfort, and overheated to the best of American standards. They were entirely insulated from the ice out of which they were hollowed, and included such amenities as a cinema and a generously-equipped hospital, complete with X-Ray unit. The leader was a delightful young American naval doctor called Maclean; there were the two New Zealanders, one of whom I had met before; and there was the Russian representative, who, I was told, was unaccountably shy, like the Beaver in *The Hunting of the Snark*, when he arrived, but who by now was thoroughly at home, and the life and soul of the party.

We had intended to lunch there; but the weather was fast deteriorating, and we contented ourselves with a cup of coffee and a slice of ham. We just had time to be towed on a sledge behind a motor-tractor to the flagstaff which marked the Pole, round which we walked quickly to enable us to boast that we had paced a circle round the world, and trespassed on all the Antarctic sectors. Then the Admiral with great courtesy broke out my standard on the flagstaff, to celebrate the fact, of which I trust my grandchildren will be proud, that I was the first Head of State ever to visit the South, or indeed any other, Pole. Photographs were taken in the howling wind (and, golly, it was cold); then back we went to the aircraft, and to a few heaven-sent whiffs of oxygen.

Our landing had been hairy, but our take-off was hairier. I sat behind the pilot and listened through a head-set to all the chat on the intercom. I was peering over the pilot's shoulder, counting the numbered barrels that marked every hundred yards of the strip, and owing to the driving ice particles I could never see more than one at a time. Looking intense, and no wonder, the pilot concentrated on keeping the aircraft straight, correcting after every barrel, while the co-pilot watched his instruments for him and called out each increase in speed. The skids with which the aircraft was fitted instead of wheels were fairly sticky, but after 2000 yards we were airborne. We had been at the Pole for only fifty minutes in all, but so far as I was concerned it was ample.

That evening, back at base, I made a formal signal to the Queen reporting the day's events and the courtesy done me by Jim Reedy. The reply next day commanded me to convey her thanks to him. I showed it to him in his own mess, where I was his guest for luncheon. He went quite pink with surprise and pleasure, and I made him keep the signal for his personal archives.

Another day we flew to Cape Crozier, on the other side of Ross Island at the foot of Mount Terror, to see a colony of

Emperor Penguins; we had already seen some of the smaller Adélie penguins at Cape Royds. We walked from where the helicopter landed to a large hollow in the ice about a quarter of a mile across, protected by an ice wall fifteen to twenty feet high, in the lee of which the penguins were sheltering from a penetrating wind: I would put their number at a couple of thousand. They strike absurd attitudes: sometimes holding their chins in the air; sometimes letting their necks drop, so that their chins rest on their bosoms as though they were doing an exaggerated bow to royalty; sometimes holding out their wings in what looks like a gesture of despair. They hang about mostly in large crowds, but sometimes you see one by himself apparently lost in contemplation, or two going off for a solemn walk together like a couple of university dons. To cross a crevasse they flop on to their bellies, and appear to be swimming on the ice. The chicks are brown and fluffy, with enormous paunches, and their parents protect and comfort them by holding them between their legs.

The Emperor lays only one egg a year, in the middle of winter; the male incubates it by sitting patiently on it through-out those cold and miserable months, while the female forages for them both. Their chief enemy is that ferocious bird the skua, which goes for the chicks; and this may be the reason why they choose the winter for breeding, when the skuas have departed for warmer climes: by the time they return, the chicks have grown a little, and are less vulnerable. I could happily have spent hours watching these creatures. When we walked back to the helicopter, we were accompanied by several of them, seeing us off as polite hosts should.

On another morning we visited a colony of seals off Weddell Island. There was a long crack in the ice which they were using for ingress and egress. We tried to induce a mother seal, complete with pup, to dive back down through the hole; we pushed her this way and that as hard as we could, but had to acknowledge defeat. As we watched her lying triumphantly with her head away from the hole and her tail flippers right beside it, another seal stuck its head up out of the hole as though he were a periscope, looked round, spotted the tail flippers only six inches away, gave them a playful nip and disappeared down the hole again. The mother seal gave an ear-splitting yelp, leapt forward eight feet in one hop, and turned round to see who was responsible: her eye fell on me, and she gave me a reproachful look. There were ten witnesses of this; and when we told Professor Rae, an American expert on seals, at McMurdo the following day what had happened, he was mortified that we should have witnessed it and not he, who had been studying seals for years and had never seen the like.

At 9 p.m. on 13 November we took off for Christchurch, and a few hours later flew into night: we had almost forgotten what it was like after the non-stop sunshine of the last week. We landed in darkness at 4.30 a.m., transferred to the vice-regal DC3, and were back in Government House in Wellington in time for breakfast, a strange transformation indeed. I had been told before going south that the two things which would impress me most were the colours and the silence. The first was certainly true: I had not expected anything like such variety. The second I didn't experience: there was nearly always the sound of aircraft or of generators running. What impressed me most was the quality of the men. Six weeks later, at 3 p.m. on Christmas afternoon, by arrangement with the Post Office, I telephoned greetings to them from the Bay of Islands; I could see them in my mind's eye, gathered round the loudspeaker in the little mess which had become so familiar to me. I made this my annual practice on Christmas afternoon for the remaining years of my tour of office, and took a final farewell of the current party by the same means on my last day as Governor-General.

In June 1966, we flew up to visit the New Zealand forces serving in South-East Asia, and to see their families. The 'confrontation' with Indonesia was at its height, and there was also a military involvement in Vietnam, where New Zealand was represented by a battery of artillery. I regretfully allowed myself to be dissuaded for political reasons from including in the tour a visit to Vietnam: the more sadly because I had seen and addressed that splendid body of gunners at Waiouru, the Aldershot of New Zealand, a week or two before they sailed for what we all knew would be a gruelling campaign. For much the same reasons, I had to refuse an invitation from the Government of Thailand to spend three days in Bangkok.

But apart from the gunners in Vietnam, there were more than enough New Zealand forces in Malaysia to justify a visit. There was a Leander class frigate, *Otago*, and two mine-sweepers on patrol duties; a battalion of infantry deployed on active service along the Indonesian frontier in Sarawak; a detachment of Special Air Service, working closely with the British SAS under the over-all command of Michael Wingate Gray, who had been my Adjutant in The Black Watch eighteen years before; and two squadrons of RNZAF, one of Canberra fighter-bombers, the other involved in supply-dropping. Of these squadrons, the British Commander-in-Chief Far Eastern Air Force, under whom they were serving, said: 'They are as good as any, and better than most'; he added that in two years of supply-dropping in the most testing conditions they had had only one 'abortive mission', a record unsurpassed by any of their friendly rivals in the RAF.

We flew in the RNZAF's one and only DC6 in the most sybaritic comfort. Our fellow-passengers were fifty reinforcements and married families; but in the after-cabin, which was reserved for our party, was a table and chairs, and the ultimate luxury, discreetly hidden behind curtains, of a huge double-bed. Lord Casey the Governor-General, one of the most distinguished Australian statesmen of all time, whom I had known during the war as Minister of State in Cairo and as Governor of Bengal, came down from Canberra for an hour's talk at Melbourne as we passed through. We spent one night in Melbourne and the next in Perth, in their respective Government Houses: both incumbents were long-standing friends and contemporaries of mine in the British Army, and all three of our wives must have been bored stiff with the reminiscing that went on.

Next day we lunched and refuelled on Cocos Island, an atoll with several islets dotted round the lagoon. Until the Japanese over-ran it in 1942, it had been the private kingdom since 1820 of the Clunies-Ross family, in much the same way as Sarawak was the private kingdom of the Brookes; and the current ruler resented the fact that his sovereignty had never been fully restored to him after its liberation. I had been looking forward to meeting him, the sixth generation of his dynasty; but he was away visiting his children at school in England. I was told, rightly or wrongly, that he usually refused to see dignitaries, such as I temporarily was, whom he associated with the 'establishment' that had diddled him out of his inheritance: I suspect that I would have taken exactly the same line if I had been in his boots. The British and Australians between them had for good strategic reasons built this large airfield, complete with married quarters and all the other appurtenances, on his biggest island; and although they paid him a good rent for it, and left him in undisturbed possession of the others, on one of which he lived, he was said still to resent the incursion, and the enticing away of a high proportion of his labour force to service it. The people appeared to be a conglomeration of Malays, Indians, Arabs and Burmese, amounting to about five hundred in all. There was an Australian 'Official Representative', and it was with him and his wife that we lunched. We also visited the little school run for the children of the airport staff. Quite improperly, I gave them a half-holiday in the name of the Queen, and sent off a note to Dick Casey apologizing for having thus trespassed on his preserves.

As a military aircraft, with 'confrontation' in full flower, we were not allowed to overfly Indonesia, but had to go right round the northern tip of Sumatra, and so down the Malacca Strait to Singapore, which we reached at 10 p.m. local time, eight hours out from Cocos. Our convoy of cars was preceded through the streets of Singapore by no fewer than eleven police motor-bicyclists with their sirens blaring, which can hardly have endeared us to people who were settling down to sleep.

Next day I made a round of calls, beginning with the President, and including an hour of useful talk with the Prime Minister Lee Kuan Yew, whom I have never known to be other than stimulating and enlightening. There followed a briefing at the British HQ, where the Political Adviser began his spiel by saying: 'This is a far cry from where I *last* briefed Your Excellency!' I suddenly recognized Jock Given, whom I had last seen in the Persian Gulf during my incarnation as an unwelcome journalist. A less happy note was struck by the

Army Chief of Staff, standing in for John Grandy who was unfortunately away in Hong Kong. I had asked him about the quality of a certain Malay General, and he replied: 'He's not really fit to be anything but a Brigadier.' The dozen staff officers supporting him remembered as well as I did what he had forgotten: that this was the final peak which I myself had reached in my military career. So when I responded with: 'Thank you very much!' they all laughed, while he blushed and stuttered in his confusion. I felt rather a cad.

Various junketings and visits, including one to the New Zealand Air Force Squadrons, occupied the next day or two, until the afternoon we flew up to Kuala Lumpur. The airfield that I knew of old on the edge of the town had been superseded by the large new modern one ten miles out, which had only just been opened. Here we were met by a crowd of about two thousand, an exceedingly smart Guard of Honour and a band, the whole of the Diplomatic Corps, and my old friend the Tunku – H. H. Tunku Tun Haji Abdul Razak bin Hussein, to give him his full style and title, Prime Minister and already, although only in his sixties, the Grand Old Man of Malaysia. Of the royal house of Pahang, the large state on the eastern coast of Malaya, he had dominated Malay politics ever since he entered them after a number of years in the Malay Civil Service, overwhelming in the first elections after independence his chief rival, another old friend of mine, Dato Onn, of the royal house of Johore. Before our engines had completed their diminishing hum into silence, the Tunku was at the foot of the steps, smiling from ear to ear and crooning his welcome. He led me to the hither end of the longest red carpet I have ever seen. It stretched all the way to the terminal, but unfortunately it was as narrow as a stair-carpet; and I realized that if I were to walk on it, there wouldn't be room for the Tunku. I didn't care to monopolize it: so in the end I was walking along one side of it, while the Tunku walked on the other, and the carpet itself remained untrodden and virgin.

Two or three splendid days followed. We were luxuriously housed in the Istana, which I had known twelve years before when it was 'King's House', the residence of the British High Commissioner: many of the old servants were still there to welcome me back. We were received by the King, who under the Malaysian constitution is elected for a term of five years from among the Sultans or Rajas who rule the eleven states which constitute Malaya (as opposed to Malaysia: Malaysia comprises mainland Malaya, Sarawak and north Borneo: Brunei has always refused to join, and Singapore, which was part of it when it was set up in 1963, broke away in 1965). The King, or Yang di-Pertuan Agong, of the moment was in private life, so to speak, Sultan of Trengganu, and rejoiced, or certainly should have rejoiced, in the name of His Majesty Sultan Sir Ismail Masiruddin Shah Ibni Almarhum Sultan Zainal Abiddin, KCMG. He has retired long since to Trengganu, but we still remain in Christmas-card touch.

Both audience and meal were highly formal, and expertly organized by a dignified Chamberlain. Every time he addressed the King or made an announcement, he clasped his hands, raised them high above his head, and said his piece in a sonorous voice. When the moment came for the King and me, sitting side by side on chairs which were almost thrones, to exchange presents, the Chamberlain and Andrew Parker-Bowles, as ADC-in-waiting, marched up to us side by side the whole length of the audience chamber bearing our respective gifts on huge silver trays. They each sank on to one knee: I took my present from Andrew's tray and gave it to the King; he took his from the Chamberlain's tray and gave it to me; I put his present on to Andrew's tray, and the King mine on to the Chamberlain's, and Andrew and the Chamberlain then walked backwards to the far end of the room whence they had come. The Chamberlain from his long experience steered a perfect 'reciprocal'; Andrew, who had not been indoctrinated in this particular art during his career on the Horse Guards' Parade or elsewhere, collided stern-first with a television camera, but contrived to preserve both his composure and my new possession.

One day we were flown down to Penang and back. It was oppressively hot for the morning's functions, and the afternoon swim was the more welcome. Back at Kuala Lumpur airport, we were met by the Tunku's huge Rolls-Royce, which had a television set in the back. Just for fun, we switched it on, and found ourselves watching our own activities in Penang of only four hours earlier. At dinner with the Tunku we found ourselves eating birds'-nest soup, and tiny birds so small that one was expected to crunch them up, bones and all, as though they were sardines. I could not help remembering Hilaire Belloc's couplet:

> Birds in their little nests agree
> With Chinamen, but not with me.

But we suffered no ill effects: far from it.

The Tunku and his Deputy Prime Minister Tun Razak (who eventually succeeded him, but died in office in 1975) saw us off at 8 a.m. one morning. The Tunku's hospitality was still not exhausted, and we were driven to Malacca and the New Zealand base camp at near-by Terendak in his splendid Rolls: once again, we were able to witness our send-off on its television. We spent four hours there visiting the grass-widows and their families, the school, the Maori meeting-house and so on; their men-folk were on operations in Sarawak. And to Sarawak I flew to see them the following day, the first time I had ever been there. I found Kuching the capital a picturesque little town, though marred by recent concrete buildings. It is bisected by a river, 400 yards wide, which we crossed in a smart sampan propelled by an outboard motor to reach the Palace, the former home of the Brooke Rajahs and now the abode of the Governor.

The Governor had a name almost as euphonious as that of the King: Tun Dato Abang Haji Openg bin Abang Sapi'ee, OBE. He was a Dyak, and by an odd chance I had met him before. In Coronation Year my wife and I had flown over from Paris, where we were stationed, to attend; and on Derby Day, just afterwards, Alan Lennox-Boyd, then Minister of State for Colonial Affairs, and my wife's brother Harry Grenfell had hired a couple of open-topped double-decker buses to take a number of Commonwealth visitors for the Coronation down to Epsom for a luscious picnic luncheon on the course, and to see the race: my wife and I had been of the party. My chief recollection of the day was of the ill-fated Kabaka of Buganda borrowing half-a-crown off me before luncheon to go and see a strip-tease act in a tent fifty yards from our picnic site. I didn't grudge him that, but I did rather grudge the second half-crown which he borrowed off me after luncheon to go and see it again. It turned out that Tun Dato Abang had been a member of that same party, and that he regarded it as one of the red-letter days of his life.

The Palace was an extraordinary edifice. Most of it was local in character, two-storeyed, with fine, long, airy, well-proportioned rooms; but the rest of it was of the worst type of Scottish baronial, with the inscription 'AD 1870' over the arched stone front door. After luncheon we returned in the sampan across the river, where I was electrified to see two small children, a boy and a girl, holding up a large placard inscribed *'Haeremai ki te Kawana Tianara!'* which means 'Welcome to the Governor-General!' in Maori. I walked over, and found behind them a smiling, chubby Maori woman. She had married a Sarawaki Chinese who had come to Victoria University in Wellington as a Colombo Plan student eight years before.

That afternoon I flew by helicopter with Bill Cheyne, the British brigade commander, to the frontier area where the 1st Battalion of the Royal New Zealand Infantry Regiment was deployed in active operations. Bill, a Seaforth Highlander, had been my pupil at Sandhurst before the war, and had had the misfortune like Freddy Burnaby-Atkins and many another, to be taken prisoner with the rest of the Highland Division at St Valéry in 1940. Despite this interruption to his professional career, he had made a great mark in the post-war Army, and was confidently expected to rise to its highest ranks: unfortunately he died from a swift and fell illness in 1970. At this moment his reputation was at its highest, and he was regarded as a supreme expert in Malaysian jungle warfare. He told me that out of the twenty or so battalions which had passed through his hands in his present appointment he rated this New Zealand battalion as equal top with one other. He refused to share my overnight stay with it because, as he put it, he didn't want to be a 'washer' between me and mine.

I reckoned that I knew enough from my own experience to

gauge whether or not a unit involved in jungle warfare was proficient or otherwise. I was perhaps more probing than a Governor-General, even though also titular Commander-in-Chief, ought to be. But I did investigate that battalion, under its Maori commanding officer Lieutenant-Colonel Brian Poananga*, as thoroughly as I knew, and found it hard to fault; I also found it difficult to dissent from Bill Cheyne's judgement, although I hadn't seen the other units on which he based his criterion. It was a tip-top battalion whose morale was still at sky level, despite the thousands of collective miles they had patrolled in tough conditions – the temperature was 104° at noon on the day I spent there – without the satisfaction of a clash with the opposition.

HMNZS *Hickleton*, on the other hand, the patrolling minesweeper which I inspected along with her sister-ship *Santon* and the frigate *Otago* in Singapore the following day, after a nostalgic night sleeping in the jungle with familiar sounds all around me, had a 'contact' on her way to Singapore. Sailing in through the Malacca Strait for her rendezvous with me, she had encountered four sampans, which she challenged for the routine stop and search. Three complied, and were found to be innocent. The fourth continued on her way, and *Hickleton* as she overhauled her fired three rifle shots across her bows. With commendable, if mistaken, gallantry the sampan then opened fire on *Hickleton*, sending a rain of bullets through her bridge. *Hickleton* replied with three bursts from twin machine-guns, and the sampan, evidently hit in her petrol-tank, blew up. Her crew of four, of whom two were picked up, were in Indonesian uniform; her commander, a lieutenant, was killed. For political reasons the story was suppressed; but the sampan's mission must have been sinister: she was in Malaysian territorial waters when she failed to obey the order to stop.

The British commander Far Eastern Fleet, Admiral Sir Frank Twiss, who was afterwards for seven years Black Rod in the House of Lords, told me a pleasant story of a similar incident which had befallen one of his own ships a few months earlier. Some of the officers were having a pre-luncheon glass

---

* Now Major-General.

of gin in the ward-room when an Indonesian vessel opened fire, and a stray bullet came whizzing through. (I had always assumed that our ironsides were tougher than that, and that their ward-rooms at least were impervious to bullets.) A Chinese steward was serving drinks, and later they congratulated him on his *aplomb*, and on the fact that he hadn't turned a hair. 'I not flightened,' he said; 'I knew it was only plactice.'

On the way back to New Zealand, we stopped one night in Adelaide, to pay a pious pilgrimage at the grave of my grandmother, Dalhousie's daughter, who had died and been buried there in 1871 during my grandfather's time as Governor. We found it well tended; but the altar-cloth of Indian material which she had given to St Andrew's Church, in whose kirkyard she lay, was in shreds. I reported this to my brothers and sister, and between the four of us we replaced it with a new one.

So ended our last sortie from New Zealand, apart from final farewells to western Samoa and Rarotonga. The latter was unduly prolonged by a cloudburst which flooded the airfield, and delayed our return by forty-eight hours. It also expanded the Fergusson connection with the Cooks, in that my eighteen-year-old nephew, my brother Simon's son Alexander, then working on a sheep-station in Hawke's Bay, had been allowed by his employer to come with us. He was far more fussed than I was at over-staying his permitted leave.

On 20 October 1967, fifteen months after our tour in South-East Asia, our time in New Zealand came to an end. We took off from the Wellington Airport which stretches out into the sea from a beach where as a boy I used to gather shells with my parents, and which bears the appropriate name of 'Rongotai': Maori for 'Hearken to the Tide'. We were accompanied by one residuary ADC, James Osborne of my own Regiment, and by the Official Secretary, David Williams, who had smoothed my path and covered up all my short-comings for the last five years, as he had done for half the tenure of my predecessor and was to do for both my successors, until he retired in 1977. I have always maintained that seven generations of careful selective breeding under the best scientific auspices and all the most up-to-date knowledge of genetics could not have produced as good an Official Secretary as David Williams.

There could be no more difficult task than being the inter-
mediary between Government House and the Government, and
David Williams discharged it for almost twenty years without
leaving a scar on either side. He was accompanying us now to
meet for the first time his opposite number in Canberra, where
we bade him a sad farewell two days later. For three out of our
five years, we had also enjoyed the congenial and devoted
services of Freddy Burnaby-Atkins as Comptroller; but the
War Office, implacable as ever, had refused to extend his tour,
and insisted on posting him as Military Attaché to Morocco
three months before my time was up. It is some measure of the
popularity of him and his wife that they and their family were
seen off from Wellington Airport by half the Cabinet and
most of the Diplomatic Corps.

From early in the year, a stream of generous invitations had
been reaching us through their Ambassadors or High Commissioners in Wellington from the various countries through
which we might be passing on our homeward journey, to
spend a few days in them as their guests. We found these hard
to resist. For one thing, it was very friendly of them; for another,
we thought it unlikely (though in this we were to be proved
wrong) that we should ever have the chance to see the world
again, apart from the occasional modest sortie to France;
and for a third, there was something attractive in the idea of
filling in the time while our heavy luggage pursued its leisurely
way back to Britain by sea. We therefore accepted no fewer
than seven of these invitations, and planned for good measure
additional private stops in Istanbul, Rome and Paris. We were
not rewarding guests for Charles and Natasha Johnston in
Canberra, where he was the British High Commissioner: after
all the physical and emotional strain of the last few days, we
were as whacked as when, three years earlier, we had arrived
at Government House, Fiji; but three days of their sympathetic
hospitality restored us, and we arrived at Bangkok in good
shape.

Bangkok was followed by Singapore and Kuala Lumpur,
where once again the Tunku did us proud. He granted us one
afternoon off, to go and see Gathorne Medway, my first
cousin once removed, a dedicated naturalist half-way through

his nine years as lecturer in Zoology at the then University of Malaya, having already spent several years in Sarawak. He was living in a tiny abandoned stone house which he had discovered in the jungle twelve miles out of Kuala Lumpur, with aviaries and a selection of tame birds and beasts all round him: supported by an elderly Dyak called Uncle Ned who had been with him in Sarawak, and sustained by a varying number of aboriginal servants who came and went as the spirit moved them but never left him uncared for. To the horror of the elegant servants, he called for us at the Istana in a huge, ancient car which looked more like an elongated bucket; the back of it was full of skins, carcasses and assorted tinned provisions from his weekly shopping. Once again, through no wish of mine, we were preceded by eleven police outriders on motor-cycles. Gathorne said: 'There's a back-road here: I know how to give them the slip!' and turned up it. Within a minute they had caught us up, and chased us with menaces back on to the official route. Once at Gathorne's, however, I was able to persuade them to go back home, satisfying their sergeant by means of a written chit that he was absolved from all responsibility for our safety.

Burma followed; then India; then Israel (we had sadly to miss Pakistan). At the last moment we had to substitute Athens for Istanbul, but a very agreeable substitute it was. At Rome we stayed with Alister McIntosh, who was serving there as Ambassador after having been for twenty-one years Permanent Head of the Prime Minister's Department as well as Secretary for Foreign Affairs: he was once described to me, although he would reject the description, as 'the man who makes New Zealand tick'. There we were met by our son, now aged twelve, who had left New Zealand some months earlier for a preparatory school in England: he shared with us our three days in Rome, and our three in Paris.

Hitherto, the whole seven-weeks' journey, meticulously planned in New Zealand, had gone without a hitch. We drove out to Le Bourget confidently expecting that an hour's flight would bring us to Heathrow, where representatives of the Queen and the Government, dear Sir Tom Macdonald the New Zealand High Commissioner who had seen us off five years before, and our relations in cohorts would be awaiting us. White, implacable December fog suddenly descended; and we had to transfer to an ignominious train. At Dunkirk, for the first time in five years – and very salutary for us it was – we had to turn to and man-handle our luggage. The ferry was packed with people from truck to keel, and there wasn't even a seat to be had. Furthermore, we had no money. We were sitting sadly on our suitcases, when the Purser came along. He took two looks at me, and said: 'Aren't you Brigadier Fergusson, who used to be at Dover?' I pleaded guilty to this charge: whereupon he produced a large key, and ushered the four of us into a first-class suite, for free.

So ended five blissful years which I had never deserved and never expected, but of which the memories will continue to illumine the rest of our lives.

Chapter Ten

LATE FLIGHTS WITH A SOFT LANDING

It took a little time to adjust to the many changes that had taken place in Britain during our five years' absence, and to becoming private citizens again. The morning after our arrival in London, I went round to White's Club, something I had been looking forward to for ages. The first person I met was Bill De L'Isle, who had been my opposite number in Australia during my first three years in New Zealand; and his salutary opening words were: 'You'll soon find that there's nothing so "ex" as an ex-Ex!' He was quite right: I'd had no money in my pocket for five years, and Wheeler the barman had to remind me precisely how to make out a cheque – I hadn't even a cheque-book as yet, and was obliged to use one of the Club cheque-forms. Meanwhile, my wife had gone with our son to take delivery of the car which had come back from New Zealand by sea: within fifteen minutes flat, not knowing the ropes, she had to take delivery of a parking-ticket as well. We also found it difficult to refrain from waving to all and sundry as we drove through the streets.

Motorways were new to us; a strange driving code was in force; the mysteries of STD had to be mastered. The increase in the number of coloured faces was much greater than we had expected. British Rail had introduced a new (and we thought ugly) standard lettering, and thrust its officials into unfamiliar headgear. We felt insecure at not being slaves of a strict programme. For a month we paid visits to various relations before returning in joy one sunny January morning to our home, stopping in the village of Ballantrae for an informal welcome by the Lord-Lieutenant and the schoolchildren, few of whom can have remembered us. Piled in the hall of the house were 450 items of luggage, varying from huge packing-cases to boxed pictures and rolls of carpets. It was a good two months before we got the place straight, the pictures hung, the books on their proper shelves.

We had brought the boat *Te Aaka* home with us, and during the glorious summer that followed, hot, calm and windless, we spent much time on the water, nipping over to Ailsa Craig or Arran, and enjoying being back, though often yearning for the Bay of Islands. I found myself busy too: I took over the Colonelcy of my Regiment and the chairmanship of the London Board of the Bank of New Zealand, and found myself one of the four non-party members of Sir Alec Douglas-Home's committee probing the subject of devolution for Scotland. There was some sense of anti-climax after the joys of New Zealand, but it looked as though life would hold plenty of interest without being too exacting. We thought that our roots had grown finally, firmly and forever back into our native soil; but we were wrong.

In October 1968, ten months after our return from New Zealand, I was asked to fly out at short notice to take over the job of senior British representative on the International Observer Team which was monitoring the civil war in Nigeria. I pointed out that I had no knowledge whatever of Black Africa in general or Nigeria in particular, but I was told that this was all to the good: I would be bringing a fresh mind to the problem, and could not be suspected of having any axe to grind, or any former loyalties to confuse me. I was soon to learn, from the flood of letters which began as soon as my appointment was announced and continued to reach me long after I came back to Britain, that many British people who had lived long years in the country had become fiercely partisan for this or that ethnic group.

The war was the more tragic because when Nigeria achieved Independence in 1960 the future seemed so auspicious: although those who knew the country best had plenty of misgivings. The quality of British administrators had always been high, and there was a strong cadre of indigenous officials who had not only been at British universities, but had actual experience of administrative responsibility. In his speech on Independence Day, Sir Tafawa Balewa Abubakar, the first Prime Minister, had included his famous sentence which to my mind remains as the epitaph of British colonial rule at its best: 'The British came first as masters, then as teachers, then as partners, but always as friends.' Nigeria had come to be regarded as one of the show-pieces of British colonial policy: beginning with the imposition of law and order, the abolition of inter-tribal strife and barbarous practices, the establishment of first-class schools and universities, and the development of its enormous economic potential.

The origins of the civil war are complicated, still disputed, and well outside the scope of this narrative. It need only be said that there are three major ethnic groups in the country, with innumerable minority tribes dominated by each: the Moslem north, with its Emirs and Sultans still enjoying residual powers and reminiscent of their equivalents in Arabia; the Yorubas of the west; the Ibos in the east. These last, a likeable and energetic people, who took to modern education like ducks to water, have sometimes been described as the Scotch or the Jews of Nigeria, in the pejorative but grudgingly admiring sense so often applied to both those labels. They engaged with conspicuous success both in business and in the public service, far beyond, as well as within, the bounds of their own ancestral territory; and met with the inevitable jealousy which such success provokes. Some of those I met seemed to have a touch of arrogance about them, but I could easily see why they had captured the sympathy and affection of so many of my own countrymen.

The seeds of separation began sadly to germinate soon after Independence. The accounts of what finally sparked off the war are still at variance, but certain facts are beyond query. There was a series of assassinations and massacres and *coups d'état*; and among those assassinated was one of the leading northern Sultans, Sir Tafawa Abubakar and General Ironsi-Johnson, who had been my guest in New Zealand some years before, when he came to Government House as one of a dozen visiting students from the Imperial Defence College, of which I was myself an 'Old Boy'. Colonel Ojukwu, the Military

Governor of the eastern region, was himself an Ibo, educated at an English public school and at Oxford, and the son of an Ibo businessman successful enough to have become a million-aire and to have been accorded the honour of knighthood. Ojukwu himself had passed high into the Civil Service, but soon decided that he would find a more influential future in the Army, and transferred to it, by way of the now defunct British Officer Cadet Training Unit at Mons Barracks, Alder-shot. This existed to train potential officers for Short Service Commissions, as opposed to Sandhurst, which trained Regulars. It always amused me when General Gowon, the Head of State and at one time a close friend of Ojukwu, who had him-self been at Sandhurst, never failed to say in any conversation: 'Of course, Ojukwu was only at Mons.'

The moment came when Colonel Ojukwu declared the eastern region an independent state, under the name of 'Biafra'. From the way in which his supporters in Britain and elsewhere were soon to talk of it, one would have been justified in assum-ing that this was an ancient name for the area which he had resurrected; but it was in fact even less appropriate than the resurrection of the name 'Strathclyde' for the region of Scot-land which has laboured under that appellation since 1975. The question of who fired the first shots of the war, and whether the actual date was the 5th or the 6th of July 1968, will prob-ably never be established. It is more than likely that the initial exchanges were fortuitous, unplanned and at something like platoon level; but war was inevitable, and the point is academic. Certainly both sides were poised for fighting, with Ojukwu's the readier of the two.

We of the Observer Team were always careful to remain, and to be seen to remain, impartial. We avoided using the term 'rebels', which would imply a bias towards the Federal Government, or 'Biafrans', which would imply recognition of the sovereign status which they claimed. The word we adopted was 'Secessionists'. The Secessionists, then, delivered an immediate blow, which might be described in boxing parlance as a 'straight left', across the River Niger, thrusting for the Federal capital of Lagos, and coming within 130 miles of it at a place called Oré. Here they were stemmed, and eventually pushed back across the Niger, though not before giving the Federals a nasty fright. The unfortunate Colonel commanding the Secessionist column was shot for alleged treachery. At much the same moment, the Federals brought off an amphibious 'right hook', landing at the mouth of the Calabar River, and advancing rapidly overland to the oil port of Port Harcourt, cutting off the Secessionists from the sea once and for all. This model operation was carried out by a forceful little Yoruba Colonel called Benjamin Adekunle, but nicknamed 'the Black Scorpion' – a soubriquet in which he delighted.

The first round, therefore, went to the Federals; and the war might have ended then but for several factors which were not foreseen by most people at the time. One was the determination, courage and ingenuity of Colonel Ojukwu and his followers. Another was the active support of the French, which was then, and subsequently, thought to be due to their hopes that a Secessionist victory would transfer to them the oil concessions then enjoyed by British firms (and there were political considerations too). The third was the enlistment by Colonel Ojukwu of the services of a brilliant public relations firm called Markpress, based in Geneva and run by an American. Their propaganda campaign, which won liberal sympathies for 'Biafra' all over the world and the support of many countries in the United Nations, was, in the old phrase, 'worth a guinea a minute'. How much it actually cost, I have no notion; but it was certainly a good investment.

It was probably Markpress who first spread the word that the Federal Government was bent on 'genocide': a word of which the official United Nations definition is: 'The committing of certain acts with intent to destroy – wholly or in part – a national, ethnic, racial or religious group as such.' Smarting under this accusation, and clear in its conscience, the Federal Government issued an invitation which I believe to be without precedent. It invited four countries, Britain, Poland, Canada and Sweden, to send representatives to investigate these charges. The invitations to Canada and Sweden were particularly courageous, since the feeling in both these countries was strongly and stridently in favour of the Secessionists. All four Governments accepted; and at that point both the United Nations and the Organization of African States asked to be allowed to send observers also, to which the Federal Government agreed. It was thought at that time that the war would be short, and that the team would not be required to operate for more than two or three months at the most; but by October the fighting had ground to a halt. The original British senior observer, my old friend Henry Alexander, who had been both a cadet and an instructor at Sandhurst with me, and on Wingate's staff when I was commanding a Chindit brigade in Burma, had already exceeded the leave of absence which his civilian firm had granted him, and a replacement for him was urgently needed.

And so in October I exhumed my old bush-shirts and tropical uniforms, which smelled strongly of moth-ball, and flew out to Lagos, accompanied by David Arbuthnott of my own Regiment in loyal support. David, by then a major, had first joined The Black Watch during my time in command; his father, Major-General Lord Arbuthnott, had been Adjutant when I was a subaltern, and Colonel of the Regiment at one remove before me. After an overnight flight from London, we were met at Ikeda airport — a dismal place which we were to come to know all too well – by some of my new colleagues, and driven to the huge modern hotel in Lagos which the Government had designated as our base, where I met the rest of them.

The heads of the three original missions other than the British comprised two Major-Generals, Bill Milroy of the Canadian Army, with a distinguished career still ahead of him, and Baron Arthur Raab of Sweden, the *doyen* of us all in terms of age; and Colonel Alphons Olkiewicz of the Polish Army, a real charmer with surprisingly grey hair for such a youthful face, and a great sense of humour – which, heaven knows, we all needed. Having been taken prisoner as a young officer in 1939, he had by a curious chance been liberated from his prisoner-of-war camp by Henry Alexander in 1945; and he had had previous experience as a United Nations observer in Vietnam. A third Major-General, the Ethiopian Negga Tebegn, headed the OAS group, made up of his ADC and two Algerians. As a boy of twelve, he had witnessed Wingate's entry into Gojjam at the head of his partisans in 1941, and despite his youth had joined his force: among a lot of esoteric Ethiopian ribbons, he proudly sported on his breast those of the Africa Star and the Victory Medal. His wife Ruth, who joined him in Lagos for a month, was a grand-daughter of the Emperor. Finally, the UN team was headed by Nils Gussing, an able Swedish civilian who had done similar jobs all over the world. They were a pleasant bunch, and so were their subordinates; there were eighteen of us in all.

I was fortunate to be inheriting Henry Alexander's No. 2, Duggie Cairns. They had served together both in Ghana, when Henry had been commanding Nkrumah's forces, and in the UN operation in the Congo: Henry had enticed him back from civilian life to share in this curious assignment. He had long experience of West Africa, and proved to be a jewel. He was to die from a swift onslaught of cancer in 1978, a year after Henry.

So began what were perhaps the five most frustrating months of my life. At the top level all was sweetness and light. General Gowon, the Head of State, aged thirty-one, was still very much the Sandhurst cadet which he was so proud to have been, the son of a Christian evangelist from one of the smaller northern tribes, whose chief hobby was playing squash. He was making quite a good fist of his unexpected elevation; he seemed dead honest and devoid of personal ambition; but he also seemed to me a poor picker of subordinates, and many of the people around him were obviously more interested in lining their pockets than in getting on with the war. Only once were we actually denied access anywhere, and that was by Benjie Adekunle; but promised aircraft would fail to turn up, vehicles would break down; and once a group of my colleagues was stranded for three days at Makurdi, which is a long, long way from anywhere.

The redoutable Benjie Adekunle was a fiery, wizened little man in his early thirties, Sandhurst-trained and a close friend of Gowon, who tolerated his excesses unduly. He couldn't keep still, and was always hopping around like a jumping-jack. Outside his office at Port Harcourt was a large painted sign, reading: 'NO ADMISSION ON PAIN OF THE DEATH!' Once he had an officer shot out of hand for ill-treating civilians; once I saw him beating up a soldier who had displeased him; once he actually threatened to have Arthur Raab flogged for arguing with him. This led to a major diplomatic incident, and he was made to apologize. I still have the notes I made of a flaming row I had with him, when he refused to allow me and two other observers up to the front. Presumably there was something going on that he didn't want us to see. Here is part of the exchange:

Adekunle: I am a soldier; I have my job to do.
Fergusson: So am I a soldier, and I have had responsibilities like you have now. I too have my job to do: it's a rotten one, and I hope for your sake you never get one like it.
Adekunle: I'm fighting a battle on all fronts, and I can't be bothered with observers at this time.
Fergusson: In fact, you only want us to observe when there's nothing worth observing?
Adekunle: If you like to put it like that, yes!

I flew back to Lagos and put in a sharp report to Gowon: I returned to Port Harcourt next day, and there was a welcoming grin where yesterday there had been a murderous scowl. Thereafter we got on well; and although he wouldn't have any other journalists near him, he not only agreed, at my request, to receive my nephew Julian Haviland and his team from Independent Television News, but gave him every facility and an exclusive interview before the cameras.

I had sympathy for the British High Commissioner Sir David Hunt and his staff, who were continually being accused of bias, misrepresentation, *suppressio veri*, *suggestio falsi*, and every other crime in the diplomatic calendar. Feelings in Britain ran higher on this subject than on any other since the Suez affair, in which I was also physically and geographically involved: old friends almost came to blows about it. Admittedly, the High Commission had no access to 'Biafra' after the war broke out, nor had we observers; but the effect of this on both the High Commission and on us was to make us lean over even further backwards to be scrupulously fair and objective. I remained as independent as possible of the High Commission, though I had to use it as my means of communication with the

Foreign and Commonwealth Office. Never at any moment did David Hunt or anybody in his office seek to put thoughts or prejudices into my mind, which is more than could be said for the Swedish Ambassador. I must confess that once, to oblige the British Defence Adviser, I ventured beyond my neutral position. He had heard a rumour that there were Russian Ilyushin aircraft on a certain airstrip, and could I confirm yes or no when I next went past it? I rejoiced in being able to report that there were only optical Ilyushins.

I was able personally to refute, through being on the spot, several of the phoney reports put out by the propagandists. They claimed that 200 prisoners had been shot in Port Harcourt jail on a certain day: unfortunately for them, I had spent that whole day in the jail with the prisoners. A prominent Canadian newspaper carried a circumstantial report, received from 'Biafra', of a massacre by Federal troops in a village called Inyang: it was extremely remote, but I managed to get there, and found that it had never even been visited by Federal troops. I happened to be in Ibadan throughout the day when 'Radio Biafra' claimed it had been bombed, allegedly by Federal aircraft pretending to be Secessionist: it wasn't.

But I did see many heart-rending sights. Among the most haunting were the thousands of small children, mostly being cared for in *ad hoc* orphanages, who had either lost or been separated from their parents: some of the little mites were too young to know their names or the names of the villages from which they came, and had little prospect of ever being reunited. Scores of villages had been evacuated to avoid the fighting; and from many the population had been removed by the retreating Ibo troops and carried with them into improvised internment camps in the jungle where there was little food for them. These included thousands from minority groups living in Ibo or Ibo-dominated areas: Efiks, Ijaws, Ibibios, Rivers people. I have never been able to fathom why the Secessionists should have crowded them into their shrinking enclave at the same moment as they were pleading to the world that they themselves were dying from starvation at the rate of 15,000 a day – a figure which was manifestly bogus: had it been true, the total population of 'Biafra' would have died several times over. Around the Federal-held fringes of that enclave there was certainly appalling malnutrition, and the death-rate especially among the children was high indeed; the dreaded deficiency disease of Kwashiorkor was rife. This was due primarily to the difficulty of moving foodstuffs to and from their normal markets when the rival armies lay athwart the usual lines of communication, and also to the interruption to the usual rhythm of seed-time and harvest.

There were those who said that the tales of non-Ibos being forcibly withdrawn into the enclave were Federal propaganda. I myself met three such parties escaping. One was of fifteen, whom I met at Kwale just west of the Niger, which they had crossed in boats under cover of darkness early that morning. The others, whom I met on consecutive days near Owerri, numbered about three hundred each. The first was headed by a schoolmaster with degrees from both Ohio and McGill Universities; he told me that a party of the same size would be emerging from the jungle next day, and I made it my business to meet them. Their leader told me, dry-eyed, that his wife had died on trek the day before, and he had buried her. I went on up to the battlefront, whither I was bound; and on my way back five hours later I was stopped by this man and another, who gave me a piece of paper. It read: 'We have to suggest to you never to announce it over the wires that you have got refugees from Ogoni. If this is done, we are sure that the Biafran government will kill all the rest of us who are still in Biafra waiting to come. We thank you for your co-operation.' It was later suggested to me by a Member of Parliament who was a supporter of 'Biafra' that this document must have been a forgery.

I only came under fire twice, once from mortars and once from small arms. The first occasion was quite funny, in that my companion was not the bravest of my colleagues: I will reveal neither his name nor his nationality; but when it came on to bomb, he got rather agitated, saying: 'This is not our job, this is not our job!' I suggested that it was an unusually good opportunity to 'observe', and that we ought to hang around in case prisoners were taken, to see how they were treated. I pocketed the keys of our Land-Rover in case he was tempted to make off with it; but he got so frantic that after twenty minutes

I gave in, and drove away down the track with him, feeling rather craven: the skirmish in any case seemed to be petering out.

Occasionally I evacuated wounded, though strictly this was 'not our job' either, or picked up lost and wandering children. Once I tried to deliver by the roadside the baby of a desperately emaciated woman who had come stumbling out of the jungle, already in labour: I was unable to save either, but an Indian doctor who came along later comforted me by saying that he could not have done any better for them. Teams from Oxfam, the Save the Children Fund and other such organizations performed wonders; and I recall a young and beautiful American nun who with the help of two Ibo women ran a makeshift orphanage near Abakaliki which changed hands more than once between the two armies: she carried on quite unperturbed, and laughed cheerfully at the many setbacks that befell her.

The war dragged on into the New Year, and neither side showed signs of moving; such fighting as there was had become desultory. I was allowed to demit office, and early in March I handed over to my No. 2, Duggie Cairns. My wife had been with me for the last few weeks, and we travelled home by way of Rabat, where Freddy Burnaby-Atkins, with whom I had visited it nineteen years before, was now Military Attaché. He and his wife did me the honour of inviting me to sack their cook for them in my rusty Arabic, and I was happy to oblige. I was thoroughly relieved to have got away from Nigeria, from an oppressive climate and a joyless job. At no time had I felt well, nor did I feel much better when I got home. The trouble was eventually diagnosed as Sprue, but it must have long been latent, since apparently Sprue is unknown in Nigeria. Several weeks of treatment, five of them in hospital, eventually put me right, but it is not an ailment which I can recommend. Nor is a burst appendix with peritonitis, which assailed me the following year.

As Colonel I had already visited my Regiment in Gibraltar, and our sister Regiment, the Black Watch of Canada, in Montreal; now our 1st Battalion was in Hong Kong, and in October of 1972 I set out to visit them there, by courtesy of the

Ministry of Defence. It seemed a pity to be returning to that part of the world without calling in on some of my old stamping-grounds in South-East Asia, and the *Sunday Telegraph* agreed to pay the expenses of a diversion from the direct route in return for a series of articles on Malaysia, Burma and Vietnam. The burst appendix was not long behind me, and my wife was reluctant for me to travel in remote areas without some sort of 'nanny'; so I asked the Regiment to provide me with somebody to meet me in Singapore and to act as ADC, partly at his own expense and partly at mine: I felt able to promise him a memorable trip. They made available Bruce Osborne, whose father and grandfather had also been in the Regiment, and whose elder brother James had shared our last two years in New Zealand and travelled home with us five years before.

Two weeks before I left, I received a tentative and informal approach on behalf of the Board of the British Council asking whether I would like to be considered as its Chairman, in succession to Sir Leslie Rowan, who had tragically dropped down dead a few weeks earlier. Having seen and admired its work in various parts of the world, and after discovering exactly what the chairmanship entailed, I was tempted. I could discern only two snags to it, apart from the fact that it would mean long and frequent absences from home: I should have to postpone the writing of various books which I was contemplating, and I should have to abstain from indulging in any controversies. I am not by nature a controversial animal, but I would have to refrain from expressing any views that I might have or form on (for instance) foreign affairs. At an enjoyable, and at times hilarious, meeting over luncheon with eight members of the Board, I said that I would be happy to accept, if asked, but would not be unduly disappointed if not.

Bruce Osborne duly met me in Singapore, where we spent three days with the New Zealand High Commissioner and I renewed old contacts with many people from Lee Kuan Yew downwards; we flew out by helicopter to spend a day in the jungles of Johore with the New Zealand infantry battalion, and drank gin with the New Zealand Navy and Air Force. In Malaysia we saw the Tunku, and stayed two nights with a cousin of mine, a rubber planter near Seremban, with whom we shot some pigeon and killed a cobra, and had a swim in the sea near Port Dickson. In Burma I introduced Bruce to old friends in Rangoon, Mandalay and Maymyo, and spent a morning on the Inle Lake: we were to have lunched with General Ne Win, but unfortunately his wife, whom I was greatly looking forward to seeing again, died suddenly the previous day. In Bangkok I received a cable from the British Council formally offering me the chairmanship, and I replied accepting. I went round to have a look at their local offices, and rejoiced in the instant dropping of the staff's collective jaw. The circulation clerk in the British Embassy had improperly sent them a copy of both the incoming and outgoing confidential cables, but they had hardly expected a visitation from their new Chairman within half an hour of his appointment. At Saigon we stayed with the New Zealand Ambassador, General Sir Leonard Thornton, who had been first Chief of the General Staff and then Chief of Defence Staff during my time in New Zealand: it was his uncle, Air-Marshal (though then merely Captain) Sir Leonard Isitt, who had been my pilot on my first-ever flight from Christchurch in 1925, when I put my foot through the canvas floor.

With Bill Thornton we spent a couple of days helicoptering around up-country, visiting Vietnamese units and one Cambodian one, in which many of the soldiers seemed to be aged about fifteen. We lunched one day at a leper hospital run by some devoted French nuns under a Breton Mother Superior of obviously aristocratic breeding, whom I would guess to be in her late sixties: she had a memorable ivory beauty, and a Christian tranquillity which had survived not only expulsion from China after many years and much humiliation, but also recent fighting around her present hospital. This was a place of peace and quiet: of small houses in which families were living happily despite the strife around them; of shady groves with sandy tracks between the trees, in which children were happily playing. Every face lit up whenever any of the Sisters came by, and pathetic stumps where fingers should have been were waved in greeting. They broached for us over luncheon a couple of bottles of Sancerre, and I felt guilty at drinking it, for I doubt if they had much of it left. After luncheon, they lent us towels, and we had a splendid swim from their beach, where the majestic rollers of the South China Sea broke in green and white glory. I have no idea of what happened to the Sisters when the more sinister rollers of the invasion from the north broke over their hospital. They were the sort of people who might well refuse all offers of evacuation.

Now that I was Chairman of the British Council, it was obviously not possible for me to contribute articles to the *Sunday Telegraph*, and I cabled them accordingly, asking only for a few months of grace in which to pay back the advance they had made me. With great generosity, they let me off this financial hook without quibble; and I only hope that the anonymous pieces that I sent them without payment during the following five or six months reimbursed to some extent their investment in me. I always found both *Telegraphs, Daily* and *Sunday*, friendly papers to work for, although such dimly-etched political views as I have are *café-au-lait* compared with their stronger brew. Certainly their respective editors, Colin Coote and Brian Roberts, treated me with generosity, indulgence and patience. I was not always as biddable when under their orders as I should have been, but they forgave my various trespasses.

I knew that I was going to enjoy my four days with The Black Watch in Hong Kong as its visiting Colonel, and I did: not only the formal ceremonial parade, but also the Guest Night in the Officers' Mess, the evening in the Serjeants' Mess, the Regimental Games, Church on Sunday (I was a foundation elder of the Regimental Kirk Session), at which I attended the baptism of various regimental children, and the ordination of two new elders. I was taken sailing and swimming by four enthusiastic yachting officers. I was flipped around the frontier in a helicopter, which made me grimly aware of the vast, watchful menace of China lying beyond it, from which a constant trickle of refugees was reaching Hong Kong every night, usually by water. I enjoyed those four days thoroughly, but the more because I knew I would be returning to something more challenging than a merely idyllic life up the hill above Ballantrae: to the chairmanship of the British Council.

The work of the British Council is not known or appreciated

in Britain as well as it should be, although overseas it is a household word. It was founded in 1934 on a shoestring, and built up largely by Lord Lloyd, the one-time Governor of Bombay and High Commissioner in Egypt. Its main function is to spread interest in the English language, in British culture, in technological knowledge throughout the world, and it has enjoyed a marked success in doing so. Paradoxically, the best publicity it has ever had in Britain was in 1977, when an egregious committee, set up by the Central Policy Review Staff under the chairmanship of Sir Kenneth Berrill, recommended (along with revolutionary changes in the Foreign Service and the emasculation of the overseas service of the BBC) the Council's total abolition. Powerful allies, many of them unexpected, and some of them foreign, emerged from every quarter to sing praises of its achievement and to thunder in its defence; and the Berrill Report sank virtually without trace, almost wholly discredited.

All that lay five years ahead of my appointment as Chairman, and ten months after it ended. We were not able to expand as widely as I wished: I wanted very much, for instance, to set up shop in a big way in the Caribbean, where we were not represented at all. In some countries we were having to retrench because of costs which were rising faster than our budget; and from others, such as Cuba and Uganda, we were rudely evicted. But on the whole we were doing well, and beginning to earn revenue in such countries as could afford to help pay for what we were doing for them, enabling us to plough it back into developing countries which needed financial support to develop their own technical and intellectual resources; and such revenue was increasing all the time.

In the course of the next four years I visited thirty-six countries, of which six were wholly new to me, to inspect and encourage Council activities, and to report back to the Board in London how we were doing, and how what we were doing might be improved upon. My wife came with me to all except Canada. In all of them I met the Ministers of Education and of Culture, and in most of them the Prime Minister and the Head of State, an indication of the esteem in which the Council was held. I have lost count of how many university campuses

I tramped, how many language laboratories I inspected, how many receptions I attended. I learned early on to make a rule that I must have one day off in seven, preferably Sunday. I nearly slew our very nice man in Ibadan, which we reached late one Saturday evening after an exhausting tour through North Africa and half Nigeria: he said that it had seemed to him a pity to waste a spare day on the morrow, and he had therefore arranged for us to drive to Ifé and back: three hours each way on a rough track in sweaty weather, with a banquet in the middle of the day. There was very nearly a vacancy for a new Council posting to Ibadan.

My explosion on that occasion got through loud and clear to Council representatives deployed in the eighty or so posts throughout the world, and thereafter our Sabbaths were recognized as literally sacrosanct. Whenever possible, we attended a church service; and this was highly rewarding, quite apart from 'spiritual edification', in that we found ourselves worshipping with many a far-flung congregation, sometimes large, sometimes a mere handful. I recall Church of Scotland services in Singapore, Madras, Colombo, Rome, Jerusalem and Paris: in both these last two I had served as an elder at different periods of my life, in the first as a Palestine Policeman, in the second as a staff officer at SHAPE. Prominent in the congregation of St James's Church in Delhi was the illustrious Anglo-Indian family of Skinner, descended from the founder of Skinner's Horse; they had many family memorial tablets on the walls. In Bangkok the Anglican chaplain had been one of my padres in Burma during the war. In Isfahan the congregation was largely American, and the service smacked rather of Moody and Sankey, with individuals rising in their seats and 'testifying' in a manner which we found embarrassing: one of our number was the charming Iranian Anglican Bishop, whose wife was the daughter of his English predecessor.

Often on our free days, usually Sundays, after catching up with correspondence and 'bread-and-butter letters', we would drive out into the country: sometimes by ourselves, sometimes with the local Ambassador or British Council Representative and their wives, sometimes for a picnic. From these occasions derive such memories as a luncheon at Delphi, looking down the firth on to the Gulf of Corinth; luncheon *al fresco* by the ancient harbour of Tyre, with caiques moored beside us; luncheon with the Khyber Rifles at Landi Khotal, where they showed us the Visitors' Book with such signatures as Curzon's and Kitchener's; luncheon in a coffee-shop at the foot of the Mexican pyramids within sight of Popocatapetl; a picnic by a tree-fringed *wadi* in the hills east of Sharja on the Persian Gulf, with heavily-laden donkeys plodding past us; another by a gentle stream fifteen miles out of Isfahan; another on a snowy hill-side near Ankara.

Our first journey of all was almost too exacting. It began with New Zealand, a happy return indeed, where I had business for the Bank, and then transformed itself into a British Council tour: Australia, Mexico, Venezuela and Brazil. When we totted it up in the end, we found that we had been away for 45 days, had slept in 25 beds, had spent 4 nights in aircraft, and crossed the Equator 4 times. Apart from New Zealand, we had been in Canberra, Sydney, Melbourne, Acapulco, Guadalajara, Mexico City, Caracas, Rio de Janeiro, Brasilia and São Paulo. It was altogether rather too hot a pace; but on this journey, as on every other, one had to balance the pros and cons between visiting as many countries as possible, however cursorily, or visiting fewer for longer. I opted for the first of these policies, and I think it paid off: largely thanks to meticulous planning within the Council, and still more to the imaginative and generous help of the Ambassadors and Representatives concerned.

In Brazil, the Council was especially strong. This was partly because we had inherited, long since, a number of long-established British institutes known as *Cultura*. When I lunched with the Foreign Minister and six of his officials, I found that all of them had learned their English under the auspices of one or other of these. This stood up well with one of our favourite boasts: that at one time not long before every Cabinet Minister in Jordan was a former 'British Council Scholar', or in other words had spent a period in Britain under our wing.

For most of our week in Brazil, we were the guests of David and Iro Hunt, late of Nigeria, in the magnificent Embassy in

Rio. In surprising conflict with the austerity which prevailed generally in Britain after the war, this huge and prestigious Residence had been purpose-built in the late 1940s, at the instigation of Ernie Bevin. (I cannot help deploring, in parenthesis, the modern substitution of the word 'Residence' for 'Embassy'. The 'Embassy' used to be where the Ambassador lived, and his place of work was the 'Chancery': now he works in the 'Embassy' and lives in the 'Residence'.) Here we stayed in style and comfort: among the last people to do so, for the days of the house were numbered. The Government had 'flitted' – to use a Scotticism – to its new and far from convenient capital of Brasilia, 600 miles inland, to which we flew with David Hunt across seemingly endless jungle to call on the President. Here the new 'Residence' was little more than a villa, where an adequate dining-room had had to be contrived by enclosing a verandah: a sad come-down from the dining-room in Rio, where forty people had sat down to dinner the night before, to enable us to meet a wide cross-section of Brazilians. The attentive reader will deduce that I am not one of those who think that the dignity of Britain overseas is best enhanced by Ambassadors regaling their guests on fish and chips and tomato ketchup from a cafeteria. I remember how ashamed I was to find that the dignified old British Embassy in Damascus, near the Hejaz Railway Station, which I first knew as our Consulate-General in 1937, had been replaced by a poky ground-floor flat, where the only guest-room did not even boast a window. In an Arab capital, where prestige counts for a lot, this was hardly a worthy setting for Her Britannic Majesty's Ambassador.

The kidnapping risk for Ambassadors in Brazil was high. Sir Geoffrey Jackson in neighbouring Uruguay had only just been released after nearly a year's incarceration by Tupamaros, and the Hunts were dogged wherever they went by heavily-armed detectives. The detectives, the Hunts and the Hunts' poodle Apollo were all on the best of terms with each other; and the detectives were ever willing to oblige by taking photographs, carrying picnic-baskets, or 'walking' Apollo.

My next journey was to Tunisia, Morocco, Senegal and Nigeria. President Bourguiba of Tunisia welcomed me as an old friend, and I told him how the carpet he had given me when I visited him with the Queen Mother now adorned my son's sitting-room at home. Our visit to Tunis coincided with Armistice Sunday; and the service in the little Anglican Church there, now well over a hundred years old, and surrounded by romantic tombstones commemorating English people who had died there far from home, was conducted by the Embassy chaplain, who happened to be a New Zealander. We were to attend other Armistice Sunday services in the course of British Council tours, in Delhi and Beirut: the latter was especially moving for me, because it was held in the War Graves Commission cemetery, and I knew several people buried there, killed in the Syrian campaign of 1941, in which I had myself taken part.

Morocco was also full of memories, but I was brought up sharp by the many political changes since my previous visits: everybody I knew seemed to have disappeared from the scene. My activities were slightly hampered by instructions that I was to hold myself in readiness for an audience with the King, which would be at short notice. The three days of my visit passed; and the summons eventually came when I was poised at Casablanca airport, two hours away, about to board the aircraft for Dakar in Senegal; and I had to return a regretful, but I hope respectful, *non possumus*.

My visit to Senegal would have been worth while if only for my meeting with President Senghor, who had corresponded with me when I was in New Zealand. I knew he was a scholar and a poet as well as a statesman; and I was even more impressed by him than I had expected to be. He was newly returned from receiving an honorary degree at Oxford, and was still in a glow from the warmth of the reception that he had had there. He told me that he was engaged in translating T. S. Eliot and Gerard Manley Hopkins into French: I ventured to suggest that he might next consider translating them into English.

My visit to Nigeria was infinitely happier than my time there during the civil war, when I had been so constricted in my movements, and had had to concentrate on the distressing events in the war zone. I had been confined to Lagos, the fringes of the 'Biafran' enclave, and a single visit to Ibadan, to investigate how the Ibo minority there was faring. This time I was able to travel more widely, including to Kano and Kaduna in the Moslem north. The traffic jam in Lagos was worse than ever: so was the blare of the motor-horns. I was almost called upon to resign from the chairmanship of the Council a year or two later, when I was asked to comment on the performance of a British orchestral quartet in Paris, which had been playing ultra-modern music: I said that it reminded me of a traffic jam in Lagos. So indeed it did, but I shouldn't have said so. What impressed me most was the degree to which Nigeria had returned to normal after the warfare of six years before. Enugu, which had once been Ojukwu's capital before he had to evacuate it, and which I had seen during those troubled times, was flourishing. It was still under the administration of Asika, the Ibo who rightly or wrongly – who are we to judge? – had remained faithful to the Federals throughout. He invited to meet us at dinner a number of Ibos who had taken to the bush during the war. All seemed to be going well, and General Gowon had given me a warm welcome back. People with longer and deeper knowledge of Nigeria than I might well have forecast his downfall a few years later, but I got no whiff of it. My own assessment of him is that he was a good man, but not subtle enough for the labyrinth of intrigue in which his lot was cast.

Nigeria and Brazil were two of the three countries where the Council was strongest on the ground; Brazil for the reason I have already mentioned. The third was India, where we toured for three weeks in 1974. When one discovered the immense importance which the Indian authorities attached to the learning of English all over the sub-continent, it was strange to remember how, only a quarter of a century earlier, efforts were being made to supplant it entirely with Hindi. Now all the constituent states were teaching English at a comparatively early age; in the former Presidencies of Bombay and Madras, children began learning it two years younger than elsewhere, at the tender age of seven. In addition to our regular out-stations in Calcutta, Madras and Bombay, we ran a number of libraries in other cities, such as Allahabad; and the statistics concerning the number of books borrowed, apart from those read on the spot, were astronomical. In India, as in other countries all over the world, the richest marrow in the Council's bones was the locally-enlisted element, all strongly Anglophile and dedicated. I recall such devoted people as Mr Jacob and Miss Majumdar in Calcutta, and Mr Macaulay in Lagos, all of whom had well over thirty years of service to the Council under their belt. And there was Mrs Nghia, a slight, delicate figure, who continued to run our library in Saigon long after our post there had closed down. We called on her only a few months before that sparkling city was overwhelmed by the bloody tidal wave from the north. I was immensely relieved to hear that the Council had managed to arrange for her and her daughter to be flown out at almost the last moment, and that they had found refuge with her sister, married to a Frenchman living in France.

We included in our Indian tour a brief visit to Poona, where we stayed in the Royal Western India Turf Club, still redolent of the Raj and run on traditional lines by a retired Indian Brigadier, a former cavalry officer. I paid my second visit to Fergusson College, thirty-two years after my first, and rejoiced to see portraits of my father and grandfather and a photograph of Kilkerran still hanging on the walls, ninety years after its foundation. Dr Mahajani, a Wrangler and Honorary Fellow of St John's College at Cambridge, who had been Principal at the time of my first visit, was present, and we dined with him that evening at Poona University, of which he was now Vice-Chancellor. We had come up from Bombay by air, but we returned by train, by the line that winds as dramatically down the western Ghats as the Taurus Express that used to carry me in 1941 between Adana and Ulukişla in Turkey. In Bombay I was called upon to repeat to an audience, which included two retired Indian officers with whom I had been at Sandhurst, the lecture on the Wingate Expeditions which I had been invited to deliver two weeks before in Delhi. That had been a nostalgic experience, since its venue had been in the large hall in Army Headquarters which had been the Map Room, next to my office, when I had been a Joint Planner there in 1942: it used to be known as 'The Cathedral'. The current Chief of the

General Staff, General Bewoor, honoured me by taking the chair; and I was shaken to discover that my audience knew a great deal more about the details of my subject than I could remember after the passage of thirty years.

I was impressed in India by the enormous affection evident among senior officers and elder statesmen towards the memory of Lord Wavell. *The Viceroy's Journal*, judiciously edited by Sir Penderel Moon, had appeared shortly before our visit, and had been read widely and avidly. Wavell had pulled no punches in his references to the people with whom he had had to deal: British, Hindu or Moslem. Far from giving offence in India, the book seemed to have put Wavell back more securely on to the pedestal where some few people had thought that his reputation might be tottering. His integrity, his sincerity, were so transparent in these notes, often jotted down late at night or in the small hours of the morning at the end of long hours of fruitless discussion, that they glowed warmly through the cold print. I remember especially the distinguished Governor of Bombay, who had long been in the service of the Nizam of Hyderabad, holding forth on the virtues and the patience of Wavell, illustrating his points by references to the book, and calling on his own memories of Wavell to reinforce them.

Other highlights of my journeys and interviews linger with me, such as the brick I dropped during an audience with the Shah of Persia. He had asked me whether Council business, of which he had spoken in generous terms, was going well; and I had told him that the forty University teachers we had recruited for him at his request were suffering from six months' arrears of pay. He said: 'I know that money was allocated for that: what on earth can have happened to it?' Of all the phrases available to me, I hit on the most tactless of all, and heard myself saying: 'Perhaps it's got stuck in the pipeline!' In the event, it didn't matter; the teachers got their arrears within a week, plus a bonus in compensation.

It was an inspiration to see the quality of the British Council people: those who had made it their career, those whom we had recruited on contract as teachers or technical advisers, the VSOs or Volunteers for Service Overseas, young people of both sexes whom we administered in many of the countries in which they served. Only rarely did I meet a misfit, such as the wife of a teacher in Indonesia, where the home-grown coffee is probably the best in the world, who complained that she couldn't find Nescafé in any of the local stores. It was in Indonesia, in Jogjakarta, that my wife and I celebrated our silver wedding: I had never even heard of Jogjakarta when I emerged with my bride on my arm from St Michael's Chester Square at 3 p.m. one November afternoon in 1950, and tried in my excitement to shake hands with my first-ever platoon piper, Pipe-Major Roy, DCM, while he was playing *Highland Wedding* for all he was worth, to the detriment of this tune. British Council people tend to stay longer in a post than their opposite numbers in the Foreign Service, and have better opportunities to get under the skin of the host country: they do not have to labour under the intolerable burden of having to attend cocktail parties for almost half the evenings in the year, to celebrate the National Days of their innumerable *chers collègues*.

What proved to be our penultimate trip (because I had an illness which put me out of action for four months) covered Germany, Austria, Yugoslavia, Cyprus, Israel and Turkey. On this journey we were pulled up almost literally short in no fewer than three countries by barriers erected by man in his foolishness, between people and people. In Cyprus there was the barbed wire dividing Turk from Greek, running through the very heart of Nicosia, close to the Ledra Palace Hotel, which I remembered as the scene of such jollity on many occasions in bygone years. In Jerusalem there was no longer any wire, but the hostility between Jews and Arabs remained almost as barbed and almost as tangible; and I felt as furtive as Nicodemus as I sought out old friends in both camps, some of whom I had known for forty years. And in Berlin there was that horrible Wall.

The Wall was erected long after I was stationed in Berlin in 1951, and I had not seen it before. I saw it again a few weeks before I write these lines, this time from a helicopter, with its watch-towers every few hundred yards, and the wide stretch of raked soil around it, ready to betray any footprint. It is menacing and sinister from the air, where you can see its whole length winding through both the city and the woodlands that surround it; and menacing in a different fashion from the ground, with the sad little memorials along its length to those who have lost their lives in trying to scale it. There is something especially cynical in the cruel device that runs along its crest: a roller that turns if you put a hand on it, and effectively prevents you from getting any sort of grip.

But within Berlin itself there survives, as it has always done, even in the darkest days, a richness of interest in music, in art, in literature, in the exchange of thinking, which even the worst moments of ordeal never looked like quenching: the sort of spirit which gave rise to the building of the Blue Church, the Gedächtniskirche (the Church of Thankfulness), on the ruins of the Kaiserwilhelmkirche, much in the same way as the new Coventry Cathedral rose on the ruins of the old. Berlin remains one of the most fruitful fields of all in which the British Council has sought to sow its seed; and it has been 'fed and watered' largely by the beleaguered Berliners.

We returned from Turkey by the Orient Express, which was in its death-throes: it expired a few months later. Gone was all its glory, gone all the luxury recorded by Agatha Christie and Graham Greene, gone the mysterious and glamorous countesses who filched from you your secret despatches. There was not even a restaurant-car, except for luncheon between Venice and Milan: so we lived off a magnificent hamper provided by the Council people in Istanbul. We were the only through first-class passengers: most of our fellow-travellers were Turkish labourers going to Germany to work.

Our final tour for the Council was in the autumn of 1976: a comparatively modest one to Italy and France: to Rome, Naples, Milan, Florence and Paris. The Mayor of Rome inhabited what must be the most beautiful municipal chambers anywhere in the world. We looked out from his balcony over the most august and famous of all Rome's ruins, and even the sound of traffic seemed to be hushed by history. He was Roman-born, a highly cultured Professor and author, a Communist, and a man of great charm, but much concerned with worries about housing, and the enormous interest that the city was having to pay on the borrowings incurred by his predecessors in office. Such pecuniary matters seemed far removed from Lars Porsena, the geese that saved the Capitol by their cackling, and even from the canonization of Blesséd John Ogilvie, the Scottish saint who was receiving his saintly accolade in Rome that week-end. We had already arranged to attend the Scots Kirk in Rome that Sunday, the third time in my life that I had worshipped there, and had therefore to refuse with regret the only invitation to a canonization that I am ever likely to receive. But we did accept the invitation to luncheon at Scots College afterwards, where I was enchanted to find that the Rector, a former officer of the Scots Guards, was a distant Ramsay cousin of my own. The place was swarming with Ogilvies, both Catholic and Protestant, including Princess Alexandra and her husband, and with Scottish Catholics of all walks of life, from Cardinal Gray downwards; and I much enjoyed hearing Mgr Colin MacPherson, the very tall Catholic Bishop of Argyll and the Isles, who hails from Lochboisdale in South Uist, matching his Gaelic with the Irish Bishop of Sligo, and claiming it to be far the purer.

The Mayor of Naples was also a Communist, and as charming as his confrère in Rome. He had been born and bred in Tunisia, and had first been introduced into Italy during the war by the British, in order to help and organize the partisans. We therefore spoke in French, since my Italian is negligible; and when I said to him: '*Alors, vous êtes en verité pied noir?*' he returned what I thought an excellent answer: '*Disons plutôt, "Pied Rouge!"* '

That ultimate journey culminated in the opening by Queen Elizabeth the Queen Mother of the new British Institute in Paris in the Rue de Constantine, in the former house of the Comte de Paris, not far from the Invalides. It was my swansong as Chairman, and a happy one for a Francophile such as myself. During the three days that the celebrations lasted, we lunched, two among forty, at the Palais de l'Elysée as guests of the President and Madame Giscard d'Estaing: the more fun for me because, as I have already said, we had had three of their children to stay at Ballantrae some years before, and still more so because her father François de Brantes, who had died in a concentration camp in Germany during the war, had been a friend of mine before it: both when I was a subaltern attached to the French Army in 1932, when I was several times a guest at his home in Touraine; and in 1939 when he was Assistant Military Attaché in London.

Thereafter I returned like Cincinnatus to my own scanty acres: not like him to the plough, for my twenty-five acres (which I decline to describe as hectares until I am forced to) are all woodland, and require minimal physical work to run, which suits my congenital idleness. I am fortunate in that I still have the chance to travel from time to time: indeed, as I write these words, I am planning my first visit to the Solomon Islands, as well as a return to Tonga and Sikkim. Even when I am based at home, my mind takes wing to distant places, for many of which I have not found space in this book. I have not mentioned, for instance, the brooding city of Benin, which for me still reeks of blood from human sacrifices of not so long ago; nor the benevolent ruins of Baalbek, still placid despite the centuries of strife that have rolled over them; nor the Disney-like towers of the Castle of Orchha in India, which I found soaring above me as I led my column through the neighbouring jungle on a leisurely training march in January of 1943; nor Pitt Island, 400 miles east of New Zealand, inhabited by a single family with its numerous offspring, settled there for five generations, and still subscribing, despite the rarity of an in-coming mail, to such publications as *Country Life*, *The Field* and *Blackwood's Magazine*. These places at least, and many others, I cannot aspire to see again.

Meanwhile, and with great happiness, I am close to Kilkerran, whence I first set out, and surrounded by people who bear surnames which have been familiar to me all my life, and which were equally familiar to my forebears. I rejoice in the peace and quiet when I step out of the house and listen. In my youth one would have heard the creaking of a farm cart: that is now no more, and one is more likely to hear the rattle of a tractor. In the spring we hear the mounting, bubbling cry of the whaup, and the bleating of the black-face lambs as they protest at their mothers shambling away from them. The dawn chorus is with us all the year round, and so is the view of the peaks of Arran, the bannock lump which is Ailsa Craig, the long arm of Kintyre with the low island of Sanda crouching below it, the North Channel which is the gateway to America, and far to the left the hills of Antrim behind Carnlough and Glenarm. After dark three lighthouses blink at us: the Craig, Davaar Island at the southern entrance to Campbeltown Loch, and Sanda. We feel cosy, and happy not to be at sea, much as I loved, and still miss, the various boats I have owned in my time.

But the sea is always with us: we are a fishing as well as a farming community. On still nights we hear the waves breaking on the shingle; on misty nights we hear the boom of the foghorn from Ailsa Craig; and on stormy nights we know that there will be salt spray on our windows next morning, for all that we are more than a mile inland, and more than three hundred feet up. There is much to be said for 'sleep after toil, port after stormy seas, ease after war', as Spenser put it; and with Kilkerran close at hand.

INDEX

Index

Index

Index

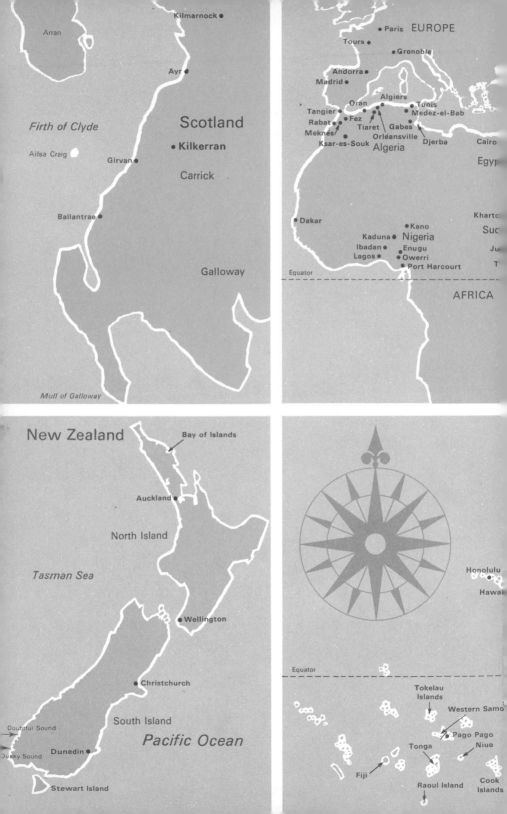